W9-BRM-442

The Complete Garlic Lovers' Cookbook

THE COMPLETE GARLIC LOVERS' COOKBOOK

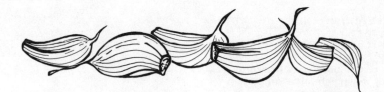

from
GILROY

Garlic Capital of the World

CELESTIALARTS
Berkeley, California

CELESTIAL ARTS
P.O. Box 7327
Berkeley, California 94707

Cover design by Ken Scott
Cover photograph by Robert R. Stein
Text design by Abigail Johnston
Interior Illustrations by Shirley Wong
Typography by HMS Typography, Inc.

Library of Congress Cataloging-in-Publication Data

The Complete garlic lovers' cookbook.

   Previously published in two volumes.
   Includes index.
   1. Cookery (Garlic) I. Gilroy Garlic Festival.
TX819.G3C66 1987   641.6'526   87-13865
ISBN 0-89087-503-0

First Printing, 1987
Manufactured in the United States of America

   4 5 6 7 8 9 0 — 91 90

DEDICATION

To the people of Gilroy
For sharing a lifestyle of
    good food, good times
    and for giving from the heart.

Contents

The People of Gilroy   1
Map   4
The Festival   5
Gourmet Alley's Recipes   7
The Gilroy Garlic Festival   15
Recipe Contest
Appetizers / Antipasti   19
Soups   55
Salads / Dressings   77
Eggs / Cheese   95
Pasta / Rice   105
Vegetables   137
Meats   177
Poultry   227
Seafood   269
Breads   293
Sauces / Marinades   313
Miscellaneous   321
Good Things to Know   337
About Garlic
Cooking Equivalents   343
Table
Index   345

The People of Gilroy

The first reviews were great! "The ultimate in summer food fairs" *(Los Angeles Herald Examiner);* "Fame is Nothing to Sniff at in Gilroy" *(Washington Post);* ". . . Call the town of Gilroy fragrant and friendly" (Copely News Service); "It was rollicking good fun and the food was super" *(San Francisco Chronicle);* "By any measure, it was a success" *(San Francisco Examiner).* The nationwide headlines, proclaiming the phenomenal success of the first Garlic Festival in 1979 caught the people of Gilroy, California, by surprise.

When a group of local residents staged the first weekend celebration of the "scented pearl" to increase community pride and help create a more flavorable image of their town, little did they know what a dramatic impact it would make on Gilroy. What they did know was how to use the area's most prominent product, garlic. They knew how to cook up cauldrons of mouthwatering garlic-laced food, how to have fun with garlic, how to motivate people and how to share this very special lifestyle. The rest is history and the Garlic Festival became a permanent fixture on the town calendar.

The response to Gilroy's harvest festival surpassed even the most optimistic expectations. Yearly attendance grew from 20,000 to 142,000 and by 1986 over one-half million visitors had trekked to Gilroy, "The Garlic Capital of the World," to share in the culinary legacy of its townspeople.

The steering committee of community leaders, determined to provide a quality event, rose to meet the challenges created by the ever-increasing numbers of garlic lovers. More garlic! More space! More food! More planning! More volunteers! All this, and a more enviable challenge: determine the best use for the monies generated at each year's event.

More garlic? No problem in Gilroy. The issue of more space? Solved with cooperation from the City of Gilroy's award-winning Parks Department and the generosity of local landowners. To meet the other needs a cross section of Gilroy residents came forward as volunteers to form thirty committees to deal with the creative aspects, detailed planning, logistics and implementation of each phase of the Festival. The Gilroy Garlic Festival Association was formed as a nonprofit, tax-exempt private corporation with a rotating board of directors. The Association's continuing goal was identified as the support of community projects, charitable groups and service organizations. Several criteria were established for the disbursement of Festival funds, but the majority of funds available is given to those groups who have directly participated in the event through commitment of time and labor. (Voila! More volunteers.) Additional monies are used for permanent improvements to city parks for all to enjoy.

From 1979 to 1986 the yearly volunteer base of the Festival grew from 50 to 4,000; participating organizations from 15 to 117; man-hours contributed increased from a few hundred to 32,200; and yearly distributed monies increased from $5,500 to $250,000.

In the light of these extraordinary facts, the media quotes now took on new meaning. "Gilroy provided an experience to warm the heart" *(San Francisco Examiner);* "Garlic now gives the town (Gilroy) a certain dignity" *(Wall Street Journal);* "Enjoy a town being proud of itself and transforming the pungent aroma of garlic into the sweet smell of success" *(The Urban Fair,* U.S. Department HUD); "Garlic Breathes New Life Into Town" *(Washington Post).* In reality the people of Gilroy have breathed new life into their town. Garlic is simply the product and the Garlic Festival is the vehicle for people to help themselves and each other.

Volunteers, matched to their Festival job by skill level, ability and/or willingness, eagerly give hours, sometimes all three days of the Festival, to help the charity or organization of their choice. They contribute their time by working man-hours for local hospitals, rape crisis and battered women centers, drug abuse prevention, sports and service clubs, rehabilitation centers for the handicapped, libraries, Special Olympics, youth, school, church, senior citizen and cultural groups as well as for the better known national organizations such as the American Cancer Society, American Heart Association and the American Red Cross.

Monies received from the Garlic Festival are used by 110 local organizations for everything from their operating budgets, to building a playground for handicapped children, to buying sports equipment or classroom materials. But are the dollars the only motivation for helping? The following quotes are the ones we are most proud of—these are from Festival volunteers:

"It is a convergence of good. It is neighbors helping neighbors in a celebration of our community. It is a timely meeting of preparation with opportunity." *Albert Valencia, South County Alternative, Inc.*

"The most rewarding and enriching experience is being actively involved in the Festival." *Eleanor Villarreal, Hope Rehabilitation*

"The togetherness created by everyone working together to create an event we are all proud of is worth so much more than the financial returns." *Richard Imler, Gilroy High School*

"The Gilroy Garlic Festival is a beautiful time when community spirit unites and takes precedence over all other activities. We have become closer as a group by working long and hard hours together." *Karen Rizzi, Childrens Home Society*

"Other benefits equally important for the kids are the teaching of teamwork, responsibility, accomplishing a task, development of pride . . ." *William Kauffold, Western Homes for Youth*

"The Festival is the epitome of people giving and sharing of themselves for a common cause. There are always more than enough willing volunteers to get the big job done." *Oscar Torres, Jr., Big Brothers / Big Sisters*

So in reality it is not only Gilroy's famous garlic but Gilroy's main resource—its people—that guarantees an enjoyable time for all who visit the Festival.

The festival of harvest is, of course, a unifying event as old as civilization itself, but to do it well is the equivalent of staging an opera or anything else that lifts the spirit. In this regard, Gilroy is approaching the first rank.

San Francisco Examiner

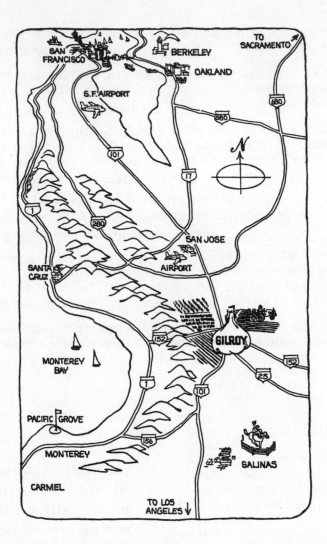

Gilroy, California, is a town of 23,000 located in the fertile Santa Clara Valley, 80 miles south of San Francisco. Its livelihood is derived from a variety of agricultural products, among which garlic is an especially important crop. It is estimated that garlic is a $53 million industry in Gilroy and within a 90-mile radius, 90 percent of the garlic grown and processed in the United States can be found. Gilroy is also the home of two of the major dehydration plants and three of the major fresh garlic shippers in the world. An estimated 100 million pounds of garlic is grown, processed or distributed through Gilroy each year. With all this in its favor and the desire to stage an unparalleled celebration of garlic that would attract garlic lovers from all over the world, Gilroy claimed the title Garlic Capital of the World during the first annual Festival in 1979.

The Festival

"The bulb's biggest booster since King Tut."
People Magazine

Whether you appreciate garlic for its flavor, its health aspects or its folklore, you'll want to travel to Gilroy and experience the annual Garlic Festival. Seeing is believing!

The ultimate in summer food fairs, the Garlic Festival features a truly international array of epicurean garlic delights. Gourmet Alley is the heart of this food showcase, where local chefs perform culinary magic over the firepits in full view of spectators. These wizards work wonders with iron skillets the size of bicycle wheels as they toss the flaming calamari or gently saute bright red and green peppers to add to the top sirloin in Pepper Beefsteak Sandwiches. Mouthwatering mountains of garlic bread, tons of scampi swimming in lobster butter sauce, delicate Stuffed Mushrooms, and cauldrons of Pasta Con Pesto all set the high standards for quality and adherence to the garlic theme that prevails throughout the Festival.

Eighty additional food booths operated by service clubs, civic and merchant groups offer a breathtaking variety of garlic creations. After sampling the aromatic offerings of the talented townspeople of Gilroy, visitors can cool their palates with the local wines, a cool drink, or garlic ice cream and desserts of local fresh fruits.

Thousands of garlic garlands and braids and the mouthwatering aromas from the outdoor kitchens create the perfect setting for the garlic displays and demonstrations. Merchandise and exhibit booths offer an array of garlic-themed articles such as fresh garlic (pee-wees to colossal), garlic braids, wreaths, leis, dry decorative arrangements, all forms of dehydrated and processed garlic (even deodorized), garlic pills, cookbooks and information on garlic uses and its health aspects, folklore, garlic hats, tee shirts, jewelry. . .just let your imagination go! It will probably be there.

And then there is "Art Alley," seventy-five booths of juried fine arts and crafts featuring many original works pertaining to the theme of garlic. Musicians and theatrical groups perform continuously throughout each day of the Festival with the emphasis on family entertainment.

Mr. Gourmet Garlic and Miss Garlic Festival will reign and Festivalgoers will be encouraged to participate in the garlic braiding and the garlic "topping" (a garlic harvesting technique which removes the tops and roots with sharp shears) and to observe the Great Garlic Recipe Cook-off, described in the next section.

But that's not all! There are also events to entertain you if you choose to arrive in the area earlier than the Festival weekend. These events are the Miss Garlic Contest, Love That Garlic Tennis Tournament, Garlic Golf, Garlic Squeeze Barn Dance, Tour De Garlique Garlic Country Bicycle Tour, and the Garlic Gallop 10K run.

Add to these ingredients a generous dash of California small town conviviality, and the result is a recipe for a truly unique summer experience whose savory memories will be with you long after the participants take their garlic braids, cookbooks, and totes full of garliciana home.

People flocked to this little farming community 80 miles south of San Francisco. When the crowds weren't eating, they were singing garlic songs, swapping garlic seeds and recipes . . . buying garlic souvenirs.

Christian Science Monitor

Gourmet Alley

Gourmet Alley Garlic Bread 9

Pasta con Pesto alla Pelliccione 9

Central Coast Stir-Fry Vegetables 10

Gourmet Alley's Stuffed
   Mushrooms 10

Calamari, Festival-Style 11

Garlic Festival Pepper Beefsteak
   Sandwiches 12

Scampi in Butter Sauce 13

GOURMET ALLEY GARLIC BREAD

½ cup each butter and margarine
½ cup oil
3 cloves fresh garlic, minced
½ teaspoon pepper
¼ teaspoon oregano
½ cup white wine
3 tablespoons fresh parsley, chopped
2 loaves sweet French bread

Melt butter and margarine in pan. Add oil and garlic. Simmer over low heat for 1 minute. Add pepper, oregano and wine. Bring to a boil. Add parsley. Remove immediately from heat, and pour into large baking pan. Cut loaves in half lengthwise. Toast on grill or under broiler until golden brown. Dip toasted halves, cut side down, in butter mixture. Serve immediately.

PASTA CON PESTO ALLA PELLICCIONE

Paul Pelliccione, one of the head chefs of Gourmet Alley, shares his fabulous recipe for pasta con pesto as it was prepared for the Garlic Festival.

Courtesy of: Paul Pelliccione, Gilroy, CA

2 cups packed fresh basil leaves, washed and well drained
1½ cups grated Romano cheese, plus additional cheese, if desired
½ cup olive oil
½ cup melted butter
6 large cloves fresh garlic, crushed
1 lb. spaghetti, flat noodles *or* similar pasta, cooked according to package directions

Place basil, 1 cup of the cheese, oil, butter and garlic in blender. Begin blending, turning motor on and off. Push pesto down from sides of blender with rubber spatula and continue until you have a very coarse puree. Makes about 1½ cups pesto. Spoon 1 cup pesto sauce over freshly cooked spaghetti. Mix quickly with two forks. Add ½ cup cheese and mix. Serve with additional pesto sauce and cheese. Cover and refrigerate any leftover pesto up to a week, or freeze in small portions. The surface will darken when exposed to air, so stir the pesto before serving.

CENTRAL COAST STIR-FRY VEGETABLES

¼ cup carrots
¼ cup celery
¼ cup yellow crookneck
    squash
¼ cup zucchini
¼ cup broccoli
¼ cup cauliflower
2 tablespoons oil
3 large cloves fresh garlic,
    minced
½ teaspoon salt
¼ teaspoon pepper
    Pinch red chili pepper
¼ teaspoon *each* basil and
    oregano
¼ cup dry white wine
1 tablespoon fresh parsley,
    chopped
¼ lemon

Cut carrots, celery, squash and zucchini into ½ x 2-inch pieces. Break broccoli and cauliflower into small pieces. Heat oil until almost smoking. Add vegetables; stir to coat with oil. Add garlic, salt, peppers, basil and oregano. Simmer 1 minute. Add wine and simmer 2 minutes or until vegetables are cooked *al dente*. Add parsley and squeeze in juice of lemon and serve immediately.

GOURMET ALLEY'S STUFFED MUSHROOMS

Rancher / Chef Jim Rubino shares his recipe for the stuffed mushrooms that were a hit at the Festival's Gourmet Alley. These mushrooms make great finger appetizers for company (but don't forget your family too). Prepare them the day before or at the last minute but be sure to make plenty for they'll quickly disappear.

Courtesy of: Jim Rubino, San Martin, CA

20 fresh mushrooms
½ cup finely chopped fresh
    parsley
¼ cup (1½ oz.) freshly
    grated Parmesan cheese
4 cloves fresh garlic
2 tablespoons soft butter

Clean mushrooms and remove stems. Combine parsley, cheese, garlic and butter in a firm stuffing mixture. Place approximately 1 tablespoon stuffing into each mushroom. Place mushrooms on a flat baking pan on a rack 6 inches under a preheated broiler. Broil for 4 to 5 minutes until mushrooms are cooked *al dente* and still firm. Do not overcook.

CALAMARI, FESTIVAL-STYLE

One of Gourmet Alley's greatest attractions is watching the preparation of calamari. Some argue that eating it is even better. Here is Head Chef Val Filice's recipe for calamari as it is served at the Festival.

Courtesy of: Val Filice, Gilroy, CA

3 lbs. calamari (squid), cleaned and cut
⅓ cup olive oil
¼ cup white sherry
¼ cup white wine
1 tablespoon crushed fresh garlic
½ lemon
1 teaspoon dry basil *or* 1 tablespoon fresh
1 teaspoon dry oregano *or* 1 tablespoon fresh
¼ teaspoon dry crushed red pepper
Red Sauce (below)

In large skillet heat olive oil at high heat. Add wine and sherry and saute crushed garlic. Squeeze the juice of ½ lemon into pan and place lemon rind in pan. Sprinkle herbs over and add calamari. Saute calamari for approximately 4 minutes on high heat. Do not overcook.

Red Sauce

1 lb. whole, peeled tomatoes, canned *or* fresh
1 tablespoon olive oil
½ green pepper, chopped
1 stalk celery, chopped
1 medium-sized yellow onion, chopped
3 cloves fresh garlic, minced

Mash tomatoes with potato masher and set aside. In medium-size pan heat oil, add chopped ingredients and saute until onion is transparent. Add mashed tomatoes and simmer for 30 minutes. Pour red sauce over calamari and heat for 1 minute.

GARLIC FESTIVAL PEPPER BEEFSTEAK SANDWICHES

The aroma of gently sauteing garlic brought on hunger pangs and set mouths watering. Those who attended the Garlic Festival are still talking about the Pepper Beefsteak Sandwiches served in Gourmet Alley. Chef Lou Trinchero and his team of cooks served 700 pounds of top sirloin, 250 pounds of green peppers and 750 loaves of French bread. Thank goodness Lou has worked the recipe down to one which will "feed 4 generously." You'll want to have plenty because they are unbelievably delicious.   *Courtesy of: Lou Trinchero, Gilroy, CA*

8 bell peppers, seeded and sliced in quarters
1 medium-sized onion, chopped
3 cloves fresh garlic, minced
   Salt and pepper to taste
   Olive oil
¾ lb. top sirloin steak, barbecued or broiled to desired degree of doneness
8 French rolls, halved and basted with garlic butter
   Garlic butter (see Miscellaneous section)

In skillet saute peppers, onion, garlic and salt and pepper in olive oil until tender. Brush rolls with garlic butter and heat in the oven or toast lightly under the broiler or over the barbecue. Slice steak thin and place on bottom half of roll. Top with pepper-garlic mixture and other half of roll. Makes 8 sandwiches.

The festival, which celebrates the end of this year's garlic harvest, really is smalltown Americana at its best.

Keith Muroaka
The (Santa Cruz) *Sentinel*

SCAMPI IN BUTTER SAUCE

A Festival favorite, Scampi in Butter Sauce is another Gourmet Alley delicacy. The recipe here is courtesy of Val Filice who has served this exceptional dish to the delight of friends and family for years. Scampi, by the way, are a close relative of the shrimp but have no exact equivalent outside Italian waters. Substitute prawns or shrimp of medium to large size.

Courtesy of: Val Filice, Gilroy, CA

Butter Sauce
- ½ to 1 cup butter
- 1 tablespoon finely minced fresh garlic
- 8 oz. clam juice
- ¼ cup flour
- 1 tablespoon minced parsley
- ⅓ cup white wine
  Juice of ½ lemon
- 1 teaspoon dry basil
  Salt and pepper to taste
- ½ cup half-and-half

Melt butter with garlic in small saucepan over medium heat; do not let butter brown. In a separate bowl, mix clam juice, flour and parsley, blending until mixture is smooth. Pour flour mixture into garlic butter and stir until smooth and well blended. Stir in wine, lemon juice, herbs and spices, stirring constantly. Gradually add half-and-half and stir until thickened. Simmer for 30 to 45 minutes.

Scampi
- 2 tablespoons butter
- ⅓ cup olive oil
- 1 tablespoon minced fresh garlic
  Juice of 1 lemon (retain rind)
- 1 tablespoon fresh chopped parsley *or* 1 teaspoon dry
- ½ teaspoon crushed red pepper
- 1 tablespoon fresh basil *or* 1 teaspoon dry
- ¼ cup white wine
  Dash of dry vermouth
  Salt and pepper to taste
- 3 lbs. deveined and cleaned scampi (prawns)

Melt butter in large saucepan on high heat and add oil. Combine remaining ingredients keeping scampi aside until last minute. Add scampi and saute until firm and slightly pink. Do not overcook. Pour 1 cup of scampi butter over scampi. Refrigerate the rest for later use.

The Gilroy Garlic Festival Recipe Contest

From the beginning, the Garlic Recipe Contest held each year in connection with the Gilroy Garlic Festival was intended to be first and foremost a wonderful adventure in garlic cookery rather than a commercial enterprise. Because the Festival's primary purpose is to support local charities, it was decided to keep the prizes relatively small so that more of the proceeds from the Festival could be contributed to charitable organizations. Top prize is only $500, which is extremely small when compared to other national contests. In addition, the entrants who qualify each year for the final Cook-off, held during the Festival, are expected to pay their own way to Gilroy to be a part of this event and to bring their own pots, pans and ingredients.

One might think that these conditions would discourage entries in the contest, but such is not the case. Nearly 1000 entries pour in every year from garlic lovers throughout the United States who want to share their great garlic cooking discoveries with others who would truly appreciate them.

Contest rules specify that recipes must call for 3 cloves of fresh garlic or the equivalent in dehydrated or processed garlic. Recipes must be original, and only amateur chefs are permitted to enter the contest. When recipes are received at the Festival office, the volunteer committee chairman and committee members sort through the recipes eliminating those which do not meet the specific rules of the contest.

Those recipes which qualify are then sent to a select group of professional home economists in San Francisco who themselves are in the business of developing new recipes for food clients and who understand all the problems related to such endeavors. They carefully read and compare recipes, searching for the unusual technique or combination of ingredients that might make a particular recipe a winner. If there are any questions about a recipe it is prepared exactly as specified by the entrant and then taste-tested to ensure that it qualifies to be in the finals. Once the prejudging is done, the finalists are notified to be sure that they will be able to participate in the Cook-off where the winners will be selected.

Judges who serve at the Cook-off are always chosen from the professional food world for their knowledge and personal food expertise. Many have judged the most important cooking contests in the country yet all agree that the Garlic Recipe Contest is the most fun. Past years' judges have included:

First Contest, 1979: Shirley Sarvis, free lance food writer and consultant; Anthony Dias Blue, syndicated food and wine critic; Harvey Steiman, *San Francisco Examiner* food editor; Marjorie Rice, food editor of the *San Diego Tribune*; Rita Leinwand, food editor *Bon Appetit Magazine*.

1980: Jane Benet, food editor *San Francisco Chronicle*; Jean Lebbert, staff food editor *Sunset Magazine*; Jeff Morgan, food columnist; Betsy Balsley, food editor *Los Angeles Times*; Mary Phillips, food editor *San Jose Mercury & News*.

1981: Phyllis Hanes, food editor *Christian Science Monitor*; Vern Lanegrasse, syndicated columnist and television personality; Gail Perrin, food editor *Boston Glove*; Dorothy Sorenson, food editor McClatchey Newspapers; Jan Weimer, food editor *Bon Appetit Magazine*.

1982: Carol Haddix, food editor *Chicago Tribune*; Larry Gonick, syndicated food cartoon-columnist; Kit Snedaker, food editor *Los Angeles Herald-Examiner*; Sharon Cadwallader, syndicated food columnist; Jim Neil, fireman chef on TV's *People Are Talking*; Helen Dollaghan, food editor *Denver Post* and Danny Kaye, noted entertainer and film personality as well as accomplished amateur chef.

1983: Marian Burros, food writer *New York Times*; Joe Carcione, syndicated television personality; Maggie Crum, food editor *Contra Costa Times*; Marilyn Hansen, food editor *Family Weekly*; Sharon Sanders, food writer *Chicago Sun-Times*; Jim Neil, fireman chef TV's *People Are Talking*.

1984: Ellen Brown, food editor *USA Today*; Al Hart, *KCBS Radio Kitchen*; Jackie Olden, *KNX Radio Food Hour*; Lou Pappas, food editor *The Peninsula Times Tribune*; Dian Thomas, the *Today Show*.

1985: Terry Lowry, *A.M. San Francisco*; Sue B. Huffman, food and equipment editor, *Ladies Home Journal*; Toni Griffin Allegra, food editor, *San Diego Tribune*; Gloria Glyer, editor, *The Sacramento Union*; Barbara Gibbs Ostman, food editor, *St. Louis Post-Dispatch*; Fred La Cosse, *A.M. San Francisco*, Master of Ceremonies.

1986: Joyce Christensen, food editor, *Long Beach Press-Telegram*; Paula Hamilton, food editor, *The Tribune* (Oakland); Barbara Hansen, food writer, *Los Angeles Times*; Joanne Hayes, food editor, *Country Living Magazine*; Rosina Wilson, food writer, *San Francisco Focus*; Jim McNeil, fireman chef on TV's *People Are Talking*, Master of Ceremonies.

All recipes entered in the contest become the property of the Gilroy Garlic Festival Association. All of the recipes received each year are filed by category and made available to community members for testing in their own kitchens. Local cooks select recipes at random which they feel will appeal to their families or the more ambitious may choose to have a "garlic party" at which they prepare an entire meal of garlic-laced delicacies. Evaluation forms are provided which include information as to number of servings, ease of cooking, ease of obtaining ingredients, clarity of directions, overall evaluation and appeal and most importantly, free-lance comments. There's no mistaking comments such as, "Yuck! I wouldn't serve this to my dog" or "My family loved it" or "Our absolute favorite."

The Complete Garlic Lovers' Cookbook is a collection of the best of these tested recipes plus the recipes of the winners and finalists in the contests from 1979–1986.

Garlic-laced specialties were prepared in gigantic pans from morning to night as wave after wave of festival goers followed their noses to the bustling outdoor kitchen area.
Vacaville *Reporter*

Appetizers/Antipasti

Oysters Gilroy	22
Escargots Carmela	22
Baked Stuffed Garlic Clams	23
Marion and Linda's Baked Stuffed Clams	24
Garlic-Shrimp Hors d'Oeuvre	24
Shrimp Appetizer Supreme	25
All-American Egg Rolls	25
Appetizer Garlic Puffs	26
Aphra de Jacques	27
Texas Surprise	28
Garlic Squares	29
Garlic Fritters	29
Parsley-Garlic Finger Sandwiches	30
Garlic-Spinach Snacks	30
Whole Garlic Appetizer	31
Wowchos	32
Zucchini Appetizer Angelino	32
C.C.U. Garlic-Stuffed Jalapenos	33
Vessey's Deep-Fried Garlic	33
Zucchini and Mushroom Hors d'Oeuvres	34
Pesto Mushrooms	34
Garlic Mushrooms Morgan Hill	35
Italian Sausage Stuffed Mushrooms	35
Mushrooms of the Auvergne	36
Mushrooms a la 'Rissa	37
Artichoke Hearts Marinati	38
Rose Emma's Eggplant Relish	38
The Greatest Guacamole Ole!	39
Creamy Garlic Guacamole	39
Garlic Guacamole	40
Slender Cheesy Spread	40
Auntie Peggy's Garlic Spread	41
Stinky Cheese	41
"Too Easy"	42
Creamy Garlic Herb Cheese	42
Toasted Almond Cheese Ball	42

Roasted Garlic Puree Dip   43

Dragon Dip   43

People Always Ask for this
    Recipe Party Dip   44

Antipasto Aglio   45

Garlic Artichoke Dip   45

Eggplant Dip Solano   46

Manny's Portuguese Garlic Dip   46

Dave's Favorite Garlic Dip   46

Garlic Herb Dip   47

Mexi-Gilroy Garlic Dip   47

California Crab Dip   48

Fresh Garlic Vegetable Dip   48

Tennent Garlic Dip   49

Dip with a Zip   49

Garlic Veggie Dip   49

Peanuts and Slivers   50

Mock Caviar   51

Ripe Olives with a Hint of Garlic   51

Great Garlic Olives   51

Bagna Cauda   52

Sunflower Snaps   52

Garlic-Spiced Walnuts   53

David's Preserved Peppers   53

Garlic Popcorn Balls   54

Garlic-Basil Popcorn   54

QUICK AND EASY APPETIZERS

For an easy cheese spread, combine cream cheese, grated sharp cheese, seasoned salt and minced garlic with enough mayonnaise to moisten. Shape into a ball or log and roll in chopped nuts. Serve with crackers.

You can make aioli—the French garlic mayonnaise—in a hurry. To a cup of ordinary mayonnaise, add 2 or 3 finely chopped fresh garlic cloves. Serve as a dip for vegetables or as a sauce for meats or fish.

Stuff ripe or green pitted olives with almonds. Place stuffed olives in a jar with liquid from kosher or spicy pickles and 5 or 6 cloves of fresh garlic. Chill for 24 hours.

Spinach dip is lovely with crackers or vegetable sticks. Cook a package of frozen spinach, squeezing out water. Add chopped green onions, minced parsley, two cloves of minced garlic and enough mayonnaise to make thick dip consistency. Add salt to taste.

Peel fresh garlic cloves and saute in a small amount of oil sprinkled with oregano. Turn often until well browned. Drain on paper towels and sprinkle with coarsely ground salt. Serve warm for nibbling with cold beverages.

Finalist In 1984 Recipe Contest: JUDGE STEVEN E. HALPERN, Emeryville, CA

The unusual anise-like flavor of the Pernod used in this recipe helps to create a sauce of intriguing complexity which blends very well with the oysters. An excellent first course for a very special dinner.

OYSTERS GILROY

12   medium cloves fresh
     garlic, unpeeled
½   ripe avocado
¾   teaspoon salt
⅛   teaspoon black pepper
1/16 teaspoon cayenne pepper
3   tablespoons Pernod
2   tablespoons Worcester-
     shire Sauce
2   tablespoons heavy cream
4   tablespoons melted
     butter
2   dozen medium-size
     oysters in half shell
     Rock salt

Wrap garlic in aluminum foil and bake in 325-degree oven for ½ hour. Cool to room temperature. Pinch cloves and squeeze out garlic. Add to food processor with remaining ingredients except butter and oysters and process until mixture is thoroughly pureed. Then add butter in slow stream until incorporated into puree. Place oysters in half shell on bed of rock salt in baking pan. Bake at 450 degrees on middle level of oven for 6 minutes. Remove. Cover each oyster with puree and return to oven for 1 minute. Serve with sourdough bread and dry white wine. Makes 4 to 6 appetizer servings.

ESCARGOTS CARMELA

What garlic cookbook would be complete without a recipe for garlic-buttered snails? This variation was an entry in the first Great Garlic Recipe Contest and Cook-off. You might try a light sprinkling of Parmesan cheese on each snail before baking. Serve with plenty of hot French bread to sop up the garlic butter!

Recipe contest entry: Carmela M. Meely, Walnut Creek, CA

4   oz. butter, softened
1   tablespoon chopped
     parsley
3   cloves fresh garlic,
     minced
1   minced shallot
     Pepper
     Salt
     Pinch ground nutmeg
1   tablespoon white wine *or*
     champagne
1   dozen snails and shells

Cream butter; add all ingredients, except snails, and mix until well-blended. Put a bit of butter into each snail shell; add snails and cover each with a dollop of butter mixture. Bake at 350 degrees for 10 minutes. Makes 1 dozen.

Finalist in 1984 Recipe Contest: ROSINA WILSON, Albany, CA

This marvelous hors d'oeuvre is festive, elegant and absolutely a snap to prepare. Serve with a dry California or Italian white wine such as Sauvignon Blanc or Soave. Or serve champagne to heighten the mood of the festivity.

BAKED STUFFED GARLIC CLAMS

20 to 30 cloves fresh garlic
 3 cans (6½ oz. *each*) chopped clams, drained (about 1½ cups) or the equivalent in steamed, chopped fresh clams
 ¾ cup butter, softened
 1 tablespoon fresh oregano *or* 1 teaspoon dried
 ⅓ cup frozen *or* fresh cooked spinach
 ¼ cup sherry
 1 cup French bread crumbs
 ¼ cup minced parsley
 2 tablespoons lemon juice
 2 teaspoons pignoli (pine nuts) *or* chopped walnuts
 ½ teaspoon salt
 ¼ teaspoon *each* nutmeg, black pepper, and cayenne pepper

Garnishes
 Sliced large fresh garlic cloves dipped in olive oil, pignoli, cayenne pepper and lemon wedges

Mince or press garlic to make ¾ cup. In large bowl, mix garlic and other ingredients, except garnishes, and spoon generously into clam or scallop shells. Decorate each with a slice of garlic, pignoli and sprinkle of cayenne pepper. Bake at 375 degrees for 25 to 30 minutes until bread crumbs turn golden brown and centers are cooked through. Serve piping hot with lemon wedges. Makes about 8 servings.

MARION AND LINDA'S BAKED STUFFED CLAMS

Rated excellent by all who have tried them, these stuffed clams can be made ahead, frozen and popped in the oven just half an hour before serving time.   *Recipe contest entry: Marion Molnar and Linda Hussar, Gilroy, CA*

8 slices bacon
1½ tablespoons oil
3 cloves fresh garlic, minced
2 tablespoons chopped parsley
1 tablespoon chopped onion
⅓ cup plus 2 tablespoons dry bread crumbs
Pinch of oregano
Dash of pepper
Salt, if necessary, but very little
2 cups chopped clams, fresh-steamed *or* canned
⅔ cup clam liquid
3 tablespoons grated Parmesan cheese

Render fat from bacon, and reserve 1½ tablespoons drippings. Drain on paper towels. Combine drippings and oil in pan and gently saute garlic, parsley, and onion. Add ⅓ cup bread crumbs, oregano, pepper, and salt if needed. Heat not more than 3 minutes. Add clams and clam liquid and mix well. Spoon into individual baking dishes or clean clam shells. Sprinkle with cheese and remaining bread crumbs. Dust with paprika and sprinkle with pieces of reserved bacon. Bake at 350 degrees about 25 minutes or until tops are brown and bacon crisp. Baking time will depend on the size of serving. Stuffed clams may be made ahead of time and frozen, then baked 35 minutes. Makes 4 to 6 servings.

GARLIC-SHRIMP HORS D'OEUVRE

Even those who claim not to like garlic will help themselves to seconds when you offer them this tasty appetizer spread.

Recipe contest entry: Jan Larsen, Kings Beach, CA

2 cups chopped fresh cooked shrimp
4 tablespoons finely chopped fresh garlic
2 tablespoons finely chopped celery
1 teaspoon vinegar
¼ teaspoon white pepper
3 tablespoons mayonnaise

Combine all ingredients, adjusting mayonnaise if necessary to achieve spreading consistency. Serve on crisp crackers.

SHRIMP APPETIZER SUPREME

This excellent shrimp appetizer could be served as a main dish with either rice or noodles. *Recipe contest entry: Susan Strommer, Los Angeles, CA*

2 lbs. extra-large shrimp
1 teaspoon salt
½ teaspoon pepper
4 tablespoons lemon juice
3 cloves fresh garlic, crushed
4 tablespoons mayonnaise
1½ cups fine dry bread crumbs
1 teaspoon crushed basil leaves
2 teaspoons chopped parsley
½ teaspoon dill weed
½ cup melted butter
4 tablespoons olive oil

Shell and devein shrimp. Mix salt, pepper, lemon juice, garlic and mayonnaise. Stir in shrimp and refrigerate for 1 to 2 hours. Mix bread crumbs, basil, parsley and dill. Coat each shrimp with crumbs and place in single layer in shallow baking dish. Stir melted butter and olive oil into remaining marinade. Pour over shrimp. Bake at 400 degrees for 15 minutes. Makes 6 to 8 servings.

ALL-AMERICAN EGG ROLLS

Chinese egg roll wrappers, Polish sausages and French mustard combine with garlic for an "All-American" appetizer.
Recipe contest entry: Patricia Trinchero, Gilroy, CA

1 quart cooking oil
15 cloves fresh garlic, peeled
½ cup mayonnaise
½ cup softened cream cheese
2 heaping tablespoons prepared mustard
4 Polish sausages
1 egg
¼ teaspoon milk
8 large egg roll wrappers
Chopped parsley

Heat oil in frying pan to medium-high, about 350 degrees. Combine garlic, mayonnaise, cheese, and mustard in blender until smooth. Remove from blender. Cut each Polish sausage into two shorter halves and score lengthwise. Beat egg and milk with fork until smooth. Place each sausage half at end of egg roll wrapper, add a dollop of mustard sauce and roll sausage into wrapper, sealing ends with egg mixture. Fry in hot oil until lightly browned on all sides. Garnish with chopped parsley and serve with extra mustard sauce. Makes 8 servings.

Finalist in 1984 Recipe Contest: ROXANNE CHAN, Albany, CA

The garlic filling used to make this appetizer can also be used to stuff cold cooked artichokes and cold, blanched green peppers or as a topping for cold sliced meats.

APPETIZER GARLIC PUFFS

1 **small head fresh garlic, separated into cloves**
   Boiling water
½ **cup butter**
1 **cup all-purpose flour**
¼ **teaspoon salt**
4 **eggs**

Cover garlic cloves with boiling water. Let stand 5 minutes. Drain and peel. Finely mince. In a saucepan, melt butter in 1 cup boiling water. Add garlic, flour and salt all at once. Cook, stirring, until mixture forms a ball. Remove from heat. Cool slightly, then add eggs one at a time, beating after each addition until mixture is smooth. Drop by teaspoonfuls on a greased baking sheet. Bake in 400-degree oven for 10 minutes. Reduce heat to 325 degrees and continue to cook for 20 to 25 minutes or until golden. Remove from oven and cut in half. Cool. Fill with Garlic Filling. Makes about 20 appetizer puffs.

Garlic Filling
1 **small head fresh garlic, separated into cloves**
   Boiling water
2 **cups whipped cream (about ½ pint)**
1 **cup grated Parmesan cheese**
1 **green onion, finely chopped**
2 **tablespoons *each* chopped pimento, black olives and roasted almonds**

Cover garlic cloves with boiling water. Cook until cloves are soft. Peel and mash. Stir mashed garlic into whipped cream along with remaining ingredients.

Second Prize Winner 1984 Recipe Contest: KATHE HEWITT, La Jolla, CA

This prize-winning cook named her recipe to approximate the word "aphrodisiac," because her husband claimed eating it made him amorous. Who knows? Legend attributes garlic with many such tantalizing properties and this dish certainly cast a spell on the judges!

APHRA DE JACQUES   *Fried Jack Hors d'Oeuvres*

1½ lb. Monterey Jack cheese
    (7 x 3-inch block)
30 cloves fresh garlic
 4 cups peanut oil (more as
    needed)
 1 tablespoon Italian
    seasoning
 3 eggs, beaten
 2 cups all-purpose flour
 3 cups French bread
    crumbs*
 3 tablespoons chopped
    fresh parsley
 1 small jar marinara sauce

Slice cheese into 30 slices about ¼ inch thick. Peel garlic and slice each clove lengthwise into about 6 ovals. Heat oil in deep, heavy saucepan over medium-low heat. Add garlic ovals and simmer 5 to 7 minutes, being careful not to burn or brown cloves. Remove slices as they float to surface and are light brown in color. Drain on paper towel. Reserve oil for cheese. Mince garlic and mix with Italian seasoning. Spread half the cheese slices evenly with garlic mixture. Press remaining cheese slices on each to make 15 bars. Dip flour-coated pieces into egg again, then into bread crumbs mixed with parsley. Be sure to cover sides. Reheat oil to medium-high and fry cheese in oil a few pieces at a time until lightly browned (takes about 2 minutes). Skim particles from oil as they accumulate. Drain cheese on paper towels and keep warm until all are fried. Serve with toothpicks and Marinara Sauce for dipping. Makes about 15 pieces.

* Use day old bread and prepare crumbs in food processor. Dry packaged crumbs may be used but are not as attractive when fried.

Finalist in 1982 Recipe Contest: KAREN MAHSHI, Concord, CA

Another two-time finalist in the recipe contest, this creative cook devised a recipe guaranteed to delight garlic lovers everywhere. Whole cloves are cooked inside spicy meatballs, which can be prepared ahead and frozen before baking, to have on hand to prepare for a few drop-in friends or a crowd. If you freeze the unbaked appetizers, do *not* thaw, just add 5 to 10 minutes to the baking time.

TEXAS SURPRISE

50 to 60 cloves fresh garlic, peeled
12 oz. sharp Cheddar cheese
⅓ cup fresh parsley leaves (stems removed)
1 to 2 jalapeno peppers (optional)
6 cloves fresh garlic
6 oz. hot pork sausage
6 oz. mild pork sausage
2¼ cups buttermilk baking mix

Blanch 50 to 60 cloves garlic in boiling water 3 to 4 minutes. Drain and set aside to cool. In food processor fitted with shredding disc, grate cheese. Remove and set aside. Allow cheese and sausage to come to room temperature before mixing. In dry food processor bowl, chop parsley and peppers, if used, using steel blade. Use garlic press or side of wide-bladed knife to crush 6 cloves garlic. Add to processor, along with sausages and baking mix. Process until well mixed. Add cheese, and process only until well combined. Shape into 50 to 60 small balls, inserting a whole blanched garlic clove in each. At this point, balls may be frozen for baking at a later time. To bake at once, place balls on ungreased baking sheet. Bake at 325 degrees 20 to 25 minutes or until golden brown. Serve hot as an appetizer, plain or with a bowl of plain yogurt for dipping. Makes 50 to 60 appetizers.

GARLIC SQUARES

This baked appetizer will serve about 8 or 10 truly devoted garlic fans.

Recipe contest entry: Catherine A. Peters, San Francisco, CA

1 cup fresh garlic, coarsely chopped
1 cup onions, thinly sliced
¼ cup plus 2 tablespoons butter
2 cups flour
2 teaspoons baking powder
1 teaspoon salt
2 tablespoons finely chopped parsley
1 teaspoon dill
1 cup milk
½ cup sharp Cheddar cheese

Preheat oven to 450 degrees. Gently saute garlic and onions in 2 tablespoons butter about 10 minutes until tender, but not brown. Sift flour, baking powder and salt into mixing bowl. Cut in ¼ cup butter until mixture is crumbly like cornmeal. Add parsley, dill and milk; stir just until evenly moist. Pour into well-greased 8 x 8-inch pan. Spread garlic and onions on top, then cover with cheese. Bake for 25 to 30 minutes. Cool slightly and cut into squares.

Regional Winner 1984 Recipe Contest: HELEN MARTY, Phoenix, AZ

This is a variation of the French "beignets" so popular in New Orleans as well as in France. The garlic is included in the rich egg batter. The filling is made with sour cream flavored with Parmesan cheese and oregano. For more garlic flavor, try adding some fresh minced garlic to the filling as well.

GARLIC FRITTERS

10 large cloves fresh garlic
¼ teaspoon salt
6 tablespoons butter
1 cup water
1 cup flour
4 eggs
3 to 4 lb. fat for deep frying
¼ cup sour cream
¼ cup grated Parmesan cheese
Dash powdered oregano

Chop garlic fine and add salt. Mash into a paste. In saucepan place butter, garlic, and water. Bring to a boil. Add flour, stirring quickly into a mass. Remove from heat. Add eggs, one at a time, being certain to fully incorporate each one. Form the dough into small bite-sized mounds and deep fry at about 370 degrees until golden brown. Drain on a paper towel. Cut each fritter into two pieces. Mix sour cream, Parmesan and oregano and place ½ teaspoon of mixture on half of each fritter, top with other half. Makes about 4 dozen tasty hors d'oeuvres or snacks.

PARSLEY-GARLIC FINGER SANDWICHES

Parsley and garlic are good friends. The chlorophyll in the parsley helps to prevent the odor of garlic on the breath. Combined with mayonnaise as a spread, the two herbs make very tasty finger sandwich appetizers.   *Recipe contest entry: Mrs. George Parrish, Gilroy, CA*

2   bunches finely chopped parsley
2   large cloves fresh garlic, pressed
½   cup mayonnaise
1   large loaf extra-thin white bread, crusts removed

Combine parsley, garlic and mayonnaise; mix well. Spread mixture between two slices of bread and cut diagonally to make four finger sandwiches. Refrigerate until ready to use. These can be made early on the day to be used, but *not* the day before.

GARLIC-SPINACH SNACKS

Anyone who likes garlic and spinach should really enjoy this recipe. Can also be made ahead and frozen for later use.

Recipe contest entry: Candy Barnhart, Hollywood, CA

2   pkg. (10 oz. *each*) frozen chopped spinach
4   eggs
1   can (10¾ oz.) cream of mushroom soup
1   large onion, finely chopped
½   cup canned mushroom stems and pieces, drained
¼   cup grated Parmesan cheese
¼   cup Italian bread crumbs
8   cloves fresh garlic, minced
¼   teaspoon *each* ground oregano and dried basil
⅛   teaspoon coarsely ground black pepper

In saucepan, heat spinach in just enough water to cover until completely thawed. Drain well. Beat eggs in large mixing bowl. Add remaining ingredients and spinach and mix well. Turn into a greased 11 x 7 x 1½-inch glass baking dish and bake in a preheated 325-degree oven for 35 minutes or until set to the touch. Serve slightly warm or cold, cut into 1½-inch squares. Makes approximately 36 snacks.

Finalist in 1984 Recipe Contest: PATRICK MARKEY, Los Angeles, CA

This garlic appetizer can be held in the refrigerator for up to 10 days. It's especially good for those who enjoy snacking on tart and tangy tidbits.

WHOLE GARLIC APPETIZER

½ cup olive oil
8 whole heads fresh garlic
2 large sweet red onions, quartered
1 tablespoon whole peppercorns
4 stalks celery, chopped
4 medium carrots, sliced
¼ teaspoon *each* rosemary, thyme, oregano, marjoram, coriander, basil (fresh if possible)
¾ cup white wine vinegar
¼ cup dry white wine
½ cup water
8 to 10 bay leaves
½ teaspoon dry mustard
1 small can pickled green chiles, about 4 oz.

Heat oil in skillet. Peel outer covering from garlic heads. and take a ½-inch slice from top of each head, exposing meat of cloves, but leaving heads intact. Saute garlic, onions, and peppercorns in oil for 3 minutes. Add celery, carrots, rosemary, thyme, oregano, marjoram, coriander and basil. Saute 5 minutes, stirring. Add vinegar, wine, water, bay leaves and dry mustard. Simmer for 10 minutes. Stir in chiles and simmer for 3 minutes. Remove from heat, strain, reserving garlic and 1 cup cooking liquid. Place garlic heads in flat baking dish. Pour reserved liquid over, cover and refrigerate. Serve cold as an appetizer for spreading on French bread rounds or crackers. Also can be eaten plain as a relish course or cloves peeled and mixed in salads. Makes 8 servings.

Second Prize Winner 1983 Recipe Contest:

LEONARD BRILL, San Francisco, CA

This spiced-up recipe for nachos with whole baked garlic cloves for extra flavor had the judges rolling their eyes with delight as they awarded second place to its creator.

WOWCHOS

2 **large heads fresh garlic, separated into cloves and peeled**
2 **tablespoons oil**
Tortilla chips
¼ **cup chopped red onion**
1 **can (4 oz.) chopped green chiles**
⅓ **cup sliced pimento-stuffed olives (optional)**
1½ **cups grated Pepper Jack cheese**
Chopped cilantro
Chopped green onion tops

Coat garlic cloves with oil and bake in 375-degree oven for 30 minutes, or until soft and golden. Cover metal baking pan (approximately 9 x 12 inches) with overlapping tortilla chips. Distribute garlic, onion, chiles and olives evenly over the chips. Cover with cheese and bake at 400 degrees for 5 minutes or until cheese melts. Top with cilantro and green onion and serve. Makes about 4 appetizer servings.

ZUCCHINI APPETIZER ANGELINO

Italian squash, zucchini, is abundant the year 'round and is usually reasonably priced, which makes it a good choice to help keep the budget in line when entertaining. The aroma while this dish bakes is so good, your family or guests will be waiting expectantly for their first taste!

Courtesy of: Betty Angelino, Gilroy, CA

4 **cups unpeeled zucchini, grated**
1¾ **cups biscuit mix**
¾ **cup Parmesan cheese**
½ **cup vegetable oil**
4 **eggs, beaten**
1 **large onion, chopped *or* grated**
3 **cloves fresh garlic, minced**
3 **tablespoons minced parsley**
½ **teaspoon salt**
½ **teaspoon oregano, crushed**

Combine all ingredients in large mixing bowl and stir until well blended. Spread in greased baking dish 13x9x2. Bake in preheated 350-degree oven for 25 to 30 minutes until golden brown. Cut into bite-sized serving pieces. May be served hot or cold.

Second Prize Winner 1985 Recipe Contest:

BECKY BOEHNE, Portland, OR

Here's another one for the stout-hearted. As a matter of fact, Becky made up this appetizer when she was working in the coronary care unit of an Oregon hospital.

C.C.U. GARLIC-STUFFED JALAPENOS

1 large ripe avocado, peeled and mashed
1 pkg. (8 oz.) cream cheese, softened
2 whole heads fresh garlic, finely chopped
1 large yellow onion, finely chopped
⅓ to ½ large bell pepper, finely chopped
20 to 30 jalapeno peppers, canned in oil

Blend avocado and cream cheese with a fork. Add garlic, onion and bell pepper. Mix thoroughly. Trim stems from jalapeno peppers. Cut in halves lengthwise. Remove seeds. Fill each half with approximately 1 tablespoon of filling. Serve either at room temperature or chilled. Filling may be stored in refrigerator for up to 5 days. Makes 40 to 60 Stuffed Jalapenos.

VESSEY'S DEEP-FRIED GARLIC

Until you've tried these deep-fried garlic cloves, you probably won't believe how delicious they are or how much fun it is to serve them.

Courtesy of: Wayne Vessey, Hollister, CA

2 whole heads fresh garlic
Boiling water
1 cup biscuit mix
1 egg
½ cup beer
2 teaspoons parsley flakes
½ teaspoon salt
Vegetable oil for deep frying

Separate heads and peel garlic. Drop cloves into boiling water and, when boiling resumes, blanch for 3 to 4 minutes. The longer the cloves cook, the milder their flavor, but don't overcook, or they will be mushy. Drain and pour cold water over to cool. Meanwhile, prepare batter by combining biscuit mix, egg, beer, parsley and salt. Heat vegetable oil in deep pot or fry cooker. Dip each cooked clove of garlic in batter and fry until golden brown in color. Remove and drain on paper towels. Serve hot.

ZUCCHINI AND MUSHROOM HORS D'OEUVRES

With everyone trying to eat more nutritious foods and avoid "empty calories," this healthful, delicious and simple-to-prepare company hors d'oeuvre should help to make you a popular host or hostess.

Recipe contest entry: Linda Tarvin, Morgan Hill, CA

½ cup butter *or* margarine
4 cloves fresh garlic, minced
2 tablespoons chopped parsley
   Pepper
1 lb. mushroom caps
2 medium-sized zucchini, sliced ¼ inch thick
   Parmesan cheese
   Paprika

Combine butter, garlic, parsley and cook until bubbly. Add pepper to taste and then chill slightly so that mixture is not runny. Arrange mushrooms, cupped side up, and zucchini slices on ovenproof serving dishes. Top caps and slices with ¼ teaspoon garlic butter mixture. Sprinkle with Parmesan cheese and paprika. Cook 1 to 2 dozen at a time for 2 to 4 minutes under broiler.

PESTO MUSHROOMS

Large cheese-stuffed mushrooms are topped with tangy pesto sauce and baked for 15 minutes, just until all the flavors blend. If fresh basil isn't available, fresh spinach can be substituted.

Recipe contest entry: Jonny Butcher, North Highlands, CA

16 large fresh mushrooms
2 or more oz. feta cheese

Clean mushrooms; remove stems and reserve for other use. Place mushroom caps, hollow side up, on rimmed 10 x 15-inch baking sheet. Fill each cap with feta cheese and set aside.

Pesto
2½ cups lightly packed fresh basil leaves *or* 2½ cups fresh spinach leaves and 3 tablespoons dry basil
5 oz. Parmesan cheese, cut into chunks *or* 1 cup grated Parmesan
3 cloves fresh garlic, peeled
¼ cup shelled walnuts
⅓ cup olive oil, preferably extra virgin

In food processor with metal blade, process basil, Parmesan cheese, garlic and walnuts until thoroughly combined. With processor running, slowly drizzle in oil and continue processing 5 to 10 seconds longer until well mixed. Top stuffed mushroom caps with about 1 tablespoon pesto and bake in preheated oven at 375 degrees for 15 to 20 minutes. Makes 5 to 6 servings.

Finalist in 1979 Recipe Contest: LINDA TARVIN, Morgan Hill, CA

Linda was among the top ten finalists in the first Great Garlic Recipe Contest and her mushroom recipe drew raves not only for its flavor but for its attractive presentation with whole garlic bulbs used for decoration.

GARLIC MUSHROOMS MORGAN HILL

4 cloves fresh garlic, minced
⅓ cup olive oil
⅔ cup white wine vinegar
⅓ cup dry red *or* white wine
2 tablespoons soy sauce
2 tablespoons honey
2 tablespoons chopped parsley
1 tablespoon salt
2 lbs. fresh mushrooms

Saute garlic in oil. Add vinegar, wine, soy sauce, honey, parsley and salt. Stir until mixture is well blended and hot. Place mushrooms in heat-proof container with tightly fitting lid. Pour hot mixture over mushrooms; allow to marinate from 1 to 3 hours, or more, turning over several times. Save marinade for later use on more mushrooms or use it as a salad dressing.

ITALIAN SAUSAGE STUFFED MUSHROOMS

Italians everywhere love their mushrooms. Some like them best as an appetizer stuffed with garlic and Italian sausage.

Recipe contest entry: Carmela M. Meely, Walnut Creek, CA

18 to 20 large mushrooms
½ lb. Italian sausage (regular *or* fennel, bulk type)
½ cup chopped onion
3 cloves fresh garlic, minced
3 tablespoons oil
¼ cup bread crumbs
1 egg
¼ cup grated Parmesan cheese
Additional Parmesan cheese for garnish

Remove stems from mushrooms. Chop stems. Brown sausage, onion, garlic and chopped stems in oil. Drain well. Cool. Mix with bread crumbs, egg, cheese. Stuff mushrooms full. Bake at 350 degrees for 15 to 20 minutes. Sprinkle with extra Parmesan. Makes about 6 appetizer servings.

MUSHROOMS OF THE AUVERGNE

The creator of this recipe recommends that you set the mood for relaxed dining by playing "Songs of the Auvergne" while you put the finishing touches on this do-ahead starter course. The aroma of fresh garlic and the country songs of France are a perfect blend.

Recipe contest entry: Bob Comara, Los Angeles, CA

12 medium mushrooms
 3 to 4 tablespoons butter
10 leaves fresh spinach, washed and drained
 3 large cloves fresh garlic, minced (about ½ teaspoon)
 3 tablespoons grated Parmesan cheese
¼ teaspoon salt
¼ cup dry white wine
 2 teaspoons water

Brush mushrooms with damp paper towel to remove surface dirt and remove stems by girdling with a sharp knife. Reserve stems for other use. Place mushroom caps, tops down, in a well-buttered casserole. Blanch spinach in boiling water for 3 minutes, rinse in cold water and drain. Thoroughly combine garlic and butter. Mince spinach and blend with garlic butter. Fill mushroom caps evenly with butter mixture and sprinkle each with Parmesan cheese and salt. Cover with plastic wrap and refrigerate until ready to bake. When ready, heat oven to 300 degrees, add wine and water to bottom of casserole and bake for 20 minutes until mushrooms are cooked but still firm. Makes 12 appetizers.

MUSHROOM A LA 'RISSA

Mushrooms stuffed with a combination of nutritious ingredients are a favorite of the Mayrons' 3-year-old daughter who even likes them for breakfast and says they are "yummy."

Recipe courtesy of: Cindy Mayron, Gilroy, CA

24 fresh mushrooms
   (approximately 1 lb.)
 1 medium onion, finely
   chopped
 8 tablespoons butter *or*
   margarine
 4 to 6 cloves fresh garlic,
   chopped
 2 tablespoons soy sauce
 1 tablespoon sherry
   Dash pepper
¾ cup Grape Nuts Cereal
 8 oz. Mozzarella cheese,
   shredded

Remove stems from mushrooms and chop fine. Wipe caps with damp paper towel; set aside. Saute onion in 4 tablespoons butter over medium-high heat until crispy-brown, but not burned. Add 1 table-spoon butter, garlic, stems, 1 table-spoon soy sauce, sherry and pepper. Cook until mushrooms are soft and have changed color. Add Grape Nuts; raise heat to high. Cook, stirring constantly, until moisture is absorbed. Add 1 or 2 tablespoons cereal if needed. Remove from heat and cool. Add cheese and mix thoroughly. Stuff mushroom caps with cooked mixture and place in 9 x 13-inch baking pan. Top each with remaining soy sauce and butter. Bake at 350 degrees for 15 minutes until mushrooms are cooked and cheese is melted. Makes 24 appetizers.

The festival was one of those happy bits of Americana when the whole town turns out.
MARJORIE RICE
Copley News Service

ARTICHOKE HEARTS MARINATI

From nearby Castroville come the artichoke hearts for this popular Italian antipasto. Whole artichokes may also be steamed or boiled until tender, the marinade spooned over them and chilled for about 6 hours, then served cold.

1 pkg. (9 oz.) frozen
   artichoke hearts
2 tablespoons lemon juice
2 tablespoons olive oil
¾ teaspoon garlic salt
¼ teaspoon oregano leaves
¼ teaspoon chervil leaves
¼ teaspoon tarragon leaves

Cook artichoke hearts following directions on package. Drain and put in small bowl. Combine remaining ingredients and pour over artichoke hearts. Chill at least 2 hours before serving.

ROSE EMMA'S EGGPLANT RELISH

Eggplant is a very versatile vegetable and it's at its best when flavored with garlic, onions and tomatoes.

Courtesy of: Rose Emma Pelliccione, Gilroy, CA

3 cups eggplant, peeled
   and cut in ½-inch cubes
⅓ cup chopped green
   peppers
1 medium onion, minced
3 cloves fresh garlic,
   pressed
⅓ cup oil
1 can (6 oz.) tomato paste
1 can (4 oz.) mushroom
   stems and pieces
½ cup pimento-stuffed
   olives
¼ cup water
2 tablespoons red wine
   vinegar
1½ teaspoons sugar
1 teaspoon seasoned salt
½ teaspoon oregano
¼ teaspoon pepper

Put eggplant, green pepper, onion, garlic and oil in skillet. Cover and cook gently for 10 minutes, stirring occasionally. Add tomato paste, mushrooms with liquid and remaining ingredients. Cover and simmer 30 minutes. Turn into covered dish; refrigerate overnight to blend flavors. Serve with crackers and chips. Makes about 1 quart. Also keeps well frozen.

THE GREATEST GUACAMOLE OLE!

A few tips from the Chef: If the avocados are not quite ripe, you may chop them very fine and add a few teaspoonfuls of sour cream or mayonnaise to the recipe. Don't omit the cilantro, as its flavor is essential in this recipe. For a fiery taste, use jalapenos, but be sure to wear rubber gloves to protect your hands while preparing them.

Recipe contest entry: Catherine Miller, San Francisco, CA

4 ripe avocados, peeled and seeded
3 cloves fresh garlic, minced
Juice of 1 lime
1 bunch fresh cilantro (coriander), chopped
5 scallions, chopped
5 peperoncini (mild Italian pickled peppers), chopped *or* 1 to 2 jalapeno peppers, minced
½ teaspoon salt *or* to taste
¼ teaspoon Tabasco *or* to taste
2 medium tomatoes, chopped

Mash avocados, lime juice and garlic together with a fork. Stir in cilantro, scallions, peppers and seasonings. Stir briskly until smooth in texture, then gently stir in chopped tomatoes. Serves 8 to 10 as a dip with chips.

NOTE: This will hold for several days in the refrigerator, but is best when served the same day.

CREAMY GARLIC GUACAMOLE

Don't relegate this garlic lovers' guacamole to the chip and dip department. Use it as a topping for poultry dishes, dolloped into soups, or spread on pita or other breads before adding meat or cheese to make savory sandwiches.

Recipe contest entry: Becky Ayres, Salem, OR

1 large *or* 2 small heads (not cloves) fresh garlic
1 ripe avocado
1 pkg. (3 oz.) cream cheese, softened
3 tablespoons sour cream
1 tablespoon fresh lemon juice
¼ teaspoon salt

Place whole head(s) of garlic in baking dish, drizzle with oil and roast in 350-degree oven for about 1 hour or until garlic is soft. When cool, gently separate cloves and squeeze garlic out into blender or bowl. Peel and pit avocado, add to garlic along with remaining ingredients. Blend or mash until smooth. Serve with vegetables and chips or as a topping for Mexican dishes. Makes approximately 1½ cups.

GARLIC GUACAMOLE

This is no ordinary guacamole! It's a unique variation. Once you start eating it you won't stop until you've scraped the bowl clean.

Recipe contest entry: Chris Ursich, San Mateo, CA

1 ripe California avocado
⅛ lb. tofu, firm-style (found in fresh produce section of most supermarkets)
4 to 6 cloves fresh garlic
½ medium-sized bell pepper
2 green onions
2 tablespoons freshly chopped parsley
½ teaspoon curry powder
½ teaspoon oregano
½ teaspoon thyme
¼ teaspoon freshly ground black pepper
4 to 6 tablespoons hot sauce
   Juice of ½ lime (*or* lemon)
   Tortilla chips for dipping

Mash avocado and tofu in bowl. Squeeze garlic through press and add. Finely chop bell pepper and green onion and stir in. Add herbs and spices. Mix well. Add hot sauce. Stir in lime juice. Eat with tortilla chips. Garlic Guacamole can be refrigerated, but do not make more than a few hours in advance.

SLENDER CHEESY SPREAD

There's no joy in being on a diet, but if you have a few favorite low-calorie standby recipes, you can usually make it through the difficult times when you just "have to have something" without going too far over your calorie limit. Try this cheesy spread with all kinds of vegetables or diet crackers.

Recipe contest entry: Mrs. Gilbert Blakey, San Clemente, CA

1 carton (16 oz.) 4% fat cottage cheese
3 cloves fresh garlic, minced
1 tablespoon finely chopped parsley
1 tablespoon mayonnaise
1 tablespoon wine vinegar
   Salt and pepper to taste
   Celery salt to taste

Mix all ingredients together, cover and refrigerate overnight. Use to stuff celery, scooped-out small zucchini halves or to spread on crackers or wedges of toast. Sprinkle tops with paprika for added color.

AUNTIE PEGGY'S GARLIC SPREAD

Named for a favorite auntie, this creamy, garlic spread is enough for two whole loaves of French bread. Great as a topping for potatoes, pasta and veggies, too!

Recipe contest entry: Denise Domeniconi, San Francisco, CA

6 cloves fresh garlic, peeled
6 green onions
1 pkg. (8 oz.) cream cheese, softened
2 cups shredded Cheddar cheese
2 tablespoons mayonnaise
3 teaspoons soy sauce

In blender or food processor, mince garlic. Add onions and chop finely. Add cream cheese and mix thoroughly. Then add remaining ingredients and process until well blended. Spread on halved loaves of French bread and place under broiler until bubbly.

STINKY CHEESE

Easy to make, this excellent cheese spread is good to have on hand to stuff celery, spread on crackers, for grilled cheese sandwiches, as a topping for toasty French bread.

Recipe contest entry: Martin T. Quinlan, Woodland, CA

2 lb. sharp Cheddar or Tillamook cheese
1 lb. Monterey Jack cheese
1 can (4 oz.) whole green chiles
1 jar (4 oz.) pimentos
10 to 14 cloves fresh garlic
½ cup dried minced onion
1/8 teaspoon ground pepper
Garlic powder
¾ cup mayonnaise
1 cup water (approx.)

Grate all cheese into shallow pan or mixing bowl. Dice chile peppers and pimentos and sprinkle over grated cheese. Press garlic cloves, adding both juice and pulp to cheese. Add minced onions and pepper. Generously sprinkle powdered garlic over all. Thoroughly mix together; then add mayonnaise and blend, adding water as needed to attain a smooth mixture. Store in airtight container for at least 2 days before using. Makes about 8 cups.

"TOO EASY"

A good spread to put together in a hurry when friends or family arrive unexpectedly.
Courtesy of: Doris Lane, Gilroy, CA

2 cups grated Cheddar cheese
¼ cup (approx.) mayonnaise
1 clove fresh garlic, minced fine
1 teaspoon dehydrated parsley flakes

Combine grated cheese, mayonnaise and garlic. Mix well. Be sure it is moist. Increase mayonnaise if necessary. Refrigerate for awhile to allow flavors to mingle. When ready to serve, spread mixture on muffins or French bread and broil until cheese is melted. Garnish with parsley. May be served with rye crackers.

CREAMY GARLIC HERB CHEESE

Creamy-rich and delightfully herbed, Boursin cheese is a favorite spread for crackers. Here's an easy homemade version that tries to capture a similar flavor. *Recipe contest entry: Julie and Gary Crites, La Verne, CA*

2 pkg. (8 oz. *each*) cream cheese
1 pint sour cream
½ cup butter
3 cloves fresh garlic, pressed
¼ cup snipped chives

Mix all ingredients in blender or food processor. Chill in refrigerator several hours. Warm to room temperature before serving with crackers or as a dip for fresh raw vegetables.

TOASTED ALMOND CHEESE BALL

An attractive cheese ball, good and garlicky and all the better when it has aged a little. *Recipe contest entry: Nancy Brackmann, Pittsburgh, PA*

2 pkg. (8 oz. *each*) cream cheese, softened
2 cups grated sharp cheese
3 cloves fresh garlic, minced
Dash Tabasco
1 cup slivered almonds
1 tablespoon butter

Combine first 4 ingredients and form into a ball. In skillet, toast almonds in butter until browned. Cool and insert, one by one, into cheese ball. Wrap in foil and allow to ripen in refrigerator for at least 48 hours. May then be frozen, if desired.

Winner Best Recipe Using Most Garlic 1984 Recipe Contest:

MARY FENCL, Forestdale, MA

This is a truly versatile recipe. The puree can be used on cooked vegetables, fish, steaks, salad greens or baked potatoes. You can double the recipe if you want to keep some on hand.

ROASTED GARLIC PUREE DIP

6 large heads fresh garlic (about 72 cloves)
2 pkg. (8 oz. *each*) cream cheese, at room temperature
4 oz. blue cheese, at room temperature
¾ cup milk
2 tablespoons chopped fresh parsley
Crudites (mixed fresh vegetables, sliced for dipping)

Remove outer covering on garlic. Do not peel or separate the cloves. Place each garlic head on a large square of heavy aluminum foil. Fold up the foil, so the cloves are completely wrapped. Bake for 1 hour at 350 degrees. Remove garlic from oven and cool for 10 minutes. Separate cloves and squeeze cloves to remove cooked garlic. Discard skins. In food processor, mix cheeses, milk and garlic until smooth. Place in serving dish. Sprinkle with parsley. Serve as a dip with crudites for dipping. Makes about 5 cups.

DRAGON DIP

This garlic-cheese dip should be served warm in a chafing dish with chips, crackers or, better yet, with fresh vegetables.

Recipe contest entry: Cynthia Kannenberg, Brown Deer, WI

1 pkg. (8 oz.) cream cheese
6 cloves fresh garlic, finely minced *or* 1½ teaspoons garlic powder
2 cups grated Cheddar cheese
6 tablespoons half-and-half
1 teaspoon Worcestershire sauce
¼ teaspoon dry mustard
¼ teaspoon onion salt
3 drops Tabasco
6 slices bacon, fried crisp and crumbled

Mix all ingredients except bacon in top of double boiler. Cook, stirring, until smooth and blended. Add bacon and heat through. Place in chafing dish and serve with dippers of your choice. Makes 3 cups.

Finalist in 1983 Recipe Contest: BETTY SHAW, Santee, CA

The best part of this recipe is when all the dip is gone and all that is left is the bread which is soaked in all those delicious ingredients. Just break the bread up and pass it around!

PEOPLE ALWAYS ASK FOR THIS RECIPE PARTY DIP

1 loaf sheepherders bread
¼ lb. butter
1 bunch green onions, chopped
12 cloves fresh garlic, minced finely
1 pkg. (8 oz.) cream cheese, at room temperature
16 oz. sour cream
12 oz. Cheddar cheese, grated
1 can (10 oz.) artichoke hearts, drained and cut into quarters (water pack not marinated)
6 small French rolls, sliced thinly, but not all the way through.

Cut a hole in the top of the bread loaf about 5 inches in diameter. If you wish, make a zigzag pattern to be decorative. Remove soft bread from cut portion and discard. Reserve crust to make top for loaf. Scoop out most of the soft inside portion of the loaf and save for other purposes, such as stuffing or dried bread crumbs. In about 2 tablespoons butter, saute green onions and half the garlic until onions wilt. Do not burn! Cut cream cheese into small chunks; add onions, garlic, sour cream and Cheddar cheese. Mix well. Fold in artichoke hearts. Put all of this mixture into hollowed out bread. Place top on bread and wrap in a double thickness of heavy-duty aluminum foil. Bake in 350-degree oven for 1½ to 2 hours. Slice French rolls thinly and butter with remaining butter and garlic. Wrap in foil and bake with big loaf for the last ½ hour. When ready, remove foil and serve, using slices of French rolls to dip out sauce. Makes enough for about 10 to 12 as an appetizer.

Finalist in 1979 Recipe Contest: M.J. FILLICE, Gilroy, CA

This wonderful and imaginative appetizer is the creation of one of Gilroy's finest amateur chefs who devised it for his companions on a hunting trip. When prepared this way, garlic's assertive flavor is diminished to a delicate, nut-like taste. The recipe was selected as a finalist in the First Great Garlic Recipe Contest.

ANTIPASTO AGLIO   *Garlic Antipasto*

30 large cloves fresh garlic
1 can (2 oz.) anchovy fillets
1 tablespoon finely chopped parsley
1 tablespoon butter, melted
1 tablespoon olive oil
Dash Tabasco
¼ cup olive oil
Sardine French bread, 2 or 3 dozen thinly sliced and toasted pieces. (Sardine is a long, thin bread also called "flute." Available in most markets.)

Peel garlic cloves and slice centers ⅛ inch thick. Press ends through garlic press to yield ¼ teaspoon. Place pressed garlic in small bowl with anchovies. Add parsley, butter, 1 teaspoon oil, and Tabasco; mash to a paste. Cover and refrigerate. Heat ¼ cup oil, add garlic slices and saute to a light golden brown—almost to a potato chip fry. *Do not overfry!* Spread anchovy paste on toast. Garnish with garlic slices and WHAM-O!—the taste of tastes! Follow with a sip of robust red wine. *Salute e buon appetito!!*

GARLIC ARTICHOKE DIP

Fresh garlic combines with artichokes from nearby Castroville to produce a tasty dip which is equally good with crispy chips, preferably the lower salt varieties, or fresh vegetable dippers. And oh, so easy!

Recipe courtesy of: Barbara Hay, Gilroy, CA

3 cloves fresh garlic, peeled
2 cans (8½ oz. *each*) artichoke hearts, drained
1 cup grated Parmesan cheese
1 cup mayonnaise
Juice of 1 lemon
Dash of Tabasco
Fresh vegetables or chips for dipping

In food processor with metal blade, chop garlic and artichoke hearts until medium fine. Place in small baking dish, add remaining ingredients and mix thoroughly. Bake in 350-degree oven for 30 minutes or until golden brown on top. Serve with vegetables or chips for dipping. Makes about 6 servings.

EGGPLANT DIP SOLANO

Everyone who has tried this says it's great for a company dish, and inexpensive as well.   *Recipe contest entry: Ruth Solano, San Jose, CA*

1 eggplant
¼ onion, minced
3 cloves fresh garlic, minced *or* pressed
   Olive oil
   Salt and pepper to taste

Cook eggplant in heavy skillet over low flame, turning frequently until skin is dark and crackles to the touch. Cool, peel and mash pulp; add onion and garlic. Add oil, a little at a time, while continuing to mash pulp, until mixture is creamy in texture. Eggplant absorbs the oil, so quite a bit is needed. Add salt and pepper to taste. Refrigerate. May be used as a dip for vegetables or on chunks of pita bread as a spread.

MANNY'S PORTUGUESE GARLIC DIP

Manny says this is soooo garlicky and soooo good that it always receives raves from guests or at potlucks.
    Recipe contest entry: Manny Santos, Carmichael, CA

1 pkg. (8 oz.) cream cheese, softened
6 to 8 large cloves fresh garlic, minced (*or* more for the daring)
¾ to 1 cup mayonnaise
1 teaspoon Worcestershire sauce (*or* to taste)
   Salt and pepper to taste

Mix all ingredients thoroughly, using just enough mayonnaise to reach preferred spreading or dipping consistency. Serve with chips for dipping or crackers for spreading. Makes 2 cups.

DAVE'S FAVORITE GARLIC DIP

Everyone likes garlic dip, and sometimes the simpler it is the better it is. Serve this with chips or crackers or use to stuff celery. Great!
    Recipe contest entry: Lois Biggs, Gilroy, CA

1 pkg. (8 oz.) cream cheese
3 tablespoons milk
5 large cloves fresh garlic
   Salt
   Parsley
   Paprika

With fork, mix cream cheese and milk in small bowl until it has the texture of peanut butter. Press garlic and add to cream cheese mixture. Salt to taste and mix thoroughly. Garnish with parsley and paprika. Refrigerate until ready to use.

GARLIC HERB DIP

This creamy dip can be thinned with ⅔ cup milk or buttermilk to make a delicious salad dressing or add 2 egg yolks and ¼ cup milk and pour over chicken before baking.

Recipe contest entry: Paula Linville, Aloha, OR

1 cup sour cream
½ cup mayonnaise
4 large cloves fresh garlic, minced
4 full sprigs fresh parsley, finely chopped
2 tablespoons Worcester-shire sauce
1 heaping tablespoon finely minced onion
1 tablespoon dill weed
1 teaspoon seasoned salt
3 drops Tabasco (*or to* taste)

Combine all ingredients thoroughly, cover and refrigerate overnight or up to four days for more potent flavor. Serve with dippers of your choice. Makes about 1½ cups.

MEXI-GILROY GARLIC DIP

House Rules: "No socializing or kissing allowed until everyone has tasted this garlicky dip." And it's great for discouraging party crashers. One friendly "Hi-i-i-i" is bound to send them scurrying.

Recipe contest entry: Sylvia Barber, Danville, CA

1 cup small curd cottage cheese
1 cup mayonnaise
1 can (4 oz.) diced green chiles
1 can (4 oz.) sliced black olives
6 cloves fresh garlic, minced
4 green onions, with tops, finely diced
1 large tomato, finely chopped
Salt and pepper to taste

Mix together all ingredients, cover and refrigerate. Serve with chips or veggies. Makes 4 cups.

CALIFORNIA CRAB DIP

California is well-known not only for its garlic but for the local crab, called Dungeness. You don't have to be a Californian to prepare this unusual and pleasing crabmeat combination. Canned or frozen crabmeat can be substituted if fresh is not available.

1 cup crabmeat (fresh, canned *or* frozen)
¼ cup lime juice (*or* lemon)
1 pkg. (3 oz.) cream cheese
¼ cup heavy cream
2 tablespoons mayonnaise
1 teaspoon instant minced onion
1 teaspoon shredded green onion
1 teaspoon Worcestershire sauce
½ teaspoon salt
¼ teaspoon garlic powder
⅛ teaspoon MSG (optional)
2 dashes cayenne *or* red pepper

Marinate crabmeat in lime (or lemon) juice 30 minutes. Beat together cream cheese, cream, mayonnaise and seasonings until smooth and creamy. Fold in marinated crabmeat. For an attractive presentation, serve in a deep shell or shell-shaped bowl nested in crushed ice with an interesting arrangement of bite-sized pieces of Chinese cabbage, celery, sliced cauliflowerets, green pepper strips and thin slices of carrot. Don't forget a basket of crackers or chips! Makes about 1½ cups.

FRESH GARLIC VEGETABLE DIP

Although there are vegetables in the dip itself, fresh vegetables for dipping also work well with this single, flavorful and healthful appetizer.   *Recipe contest entry: Susan Centrone, Sepulveda, CA*

1 carrot, finely chopped
⅓ cup peeled and chopped cucumber
⅓ cup chopped zucchini
2 green onions, finely chopped
1 pkg. (8 oz.) cream cheese, softened
½ cup sour cream or Imo dressing
2 large cloves fresh garlic, minced
½ teaspoon salt
½ teaspoon dill weed
3 drops Tabasco

Combine all ingredients, cover and refrigerate. Good served with wheat crackers. Makes about 2½ cups.

TENNENT GARLIC DIP

The originator of this recipe says it will "knock your socks off it's so good." *Recipe contest entry: Barbara Anderson, Portland, OR*

1 carton (16 oz.) small curd cottage cheese
⅓ cup mayonnaise
6 cloves fresh garlic
Sea salt to taste

Whirl all ingredients in food processor or blender until smooth, cover and refrigerate. Serve with chips. Makes about 1½ cups.

DIP WITH A ZIP

Tone it down or spice it up, but serve this zippy dip with fresh, fried tortilla chips for the best taste. Good with vegetables, too, or spread on a sandwich. *Recipe contest entry: Florence M. Zimmer, El Centro, CA*

1 cup sour cream
1 pkg. (3 oz.) cream cheese, softened
5 green onions, finely chopped
4 cloves fresh garlic, minced
3 tablespoons chopped chiles (*or* to taste)
2 tablespoons salsa (*or* to taste)
2 jalapeno peppers, seeded and chopped
Salt and pepper to taste

Stir all ingredients together, cover and refrigerate until flavors have blended before serving. Makes 1½ cups.

GARLIC VEGGIE DIP

Water chestnuts are a succulent and surprising addition to this easy-to-prepare dip. *Recipe contest entry: Mrs. Milton Falk, Onaga, KS*

1 cup sour cream
1 cup mayonnaise
1 teaspoon instant minced garlic
¼ cup chopped onion
¼ cup chopped parsley
¼ cup chopped water chestnuts

Mix all ingredients together, cover and chill. Serve with fresh crisp vegetables. Makes 2½ cups.

Finalist in 1984 Recipe Contest: FERNANDA S. DE LUNA, Daly City, CA

This is one snack or party treat that will disappear faster than you can refill the bowl. Or you may just be too selfish to share them with others. A true taste sensation for the serious garlic-holic!

PEANUTS AND SLIVERS

2 lbs. peanuts, raw, shelled and skinned, about 6 cups (available in health food and nut stores)

6 whole heads fresh garlic, peeled and sliced to make about 2½ cups slivered garlic

Vegetable oil for French frying peanuts and garlic separately

Salt to taste

Place peanuts in wok that has been preheated with oil to medium-high. Make sure there is enough oil in wok to cover peanuts. Stir peanuts constantly, being careful not to burn them. As peanuts begin to brown slightly, lower heat to simmer, continuing to stir, and cook until light golden brown. Drain peanuts well in wire basket and let cool. Place garlic in skillet preheated with 1½ cups vegetable oil until it reaches medium-high. Stir garlic constantly to attain a consistent color and to prevent burning or sticking of garlic. As garlic browns slightly, reduce heat to low and continue to stir and cook until garlic is crisp and light golden brown. Drain garlic in the same manner as peanuts, breaking up any clusters. Cool. Combine peanuts and garlic and salt to taste. Store in airtight containers until ready to devour!

Finalist in 1981 Recipe Contest: BARRY WERTZ, British Columbia, Canada

Simulate elegant caviar with an imaginative imitation nestled in an iced bowl. Serve with lemon or set up with finely chopped eggs, tomato and onion.

MOCK CAVIAR

3 large cloves fresh garlic
1 can (2 oz.) can anchovy fillets
2 cups chopped ripe olives
2 large ripe avocados

Peel and crush garlic. Drain and mash anchovy filets. Drain olives. Halve, seed, peel and mash avocados. Combine all ingredients. Turn into iced bowl. Serve as spread for thin crackers or toast. Makes 3 cups. *Note:* To store, squeeze lemon juice over top, seal with clear plastic wrap and refrigerate.

One good reason for the flourishing garlic industry in California is the warm climate. In such regions garlic develops its best flavor and this is probably why it has always been popular in the cookery which has developed in countries surrounding the Mediterranean. Olives also grow well in such areas, and both garlic and olives are to be found in many fine dishes. Here are two recipes, one hot and the other cold, which combine the flavors of these two products very appealingly.

RIPE OLIVES WITH A HINT OF GARLIC

1 pint ripe olives, with liquid
¼ teaspoon (*or several shakes*) instant granulated garlic
Olive oil

Add garlic to the ripe olives and leave in refrigerator for at least four days. Measure liquid and save half. To this add an equal amount of olive oil. Place olives in this mixture, heat, and keep hot. Serve with cocktail picks.

GREAT GARLIC OLIVES

2 cans (7 oz. *each*) pitted ripe olives, drained
3 tablespoons olive oil
2 large cloves fresh garlic, minced
½ teaspoon oregano leaves

Marinate drained olives in the olive oil, garlic and oregano in a covered container for a minimum of 4 hours (the longer, the better).

BAGNA CAUDA

The name of this sauce, a specialty of the Piedmont region of Italy, literally means "hot bath." Keep it hot by serving from chafing dish.

6 large cloves fresh garlic
1 cup sweet butter
¼ cup olive oil
2 tablespoons chopped anchovies
  Vegetables and bread sticks for dipping

Peel garlic and mince fine or put through garlic press. Melt butter in small saucepan. Add garlic and oil. Cook over very low heat 5 minutes until garlic is softened but not browned. Add anchovies and continue cooking 5 minutes. Serve as a dip for raw or lightly blanched vegetables such as cucumber, fresh mushrooms, celery, zucchini, carrots, cauliflower, green pepper and green onions or bread sticks.
Variation: Blend 1 cup whipping cream and a generous dash or two freshly ground pepper into garlic-butter mixture. Simmer 2 or 3 minutes. Serve while warm.

SUNFLOWER SNAPS

It's a snap to prepare these sunflower nibbles. They are delicious as a snack and also make a crunchy addition to salads, soups, hot cereal or baked beans.   *Recipe contest entry: Camille Russell, Oakland, CA*

1 tablespoon vegetable oil
2 cups raw sunflower seeds, shelled
8 cloves fresh garlic, minced
¼ teaspoon salt
1 tablespoon soy sauce

Heat oil in large frying pan over medium-high heat. Add sunflower seeds and garlic. Stir. When a few of the seeds turn golden, reduce heat to medium, and continue stirring as needed. Stop cooking when about half of the seeds are golden. Remove from heat and add salt. After 5 minutes add soy sauce and stir. Store in a jar with a tight lid.

GARLIC-SPICED WALNUTS

One of the long-time fruit crops still being produced in Gilroy is walnuts. The addition of a little garlic flavoring together with ginger and allspice turns them into great between-meal nibbles or cocktail-time snacks.

2 teaspoons ginger
½ teaspoon allspice
5 cups water
1 lb. walnut halves
4 tablespoons melted butter
¾ teaspoon garlic salt

Add ginger and allspice to water and bring to a boil. Drop in walnuts and boil about 3 minutes. Drain well. Spread in a shallow pan and bake in 350-degree oven for 15 minutes or until lightly browned. Remove from oven and toss with melted butter and garlic salt.

DAVID'S PRESERVED PEPPERS

Chill before serving. These garlic peppers are absolutely irresistible and a great addition to appetizers, salads, antipasto plates or just for nibbling. Green bell peppers can be used if red peppers are not available, but the color is not as attractive.

Recipe contest entry: David Martin, Gilroy, CA

4 quarts water
6 tablespoons salt
2 cups white distilled vinegar
8 to 9 lb. red bell peppers
25 whole black peppercorns
15 cloves fresh garlic, peeled and halved
5 sprigs fresh dill
5 bay leaves

Boil water in large pot with salt until dissolved. Remove from heat and add vinegar. Cut peppers in half lengthwise, remove seeds and cut in ½-inch strips. Into each of 5 1-quart cleaned, washed canning jars place 5 whole peppercorns, 6 halves of garlic, a sprig dill and 1 bay leaf. Fill jars with pepper strips, pour brine over to about ¼ inch from the top of jar. Scald lid under boiling water and seal jar as lid manufacturer directs. Preserve peppers by water bath method. Place jars in deep kettle with rack and add boiling water to cover. Do not pour water directly on jars as they may crack. Cover kettle, heat water to boiling and boil gently for about 10 minutes, reducing heat if necessary. Remove jars from water bath and place upright on newspapers to cool. Store in cool place for at least 2 weeks prior to serving. Best served chilled. Makes 5 quarts.

GARLIC POPCORN BALLS

Devilishly delicious, these are a great snack to accompany beer and football.

Recipe contest entry: Linda Tarvin, Morgan Hill, CA

50 cloves fresh garlic (about 4 heads)
2 teaspoons salt
4 cups shredded Cheddar cheese (about 1 lb.)
5 quarts popped corn (about ½ cup unpopped corn)

Peel garlic and mince with salt to prevent sticking and to absorb garlic juices. Toss garlic with cheese. In large glass or plastic bowl, make alternate layers of popped corn and garlic-cheese mixture, coating popcorn as evenly as possible, especially at edge of bowl. Place in microwave oven and cook 1 minute. Shake bowl gently; turn 180 degrees and cook 1 more minute. Do not overcook. Immediately turn out onto cookie sheet, and quickly shape into plum-size balls. Set balls on sheets of waxed paper. Makes 4 dozen popcorn balls.

GARLIC-BASIL POPCORN

Popcorn rises to new heights of flavor when tossed with butter, garlic, basil and Parmesan cheese. Whether for TV snacking or as party fare, you won't be able to stop eating these crunchy morsels until they're all gone.

Recipe contest entry: S.E. Moray, San Francisco, CA

3 extra-large cloves fresh garlic, pressed
2 tablespoons butter or margarine
Pinch of sweet basil
1 tablespoon oil
¼ cup popcorn kernels
Salt to taste
2 tablespoons Parmesan cheese

Place garlic in a custard cup, along with butter and sweet basil. Heat a small amount of water in a saucepan and place custard cup in it to melt butter and infuse it with the herbs, or melt in microwave oven 30 seconds. Heat oil in a heavy iron or stainless steel pot. Drop one kernel in the oil, and when it pops, add the rest of the popcorn and cover. Shake pot now and then as it pops. When all corn has popped, add butter mixture and stir in vigorously. Add salt and Parmesan cheese and stir or shake to coat well.

Soups

Cream of Roasted Garlic Soup 57
Garlicky Tomato Saffron Soup 58
Jo's Baked Garlic Soup 59
Garlic Soup with Chicken 60
Creamy Garlic Spinach Soup
  with Garlic Croutons 61
Escarole-Garlic Soup with
  Chick Peas 62
California Garlic Soup Fondue 62
The Christophers' Garlic Soup 63
Cream of Artichoke Soup 64
Avocado Bisque 64
Garlic-Broccoli Soup 65
Garlic Tortilla Soup 65
Meatball Soup, California Style 66
Mama's Potato Soup 67
Cauldito de Ajos 67
Hungarian Peasant Soup
  with Spaetzle 68
Italian Sausage Soup 69
Spicy California Gumbo 70
Barroom Chowder 71
Great Gazpacho 72
Great Gazpacho for a Crowd 73
Bloody Mary Party Soup 74
Bulgarian Cucumber Yogurt Soup 75
Cold Beet and Cucumber Soup 75

Finalist in 1986 Recipe Contest: PATTY FILICE, Gilroy, CA

Some of the best garlic recipes come right from Gilroy. Here's one—a rich-filling soup that would go well with a light seafood or poultry entree.

CREAM OF ROASTED GARLIC SOUP

2 medium-sized heads fresh garlic
Olive oil
½ cup finely chopped onion
2 tablespoons unsalted butter
1½ cups buttermilk
½ cup cream
1 to 2 small potatoes, baked, skins removed
2 tablespoons cognac
⅛ teaspoon fresh dill
Salt to taste
Sourdough French bread cubes, several days old, sauteed in butter and garlic

Place garlic heads on cookie sheet, sprinkle with olive oil and bake in 350-degree oven for 1 hour. Let cool. Cut off end of each clove and squeeze out contents. (Garlic will be soft and creamy.) Set aside. Saute chopped onion in butter until softened. Add buttermilk and cream and simmer for 5 minutes. Pour mixture into a food processor. Rice potato and add with garlic to onion and buttermilk mixture. Puree until smooth. Return mixture to saute pan. Add cognac, dill and salt. Heat thoroughly. If soup is too thin, add additional potato. If soup is too thick, add additional buttermilk. Serve immediately, garnished with additional dill and croutons. Makes 4 servings.

Alternate in 1986 Recipe Contest: ELLEN SZITA, San Francisco, CA

This soup will bring raves whether it is served hot, cold or at room temperature.

GARLICKY TOMATO SAFFRON SOUP

6   cans (10½ oz. *each*) chicken broth
1   cup boiling water
¼   gram Spanish saffron threads
1   lb. Roma tomatoes, skinned, seeded and chopped in bite-size pieces
1   bunch (3 medium or 1½ cups) leeks, white part only, cleaned
4   tablespoons virgin olive oil
5   large cloves fresh garlic
½   teaspoon dried thyme
6   whole fennel seeds
8   large fresh spinach leaves

Place canned chicken broth in freezer so fat will rise to surface for easy removal. Bring water to boil. Add saffron threads and let steep, uncovered, off heat. Skin tomatoes by putting them in boiling water for 1 minute. Seed and chop tomatoes. Chop leeks fine. Heat olive oil in soup pot over medium heat. Do not let oil smoke. Add chopped leeks and saute just until limp but not brown. When leeks are limp, squeeze garlic cloves through press into leeks and mix over medium heat for 2 minutes. Remove from heat. Remove chicken broth from freezer and remove fat clumped at the top. Add chicken broth, saffron water including threads, tomatoes, thyme and fennel to leeks in soup pot. Simmer mixture, partially covered, for 30 minutes. Five minutes before soup is ready, add spinach. Serve hot, room temperature, or cold with hearty, crusty bread. Makes 4 to 6 servings.

The best thing to do with garlic of course, is to eat it.

Sylvia Rubin
San Francisco Chronicle

Finalist in 1980 Recipe Contest: JO STALLARD, Pacific Grove, CA

"I'll never live this down," teased grandmotherly Jo Stallard as she was crowned with a tiara of fresh garlic and draped in garlic wreaths. A vegetarian, Jo has turned her cooking talents to adapting recipes for meatless cooking. This delicious soup has always been a winner with her friends, she says, and so it was, too, with the 1980 Great Garlic Cook-off celebrity judges.

JO'S BAKED GARLIC SOUP

2 cups diced fresh tomatoes
1 can (approximately 15 oz.) garbanzo beans, undrained
4 *or* 5 summer squash, sliced
2 large onions, sliced
½ green pepper, diced
1½ cups dry white wine
4 *or* 5 cloves fresh garlic, minced
1 bay leaf
2 teaspoons salt
1 teaspoon basil
½ teaspoon paprika
1¼ cups grated Monterey Jack cheese
1 cup grated Romano cheese
1¼ cups heavy cream *or* whipping cream

Generously butter inside of 3-quart baking dish. Combine all ingredients, except cheese and cream, in dish. Cover and bake for 1 hour at 375 degrees. Stir in cheeses and cream, lower heat to 325 degrees and bake 10 to 15 minutes longer. Do not allow to boil. Mmmmm— GOOD! Serves 4 to 6.

Regional Winner in 1984 Recipe Contest: CARLA MATESKY, Canton, CT

This chunky chicken broth is enriched with a puree made from a whole head of fresh garlic. What better prescription for good health and good eating?

GARLIC SOUP WITH CHICKEN

1 whole chicken, disjointed
2 carrots, minced
2 stalks celery, minced
1 large whole onion, stuck with 2 cloves
1 whole head fresh garlic, broken into unpeeled cloves
   Chopped fresh parsley
   Salt and pepper to taste
10 cloves fresh garlic, peeled
4 tablespoons butter
2 tablespoons flour

Make fresh chicken broth by simmering chicken, carrots, celery, onion, garlic, parsley, salt and pepper in enough water to cover. When chicken is thoroughly cooked, remove it and skim fat from the broth. Simmer broth, reducing it until it is very rich. Remove unpeeled garlic cloves; squeeze cooked garlic from cloves and mash to make puree. Discard skins. In frying pan, saute the 10 peeled cloves in butter. When lightly browned, add flour and small amount of broth and mix with a wire whisk until velvety. Pour this mixture into the remaining broth, add pureed garlic, and stir. Tear chicken into bite-sized pieces and add to the soup. Sprinkle with fresh parsley and serve. Makes approximately 8 servings.

Third Place Winner in 1983 Recipe Contest:

DEBRA KAUFMAN, South San Francisco, CA

This soup has fabulous flavor, but be sure to serve it with homemade garlic croutons. Use day old sourdough French bread if you have it. Combine ¼ cup olive oil, 1 teaspoon *each* garlic powder and crushed dry parsley, ¾ teaspoon Hungarian paprika and salt and pepper to taste. Cut bread into ½-inch cubes and work garlic-oil mixture into bread. Spread cubes in shallow baking pan and bake at 325 degrees for about 25 minutes. Store in tightly covered container.

CREAMY GARLIC SPINACH SOUP WITH GARLIC CROUTONS

1 large bunch spinach, stalks removed
4 cups chicken broth (preferably homemade)
2 large carrots, grated
1 large onion, chopped
8 cloves fresh garlic, finely chopped
½ cup butter (1 stick)
¼ cup flour
½ cup light cream
½ cup whipping cream
Salt and freshly ground pepper to taste
Sour cream (optional)
Garlic croutons

Chop spinach coarsely. Combine with chicken broth and carrots in 2- to 3-quart pot. Cook 5 to 10 minutes until carrots are tender and spinach wilted. Remove from heat. Meanwhile, saute onion and garlic very gently over low to medium heat in butter, about 20 to 30 minutes. Onions should be very tender and translucent, but garlic should NOT be browned! Add flour and cook, stirring constantly 5 to 10 minutes. Combine spinach / broth and onion / garlic mixtures in food processor or blender in small batches. Puree until smooth. Clean pot and return soup to pot. Add cream, whipping cream and salt and freshly ground pepper to taste. Heat until hot, but not boiling. Garnish with a dollop of sour cream and garlic croutons. Makes 4 servings.

Regional Winner in 1983 Recipe Contest: PEG RHODES, Prescott, AZ

This soup is a nutritious, satisfying, meatless main dish . . . . and it's economical, too. Great served with toasty Italian bread.

ESCAROLE-GARLIC SOUP WITH CHICK PEAS

1 bunch escarole (about 1 lb.)
4 tablespoons olive oil
5 to 6 medium cloves fresh garlic, finely minced *or* pressed
1 medium onion, sliced
2 quarts chicken broth (fresh *or* canned)
2 sprigs fresh parsley, chopped
1 can (16 oz.) chick peas (garbanzos), drained Freshly ground black pepper
2 cups cooked rice Parmesan cheese, grated

Rinse and drain escarole to remove sand. Cut leaves crosswise into long, thin pieces. Heat olive oil in 4-quart saucepan. Saute escarole, garlic and onions in hot oil for 5 minutes. Add ½ cup of broth, cover and simmer over low heat for 25 to 30 minutes. (The leaves will shrink as they cook.) Add more broth if liquid is absorbed too quickly to avoid burning. Add remaining broth, parsley, chick peas and pepper to taste. Cover and simmer 10 minutes longer. To serve, place ½ cup *hot* rice into soup bowls; pour soup over. Pass Parmesan cheese and enjoy! Makes 4 servings.

CALIFORNIA GARLIC SOUP FONDUE

This recipe offers an excellent way to use up any leftover champagne. Better yet, open a new bottle and enjoy while you prepare this tasty garlic soup.   *Recipe contest entry: Beverly Szabo, Culver City, CA*

40 cloves (3 to 4 heads) fresh garlic, minced
3 tablespoons butter
2 cans (10¾ oz. *each*) chicken broth
2 soup cans water
½ cup extra dry champagne
4 slices French bread
4 slices Gruyere cheese Cayenne pepper Minced chives

Saute garlic in butter for 10 minutes, stirring often. Do *not* brown. Add broth, water, champagne and simmer 5 minutes. Toast bread. Ladle soup into bowls. Float bread on top of soup, sprinkle with cheese and bake at 475 degrees, uncovered, for 15 minutes. Sprinkle with cayenne and chives. Makes 4 servings.

THE CHRISTOPHERS' GARLIC SOUP

One of the organizers of the Festival, garlic grower and shipper Don Christopher, devised this recipe for garlic soup after a trip to Mexico. He relates he made it a dozen times before he was satisfied that he had it right. Now it's one of his favorites. It's delicious when reheated too. *Courtesy of: Don Christopher, Gilroy, CA*

- 6 beef-flavored bouillon cubes
- 8 cups boiling water
- 14 large cloves fresh garlic
- 2 tablespoons butter
- 2 tablespoons minced parsley
- 1 tablespoon flour
- ¼ teaspoon freshly ground pepper
- 6 raw egg yolks, beaten
- 6 thin slices Monterey Jack cheese
- 6 small slices French bread, toasted

In large bowl or saucepan, combine bouillon cubes and water, stirring until cubes are dissolved. Peel garlic and mince (can be done quickly in a blender or food processor). In heavy saucepan, over low heat, brown garlic lightly in butter with minced parsley, stirring constantly so as not to burn. Add flour and stir until slightly browned. Add broth and pepper; simmer at least 30 minutes to 1 hour. Just before serving, slowly add egg yolks, stirring constantly. Place cheese on toasted bread and place 1 slice in each serving bowl. Ladle soup into bowl and place bowl under broiler just long enough to melt cheese. (This could also be done in the microwave oven.) Serve at once. Makes 6 generous servings.

CREAM OF ARTICHOKE SOUP

This creamy soup depends partly for its seasoning on the herbs and spices in the marinade used on the artichoke hearts. Fresh garlic and onion provide just the right additional flavor balance. A lovely starter course for an elegant dinner. *Recipe contest entry: Fresh Garlic Association*

1 jar (6 oz.) marinated artichoke hearts
3 or more large cloves fresh garlic
½ cup chopped onion
2 tablespoons flour
2 cans (10¾ oz. *each*) chicken broth
1 cup half-and-half
Finely chopped parsley

Drain marinade from artichoke hearts into 2-quart saucepan. Crush garlic with press or mince and add to marinade. Add onion and cook, covered, 10 minutes over low heat. Blend in flour. Slowly stir in 1 can broth and heat to boiling, stirring. Boil 1 minute or until mixture thickens. Turn artichoke hearts into blender or food processor and add hot mixture, blending until smooth. Strain into saucepan; add remaining can of broth and half-and-half. Heat just to serving temperature; do not boil. Sprinkle each serving with parsley. Makes 4 servings, about 1⅓ cups each.

AVOCADO BISQUE

Everyone likes garlic as a flavoring in guacamole. It's equally good in this elegant avocado soup.

Recipe contest entry: Mrs. John Austad, San Diego, CA

2 bunches spinach, heated until just wilted but not cooked
2 medium-sized California avocados
4 to 5 cloves fresh garlic
1 cup half-and-half
1 cup chicken broth
1 tablespoon butter
1 teaspoon salt

Place all ingredients in blender and blend 45 seconds until creamy smooth. Pour into a saucepan and cover. Heat on medium until puffs of steam are seen at top. *Do not* allow to boil, as avocados will become bitter. Serve immediately. Makes about 1 quart.

GARLIC-BROCCOLI SOUP

This rich and creamy soup has excellent garlic flavor. It's better the second day around and may be served cold as well as hot. Add a little half-and-half the next day just before serving.

Recipe contest entry: Mrs. Jol Oberly, Memphis, TN

12 cloves fresh garlic
1 large bunch fresh broc-
coli
4 tablespoons unsalted
butter
3 tablespoons flour
1 teaspoon salt
½ teaspoon black pepper
2 cups milk
½ cup chicken broth
Half-and-half as needed
Hungarian sweet paprika

Drop unpeeled garlic cloves into boiling water for 1 minute (30 seconds for small cloves); remove from water, peel, and mince. Cut broccoli into buds and stems, discarding woody portions, and cook in boiling water until tender. Remove and drain. Melt butter in 2-quart saucepan. When butter begins to bubble, add garlic, stirring rapidly for a few seconds. Quickly add flour, salt and pepper. Stir constantly for 1 minute. Add milk and chicken broth, stirring briskly with a wire whisk until sauce is thickened. In a blender or food processor, puree broccoli with a little sauce, adding remaining sauce until all broccoli is blended. Correct seasoning to taste and thin with half-and-half to proper consistency. Serve, sprinkled with Hungarian sweet paprika, if desired. Makes 4 to 6 servings.

GARLIC TORTILLA SOUP

This recipe was created by a disabled veteran who obviously enjoys cooking....and eating well.

Recipe contest entry: Mike Conrad, Carson City, NV

15 cloves fresh garlic
1 cup water
2 cans (10¾ oz. *each*)
chicken broth
Juice of 1 lemon
2 corn tortillas, cut into
½-inch pieces
2 egg yolks
Dash of Tabasco
Pinch of cumin

Peel garlic. In blender thoroughly mix garlic and water. Place in 2-quart saucepan with broth and lemon juice; simmer for 20 minutes. Add tortillas and cook an additional 10 minutes. Remove from heat and cool slightly. Slowly add egg yolks, stirring constantly. Reheat and add Tabasco and cumin. Makes 4 servings.

MEATBALL SOUP, CALIFORNIA STYLE

This recipe is adapted from the "Sopa de Albondigas" so popular in Mexico. The Cheese-Butter, added to each serving at the very last moment, could be used to season and enrich almost any clear soup.

Recipe contest entry: Fresh Garlic Association

4   large cloves fresh garlic
½   lb. ground beef
1   large egg, beaten
1½   teaspoons salt
2   tablespoons uncooked rice
¼   cup finely chopped parsley
½   cup chopped onion
1   tablespoon oil
½   teaspoon lemon-pepper seasoning
2   cans (10½ oz. *each*) beef broth
2   cups water
1   cup carrots, cut in 2 x ¼-inch strips
1   cup celery, cut in 2 x ¼-inch strips
1   can (8¾ oz.) garbanzos, undrained
1   can (1 lb.) stewed tomatoes
    Cheese-Butter (recipe below)

Peel garlic. Mash, or put through garlic press, 1 clove garlic. Combine with beef, egg, ½ teaspoon salt, rice and 2 tablespoons parsley. Shape mixture into 20 small meatballs and set aside. Chop remaining 3 cloves garlic or mash. Cook garlic with onion in oil, over medium heat until soft but not browned in covered 3-quart saucepan. Add remaining 1 teaspoon salt, lemon-pepper seasoning, broth, water, carrots and celery. Bring to boiling. Drop in meatballs and simmer 20 minutes. Add undrained garbanzos, tomatoes and remaining chopped parsley. Continue cooking 10 minutes longer. Ladle into large soup bowls and serve with a spoonful of Cheese-Butter. Makes 4 entree servings.

Cheese-Butter
½   cup butter, softened
½   teaspoon pressed fresh garlic
2   tablespoons grated Parmesan cheese
1   tablespoon minced parsley

Blend all ingredients together. Makes about ½ cup.

MAMA'S POTATO SOUP

Don't let the homespun name of this spicy Mexican-style soup fool you. It's a great dish to serve company as well as your family.

Recipe contest entry: Edna H. Ramirez, Monterey Park, CA

2 tablespoons oil
4 cloves fresh garlic, minced
1 cup finely chopped onion
3 medium-sized tomatoes, peeled and chopped
½ cup chopped green chiles
1 tablespoon flour
2 quarts hot chicken broth
2½ cups peeled raw potatoes, cut into small cubes
2 teaspoons salt (*or* to taste)
1 teaspoon black pepper
2 medium-sized carrots, peeled and thinly sliced
1 medium-sized zucchini, thinly sliced
2 cups Monterey Jack cheese, cut into small cubes

Heat oil in 3-quart saucepan and add garlic, onions, tomatoes and green chiles; saute for 3 minutes. Stir in flour and cook for 2 more minutes. Continue stirring as you pour in the hot broth. Add potatoes, salt and pepper. Cover pan and simmer over low heat for 20 minutes. Add carrots and zucchini and cook for 15 minutes longer or until potatoes are tender. Just before serving add the cubed cheese. Makes 4 to 6 servings.

CAULDITO DE AJOS   *Little Soup of Garlic*

This light, fresh tasting soup would be very satisfying served in mugs on a cold night. The combination of cilantro and lime with the garlic flavor is most interesting.

Recipe contest entry: Anne Copeland MacCallum, San Pedro, CA

¼ cup peeled and chopped fresh garlic
¼ cup oil
Juice of 1 lime
6 cups chicken broth
Salt and pepper to taste
2 eggs
Grated rind of one lime
Cilantro (fresh coriander, also called Mexican or Chinese parsley)

Saute garlic in oil until golden. Add with lime juice to chicken broth. Add salt and pepper and bring to a boil. Lower heat and continue to simmer for 15 to 20 minutes, or until the garlic taste permeates the soup. Meanwhile, blend eggs and grated lime rind in a bowl, adding a little salt and pepper. Add egg mixture to garlic soup a little at a time, stirring constantly. Turn up heat slightly, but do not allow soup to boil. Continue to cook about 5 minutes. Serve with chopped cilantro and sliced limes for garnish.

HUNGARIAN PEASANT SOUP WITH SPAETZLE

This recipe is a family favorite, originally prepared by Helen Headlee's mother. The trick to developing the good flavor is in the slow cooking of the roux. This is a meal in itself and very, very good. Spaetzle are bite-size dumplings.

Recipe contest entry: Helen Headlee, South San Francisco, CA

Soup

2   medium onions, chopped
6   to 8 cloves fresh garlic, minced
6   tablespoons shortening *or* 4 of shortening and 2 of bacon drippings
4   tablespoons flour
2   tablespoons Hungarian sweet paprika (Szeged)
3   cups boiling water and 10 cups lukewarm water
1   cup minced parsley
5   to 6 carrots, sliced
4   to 5 potatoes, peeled and cut into large chunks
Salt to taste

Saute onions and garlic in 2 tablespoons melted fat until golden. Drain off excess fat and remove garlic and onion to bowl. Set aside. In same pan, melt remaining 4 tablespoons fat, gradually stirring in the flour and paprika. Continue cooking, stirring constantly, over low heat for 4 to 5 minutes, being careful not to burn. Stir in boiling water and cook for another 3 to 5 minutes. Pour into large kettle filled with remaining water and stir in parsley. Bring to boil. Lower heat and add garlic, onions, carrots and potatoes. Cover and simmer until vegetables are done and flavors are blended, about 30 minutes. Stir occasionally. Meanwhile prepare dumplings and add to soup when ready to serve. Makes 3 to 10 servings.

Spaetzle

3   cups flour
3   eggs
½   to ¾ cup water
1   teaspoon salt

Stir together all ingredients. Dough will be very sticky. Bring large pot of water to boil and either coarsely grate dough into boiling water or place dough on flat plate and with a sharp knife, scrape and cut off tiny bite-size pieces into the boiling water. When dumplings rise to top, drain and add to soup.

ITALIAN SAUSAGE SOUP *Very Good*

You can make a meal of this soup. Just serve with a green salad, plenty of crusty French bread and. . . red wine, perhaps.

1 lb. Italian sausage, cut in ½-inch slices
4 cloves fresh garlic, minced
2 large onions, chopped
1 can (16 oz.) Italian pear tomatoes
1½ quarts canned beef broth *or* prepared from bouillon cubes and water
1½ cups red wine (*or* water)
½ teaspoon basil
½ teaspoon thyme
3 tablespoons chopped parsley
1 medium-sized green pepper, chopped
2 medium-sized zucchini, sliced
3 cups uncooked *farfalle* (bow-tie noodles)
Parmesan cheese, grated

In a 5-quart kettle, brown sausage on medium heat. Drain fat. Add garlic and onions; cook until limp. Stir in and break up tomatoes. Add broth, wine, basil, thyme and parsley. Simmer uncovered for 30 minutes. Add vegetables and noodles. Cover and simmer 25 minutes more. Sprinkle each serving with Parmesan cheese. Makes 8 to 10 servings.

SPICY CALIFORNIA GUMBO

If you are not familiar with Creole cookery, you may not know that the term "to rope" refers to the stringy strands which okra exudes when it first starts to cook. You may also not be familiar with file powder which is a very important ingredient. It is made from the ground young leaves of dried sassafras and used both to season and thicken soups and stews.   *Recipe contest entry: Jeani Cearlock, Morgan Hill, CA*

¼ cup butter
½ lb. fresh okra
1 large onion, chopped
1½ large stalks celery, sliced
½ cup chopped green pepper
5 cloves fresh garlic, minced
2 to 3 tablespoons flour
1 jar medium-sized oysters, diced
2 cups chicken broth *or* bouillon
1½ large tomatoes, chopped
6 sprigs minced parsley
Pinch of thyme
Salt and pepper to taste
Tabasco sauce
Water
½ lb. diced ham
¾ lb. shrimp, shelled and deveined
Cooked rice
File powder

Melt butter in large pan. Add okra, onion, celery, green pepper and garlic and cook until okra ceases to "rope." Add flour and cook for 2 or 3 minutes. Add the liquid from the oysters, chicken broth, tomatoes, parsley, bay leaves, thyme, salt, pepper and Tabasco. Simmer about an hour (may need additional water). Add ham and simmer another 20 minutes. Add shrimp and oysters and simmer for 10 to 15 minutes. Remove bay leaves. To serve, put a scoop of rice in a soup bowl and add a generous amount of gumbo; sprinkle with file powder and enjoy!

BARROOM CHOWDER

Chowder originated in the New England states. Its popularity is now widely spread. There's a touch of the Southwest in this recipe which gives the soup an unusual and very good flavor.

Recipe contest entry: Barbara Blosser, Alameda, CA

¼ lb. butter
1½ cups chopped onion *or* half leeks and half onion
3 cloves fresh garlic, minced
¾ cup chopped celery, including some leaves
¾ teaspoon *each* cumin (whole seed) and marjoram
⅓ teaspoon sage
⅓ cup flour
3 cups chicken stock *or* canned broth
2 cups heavy cream
½ cup tequila
6 oz. shredded cheese (Cheddar or Fontina)
2 tablespoons chopped cilantro (coriander)
1 teaspoon red *or* cayenne pepper
½ teaspoon nutmeg
2 to 3 carrots, half shredded, half cut into ovals
Zest of 2 limes
1 lb. fresh fish, a combination of your choice, cut in chunks

Melt butter in large saucepan over moderate heat. Saute onions and garlic for 5 minutes. Add celery and cook 5 minutes more. Stir in cumin, marjoram and sage. Add flour; stir and cook 3 minutes or until bubbling. Add stock, cream and tequila. Blend. Stir in cheese. Add cilantro, pepper and nutmeg. Mix well. Add carrots, zest of limes. Then add fish and cook until fish is tender, about 10 minutes. Serve with Cheddar cheese-flavored goldfish crackers or warm bread. Makes 3 quarts of soup.

Garlic is a habit and a passion.

Kim Upton
Chicago Sun Times

GREAT GAZPACHO

The Spanish cold soup, gazpacho, is a pleasing addition to brunch or lunch and a welcome first course for dinner on hot summer days.

Recipe contest entry: Connie Rogers, Gilroy

2 medium cucumbers, peeled and coarsely chopped
5 medium tomatoes, peeled and coarsely chopped
1 large onion, coarsely chopped
1 medium green pepper, seeded and coarsely chopped
2 teaspoons chopped fresh garlic
4 cups French *or* Italian bread, trimmed of crusts and coarsely crumbled
4 cups cold water
¼ cup red wine vinegar
4 teaspoons salt
¼ cup olive oil
1 tablespoon tomato paste

In large, deep bowl combine cucumbers, tomatoes, onion, green pepper and garlic; add crumbled bread and mix together thoroughly; then stir in water, vinegar and salt. Ladle about 2 cups of the mixture at a time into a blender and blend at high speed for 1 minute, or until it is a smooth puree. Pour puree into a bowl and, with a whisk, beat in olive oil and tomato paste. Cover bowl tightly and refrigerate for at least 2 hours or until thoroughly chilled. Just before serving, stir soup lightly to recombine it.

Garnishes
1 cup small homemade croutons
½ cup finely chopped onions
½ cup peeled and finely chopped cucumbers
½ cup finely chopped green peppers

Serve the garnishes in separate small bowls so that each diner may add his / her own according to preference.

GAZPACHO FOR A CROWD

A big bowl of gazpacho surrounded by crushed ice to keep it well chilled, can be, pardon the pun, an "ice breaker" for any party. Guests can step up and help themselves, while the hostess prepares the next course.

16 lbs. tomatoes, diced
 4 medium-sized cucumbers, diced
 1 cup dehydrated green bell peppers
 ½ cup dehydrated chopped *or* minced onion
 ½ teaspoon instant granulated garlic
 1 quart soft bread crumbs
 1 gallon water
 2 teaspoons crushed red pepper
 ¼ cup salt
 2 tablespoons olive oil
 3 cups vinegar
 1 cup pimento-stuffed green olives, chopped
 ¼ cup parsley flakes
 ¼ cup dehydrated celery granules

Combine tomatoes, cucumbers, green bell peppers, onion, garlic, bread crumbs and water. Bring to a boil. Cover and simmer 1 hour. Force through a sieve or food mill. Add pepper, salt, oil and vinegar. Mix well. Chill thoroughly. Serve with olives, parsley, and celery as toppings. Makes about 25 servings.

BLOODY MARY PARTY SOUP

Cocktails in the soup bowl? Why not! This spicy tomato soup is laced with vodka poured at the table from a bottle which has been frozen into a block of ice. Dramatic and lots of fun as a starter course for a brunch or light supper.

2½ cups minced onion
2   cups minced celery
1¼ cups peeled, seeded and minced cucumber
8   cloves fresh garlic, minced
2   tablespoons butter *or* margarine
4   cans (46 oz. *each*) tomato juice
1½ cups lemon juice
3   tablespoons sugar
½   teaspoon Tabasco sauce
½   teaspoon Worcestershire sauce
1   bottle (fifth) vodka
½   cup green onion, sliced

Saute onion, celery, cucumber and garlic in butter until soft. Add tomato juice, lemon juice, sugar, Tabasco and Worcestershire; simmer 7 to 8 minutes. Chill. Place vodka bottle in No. 10 can filled with water; freeze until ice is solid. Remove can but keep vodka surrounded in ice and wrapped in a towel. To serve: portion soup into serving bowl. Garnish with green onion. Add 1 oz. jigger of vodka (from bottle in ice block) per serving of soup at table. Makes 24 servings (about 1 cup each).

BULGARIAN CUCUMBER YOGURT SOUP

All over the world, Bulgarians are known for their good health and longevity, which are often attributed to their consumption of yogurt and garlic. This soup combines both in a delicious adaptation of a classic Bulgarian recipe.   *Recipe contest entry: Annegret Yonkow, Fairfax, CA*

1 large cucumber
½ cup finely chopped walnuts
4 cloves fresh garlic, minced
3 tablespoons chopped parsley
2 tablespoons oil
1 teaspoon dill weed
½ teaspoon salt
2 cups European-style yogurt (without gelatin)
2 cups ice water
Ice

Peel cucumber and shred or chop very fine. Mix with all other ingredients except yogurt, water and ice. Cover and refrigerate for several hours to allow flavors to blend. At serving time add yogurt and water and a few pieces of ice.

COLD BEET AND CUCUMBER SOUP

Even "buttermilk haters" will like this luscious and low-calorie soup.
Recipe contest entry: Ruth Gordon, Carpinteria, CA

1 lb. can julienne beets
1 carton (8 oz.) low-fat yogurt
1 quart buttermilk
4 large cloves fresh garlic
2 unpeeled cucumbers
4 green onions with stems
Handful fresh parsley
1 chicken bouillon cube, dissolved in ½ cup water
White or black pepper to taste

Drain beets, reserving juice, and set aside in a large bowl. In blender or food processor, combine beet juice, yogurt, buttermilk and garlic. (Depending on work bowl capacity you may have to do this in portions.) Pour over julienne beets. In same blender, coarsely chop cucumbers, onions and parsley, using chicken bouillon for the liquid. Add to beet mixture. Stir well and add pepper to taste. Refrigerate overnight in covered container. Serve very cold.

Salads / Dressings

Lady Sings the Greens	79
Susie Townsend's Ex-Husbands Sesame Broccoli Pasta Salad Significantly Improved	80
Scandinavian Tripe Salad	81
Caesar Salad California Style	82
Spinach Salad	82
Garlicky Pasta Chicken Salad	83
Egg Salad with Garlic Dressing	83
Garlic Shrimp Salad	84
Spicy Marinated Shrimp for a Crowd	85
Shrimply Garlic Potato Salad	85
Lucia's Vegetable Salad	86
Rosie's Broccoli Salad	86
Eggplant Salad Trinidadelish	87
Middle East Carrot Salad	87
Garlic Green Bean Salad	88
Marian's Beans	88
Garlicky Green Goddess Mold	89
Karen's Fresh Pears with Garlic-Roquefort Dressing	90
Jeanne's Low-Fat Creamy Garlic Dressing	90
Garlic French Dressing	91
Green Goddess Dressing	91
Party-Perfect Garlic Dressing	92
Georgette's French Dressing	92
Tart 'n' Tangy Italian Dressing	93
Italian Sweet-Sour Dressing	93

Third Prize Winner 1985 Recipe Contest:

DEBBIE SHEESLEY, Sacramento, CA

No one will be singing the blues when you serve this stepped-up version of the ubiquitous tossed green salad. The secret's in the dressing.

LADY SINGS THE GREENS

4 large egg yolks
2 tablespoons Dijon-style mustard
¼ cup minced cilantro (Chinese parsley)
¼ cup bacon, cooked crisp, drained and crumbled into small bits
6 cloves fresh garlic, minced
1 cup virgin olive oil
⅓ cup red wine vinegar
Salt and pepper to taste
1 bunch spinach
1 head endive
1 head butter lettuce
1 English cucumber, thinly sliced
2 or 3 hard-cooked eggs, yolks crumbled, whites shaved
Parmesan cheese, grated
Garlic croutons

In a blender or food processor, whirl egg yolks and mustard until smooth and pale yellow in color. Whirl in cilantro, bacon and garlic. Alternately add oil and vinegar, drop by drop, until well blended. Adjust flavor with salt and pepper. Wash spinach, remove stems and pat dry. Separate endive and butter lettuce leaves, wash and pat dry. Tear greens into medium-size pieces and place in large salad bowl. Toss with enough dressing to coat. Portion out onto individual chilled salad plates. Sprinkle with Parmesan cheese. Garnish with cucumber slices, egg yolks and whites and croutons. Makes 6 servings.

Finalist in 1986 Recipe Contest: SUSIE TOWNSEND, New York, NY

With a name like this, there's no need for further description.

SUSIE TOWNSEND'S EX-HUSBAND'S SESAME BROCCOLI PASTA SALAD SIGNIFICANTLY IMPROVED

1 large bunch broccoli, trimmed and broken into florets
3 tablespoons soy sauce
6 cloves fresh garlic, *or* more to your taste, minced
4 tablespoons hot sesame oil (*or* 2 tablespoons chili oil and 2 tablespoons sesame oil)
3 tablespoons white vinegar
2 teaspoons honey
½ cup sesame seeds, toasted in a dry skillet
⅓ cup pine nuts, toasted in a dry skillet
1 bunch scallions, chopped
1 medium red onion, sliced thin
1 lb. fusilli (corkscrew pasta), cooked

Steam broccoli 2 to 3 minutes or 'til tender but still crisp. In bottom of large salad bowl, combine soy sauce, garlic, oil, vinegar and honey to make dressing. Add ¼ cup sesame seeds, pine nuts, scallions and red onion. Mix well. Then add pasta and toss until well coated. Add broccoli and toss again. Then sprinkle on remaining sesame seeds. (The salad is best only slightly chilled, better the next day. If refrigerated overnight, let it come almost to room temperature before serving.) Makes 6 to 8 servings.

Finalist in 1982 Recipe Contest: ALICE GRAY, Berkeley, CA

Long, gentle cooking brings out the flavor of this delicacy, which is prepared here in the Scandinavian manner with yogurt, sour cream and vinegar, laced with the bite of fresh garlic. The cheesecloth sack, by the way, used for holding the garlic is not a necessity, only a convenience for retrieving the cloves for mashing.

SCANDINAVIAN TRIPE SALAD

1   lb. tripe
2   quarts cold water
½   lemon
1   teaspoon salt
4   to 6 cloves fresh garlic, unpeeled
½   cup sour cream
½   cup plain yogurt
2   tablespoons white wine vinegar
1   teaspoon sugar
¼   teaspoon white pepper
    Salt to taste
    Minced chives

Rinse tripe in cold water, drain, and place in large saucepan with 2 quarts cold water. Squeeze juice from lemon over tripe and drop in the peel. Add salt and bring gently to boil, turn heat to low and simmer until tender, 20 minutes to 2 hours, depending on tripe. Meanwhile, tie garlic cloves in a little cheesecloth sack, drop into kettle and cook until very tender, at least 20 minutes. Remove garlic, cool sufficiently to handle and squeeze the garlic out of its peel into a medium-sized bowl. Add sour cream, yogurt, vinegar, sugar and pepper and mix well. Chill. When tripe is tender, rinse in cold water, drain and cool. Cut into coarse or medium julienne strips and mix with the dressing. Add salt to taste, mound into a serving bowl and chill. At serving time, sprinkle with chopped chives. Serve as an hors d'oeuvre or as the main course of a light lunch. Makes 4 servings.

CAESAR SALAD CALIFORNIA STYLE

In this version of Caesar salad, it is important to prepare garlic-flavored oil several days ahead. Combine 1 cup olive oil with 1 cup sunflower oil and 7 cloves crushed, fresh garlic. Refrigerate for a few days, then strain. Now you're ready to fix the salad.

Recipe contest entry: Barbara Goldman, Granada Hills, CA

 1 loaf white bread, cut into small cubes
 1 teaspoon granulated garlic *or* garlic powder
   Salt
12 to 14 oz. garlic-flavored oil (see recipe above)
 1 clove fresh garlic
 3 large heads romaine lettuce, torn into bite-sized pieces
   Juice of 2 lemons
 ¾ cup Parmesan cheese
 2 teaspoons Worcestershire sauce
 ¾ teaspoon pepper
 5 eggs (at room temperature), coddled for 1½ minutes

Prepare croutons by placing cubed bread in deep roaster or baking dish. Sprinkle with granulated onion and garlic and ⅛ teaspoon salt. Pour 6 oz. garlic-flavored oil over as evenly as possible. Bake in 225-degree oven for 1 hour or until done. Turn every 15 minutes. Before preparing salad, rub large salad bowl with fresh garlic. Then add lettuce and toss with 10 oz. garlic-flavored oil to coat each leaf. Add lemon juice and toss again. Add cheese, Worcestershire and ¾ teaspoon salt and pepper and 2 cups croutons. (Freeze remaining croutons for later use.) Toss salad thoroughly, but carefully. Then add eggs, toss gently and serve immediately.

SPINACH SALAD

A delicious salad with a good, garlicky bite to it!

Recipe contest entry: Lillie S. Marlork, Vallejo, CA

 1 lb. fresh spinach, washed and dried
 ⅓ cup finely diced sharp Cheddar cheese
 ⅓ cup finely chopped celery
 2 hard-cooked eggs, chopped fine
 ⅓ cup salad oil
 5 cloves fresh garlic, crushed
 2 tablespoons *each* lemon juice and vinegar
 1 teaspoon sugar
 1 teaspoon Dijon-style *or* brown mustard
 ½ teaspoon salt
   Dash pepper

Cut stems from spinach and tear leaves into large bite-sized pieces. Combine in salad bowl with cheese and celery. Prepare vinaigrette dressing by combining remaining ingredients in bottle and shaking well. Remove large pieces of garlic and pour dressing over spinach mixture. Toss lightly and refrigerate several hours before serving. Makes 8 servings.

GARLICKY PASTA CHICKEN SALAD

In this recipe, the large amount of garlic, cooked slowly in rosemary-scented olive oil, develops a rich, exquisite flavor.

Recipe contest entry: Mary Jane Himel, Palo Alto, CA

6 whole heads fresh garlic
¾ cup olive oil
4 rosemary sprigs (optional)
¼ cup fresh basil *or* 2 teaspoons dried
1 tablespoon fresh rosemary leaves *or* 1 teaspoon dried
8 oz. corkscrew pasta, cooked and drained
2 cups cooked chicken, cut in strips
½ cup sliced green onion
½ cup freshly grated Parmesan cheese
Salt and pepper to taste
⅔ cup chopped walnuts
Lettuce leaves

Separate cloves of garlic and drop into boiling water for 1 minute. Drain and peel. Place peeled cloves in small saucepan with oil and optional rosemary sprigs. Cook gently, covered, stirring occasionally, for about 25 minutes or until garlic is tender. Discard rosemary sprigs and puree garlic with ½ cup of the olive oil, basil and the rosemary leaves. Place pasta in large bowl and add garlic puree, chicken, onion, Parmesan, salt and pepper. Mix thoroughly. Add more olive oil if needed to moisten salad. Let salad sit for 1 hour at toom temperature or refrigerate, returning mixture to room temperature before serving. Toast walnuts in 375-degree oven for 10 minutes. Stir into the salad and serve over crisp, chilled lettuce. Makes 6 servings.

EGG SALAD WITH GARLIC DRESSING

For a change, use this egg-garlic dressing on a mixture of vegetables such as green beans, peas, peppers, tomatoes, cucumbers, cauliflower and broccoli.

Recipe contest entry: Betty Caldwell, Danville, IL

6 cloves fresh garlic
1 cup water
8 anchovies, including oil
6 tablespoons olive oil
2 tablespoons vinegar
1 tablespoon capers
3 drops Tabasco *or* dash cayenne pepper
Salt and pepper to taste
4 hard-cooked eggs
1 lb. watercress *or* 1 small head lettuce, shredded

Boil garlic in water for 15 minutes until tender. Mash garlic with a fork to make a paste. Chop anchovies and combine in mixing bowl with garlic and all ingredients except eggs and greens. Mix well. Slice eggs in quarters. Tear greens into bite-size pieces and arrange on platter. Top with eggs and pour dressing over. Makes 4 servings.

Finalist in 1981 Recipe Contest: LOVELLE OBERHOLZER, Concord, CA

Delicate pink shrimp and luscious green avocados and artichoke hearts are featured in this salad which is an adaptation of one served all over the Mediterranean area. For variation, chicken can be substituted for the shrimp.

GARLIC SHRIMP SALAD

9 cloves fresh garlic
¼ cup butter *or* margarine
1½ to 2 lbs. large shelled, deveined shrimp
2 large tomatoes
2 medium cucumbers
3 green onions
4 cooked artichoke hearts, halved
½ cup salad oil
¼ cup lemon juice
½ teaspoon crushed sweet basil
¼ teaspoon dried dill weed
Salt and pepper
1 avocado

Peel and mince 6 cloves garlic. Melt butter in a heavy skillet. Add minced garlic and saute over medium heat until light golden. Add shrimp and cook 2 or 3 minutes, turning continuously, just until they are pink. Remove from heat. Break shrimp into bite-sized pieces into a large bowl and add the cooked garlic. Remove skin, seed and chop tomatoes. Peel, seed and chop cucumber. Chop onions and halve artichoke hearts. Combine vegetables with shrimp. Mince remaining 3 cloves garlic and combine with oil, lemon juice, herbs and salt and pepper to taste. Beat until blended, then pour over shrimp mixture, mixing well. Halve, remove seed and skin and dice avocado into salad mixture. Serve in small bowls with crusty French bread and butter. Makes 6 to 8 servings.

SPICY MARINATED SHRIMP FOR A CROWD

Shrimp take a tangy bath in a spicy oil and vinegar marinade. When drained and arranged in lettuce cups with tomato and cucumber garnish, these marinated beauties make elegant, individual salads.

8 to 10 lbs. small shrimp in shell
1½ cups dehydrated sliced or chopped onion
1½ cups water
1 quart olive oil
1½ pints cider vinegar
1 pint capers with juice
¼ cup lemon juice
2 tablespoons sugar
2 tablespoons Worcestershire sauce
2 teaspoons salt
¾ teaspoon instant granulated garlic
Few drops hot pepper sauce

Cook shrimp, peel, devein and rinse well. Reconstitute the dehydrated onion in 1½ cups of water. Alternate layers of shrimp and reconstituted onions in large flat pan. Combine remaining ingredients and pour over both shrimp and onions. Cover and refrigerate overnight. Drain and serve in lettuce cups. Garnish with tomato and cucumber. Makes about 30 servings.

SHRIMPLY GARLIC POTATO SALAD

A hot, spicy dressing tops a combination of freshly boiled potatoes and garlic-sauteed shrimp for a new taste experience.

Recipe contest entry: Bob Dixon, Santa Cruz, CA

6 medium potatoes, preferably Red Rose
4 slices bacon, coarsely chopped
½ lb. shrimp, cleaned and deveined
8 cloves fresh garlic, minced
⅓ cup white wine
2 tablespoons brown sugar
¼ cup white wine vinegar
1 tablespoon German mustard
2 green onions, minced
1 dill pickle, chopped
Salt and pepper to taste
Lettuce

Boil potatoes with jackets on for 25 minutes or until tender. Drain. In large skillet, fry bacon until barely cooked, then add shrimp and garlic. Cook, stirring, until shrimp have cooked through, being careful not to burn garlic. Remove bacon and shrimp and set aside. Drain pan and add wine and sugar. Simmer for 1 to 2 minutes. Add vinegar and mustard and simmer for 1 minute longer. Set aside. Slice potatoes with jackets into large bowl. Pour hot liquid over and mix. Add pickle, onion, shrimp, bacon and salt and pepper to taste. Mix well and serve on crisp lettuce leaves. Makes 4 to 6 servings.

LUCIA'S VEGETABLE SALAD

A very colorful salad which is a good, crunchy contrast to Mexican food.

Recipe contest entry: Joyce Childs, Danville, CA

1 cup oil (half salad oil and half olive oil)
1/3 cup wine vinegar
3 cloves fresh garlic, finely minced
2 tablespoons capers (optional)
1 tablespoon finely minced parsley
1 tablespoon Italian seasoning
1/2 teaspoon salt
Pepper to taste
3 medium zucchini, cut in 1/2-inch slices
1 can (1 lb.) medium ripe olives, not pitted, drained
1 basket cherry tomatoes
1/2 lb. whole, small fresh mushrooms
2 or 3 jars (6 oz. *each*) marinated artichokes, drained
Lettuce

Prepare dressing by combining first 8 ingredients. In large bowl place zucchini, olives, tomatoes and mushrooms and pour marinade over. Refrigerate for 12 hours. Add artichokes and mix. Arrange on bed of lettuce in shallow bowl or platter. Drizzle marinade over. Makes 6 to 8 servings.

ROSIE'S BROCCOLI SALAD

Tart and tangy garlic marinade adds zip to steamed broccoli.

Recipe contest entry: Carla Johnson, Petaluma, CA

2 bunches broccoli
1/4 cup olive oil
3 to 4 cloves fresh garlic, pressed or minced
1/2 teaspoon salt
1/4 teaspoon oregano
1/4 cup wine vinegar

Cut off tough ends of broccoli and discard. Slice remaining stems and flowers into bite-sized pieces which should equal about 14 cups, uncooked. Steam or boil broccoli until just tender. Drain and cool. Toss broccoli with olive oil, garlic, salt and oregano. Add vinegar and toss again. Refrigerate at least 1 hour to marinate before serving. This can be prepared the day prior to serving and served chilled or at room temperature.

EGGPLANT SALAD TRINIDADELISH

Serve this salad with cold roast chicken, crusty French bread and fresh fruit for a beautiful summer meal.

Recipe contest entry: Thomas Davis, Waynesboro, MI

1 large eggplant
8 oz. shell macaroni, cooked
1 medium tomato, chopped
½ cup olive oil
¼ cup finely chopped fresh garlic
¼ cup freshly squeezed lime juice
4 tablespoons finely chopped parsley
2 tablespoons dry vermouth
1 tablespoon chopped green onion
2 teaspoons seasoned salt
½ teaspoon *each* oregano and basil
¼ teaspoon freshly ground pepper
Lettuce

Wash eggplant; prick skin several times with fork. Place on baking sheet and bake at 350 degrees for 45 minutes or until eggplant is tender. Cool and peel; cut into ½-inch cubes. In large bowl, combine eggplant, macaroni and tomatoes. Prepare dressing by mixing all remaining ingredients and pour over eggplant-macaroni-tomato mixture. Cover and refrigerate overnight. Serve on crisp lettuce leaves. Makes 6 to 8 servings.

MIDDLE EAST CARROT SALAD

A dish to serve as an accent with meat and potatoes, rice or pasta.

Recipe contest entry: Marion Marshall, Van Nuys, CA

6 large carrots, peeled and cooked
3 or 4 cloves fresh garlic, minced
1 tablespoon salad oil
1 tablespoon paprika
1 tablespoon chopped parsley
1 teaspoon salt
½ teaspoon cumin
Juice of a large lemon *or*
1½ tablespoons vinegar

Slice carrots into ¼-inch rounds. Mix all other ingredients and add to carrots. Marinate 3 to 4 hours *or* overnight. Makes 4 servings.

GARLIC GREEN BEAN SALAD

A versatile, green bean dish that can be served as a side dish or combined with shredded iceberg lettuce for a delicious, crispy and satisfying salad.   *Recipe contest entry: Sylvia V. Biewener, Burbank, CA*

2   lbs. fresh green beans
4   large cloves fresh garlic
1½ teaspoons salt
½   cup oil
½   cup cider vinegar
¼   cup minced green onions
    (use some green tops)
1   can (4 oz.) chopped green
    chile peppers

Cut beans in 2-inch lengths. Boil until tender-crisp and drain. Peel garlic and mash with salt. Add oil, vinegar, onions and chiles. Pour over beans while hot. Toss gently. Refrigerate. Makes 6 to 8 servings.

MARIAN'S BEANS

This dish is high in protein and can be used as a dip or a salad.   *Recipe contest entry: Marian Chisholm, Marblehead, MA*

4   cups red kidney beans,
    cooked
2   medium onions, finely
    chopped
2   medium green bell
    peppers, finely chopped
½   cup *each* catsup,
    mayonnaise and sweet
    relish
3   cloves fresh garlic,
    minced
2   teaspoons white horse-
    radish
¼   teaspoon *each* dry mustard and Worcestershire sauce

Rinse and drain beans. Mix with remaining ingredients. Chill and serve. Makes 8 servings.

GARLICKY GREEN GODDESS MOLD

As a spread for crackers, this molded salad also makes a great appetizer or hors d'oeuvre.

Recipe contest entry: Julius Wolf, Culver City, CA

2 envelopes plain gelatin
½ cup cold water
1 carton (8 oz.) plain yogurt
1 pint sour cream
¼ cup *each* chopped parsley and chopped green onion
5 cloves fresh garlic, minced
2 tablespoons anchovy paste
1 tablespoon white vinegar
2 teaspoons Dijon-style mustard
½ teaspoon salt
⅛ teaspoon white pepper
1 medium cucumber, finely diced
¼ cup celery, finely sliced
¼ cup toasted, slivered almonds
8 lettuce leaves
8 cherry tomatoes
8 ripe olives

Sprinkle gelatin over water to soften. Stir over low heat until dissolved. Cool slightly. Pour into blender with yogurt, sour cream, parsley, green onion, garlic, anchovy paste, vinegar, mustard, salt and pepper. Process until smooth. Pour into large bowl and fold in cucumber, celery and almonds. Pour mixture into 1½-quart mold which has been rinsed with cold water; chill until firm. Unmold onto lettuce leaves and garnish with tomatoes and olives. Makes 8 servings.

KAREN'S FRESH PEARS
WITH GARLIC-ROQUEFORT DRESSING

The man of the house is of Danish ancestry and grows garlic and comice pears. What better combination to keep him content than Roquefort cheese and fresh garlic dressing on fresh comice pears? A classic combination that makes a terrific salad.

Courtesy of: Karen Christopher, Gilroy, CA

½ cup mayonnaise
1 tablespoon cream
1 tablespoon lemon juice
2 cloves fresh garlic, pressed
1½ oz. Roquefort *or* blue cheese, crumbled
8 fresh comice pears
   Lemon juice
8 lettuce leaves

Mix together mayonnaise, cream, 1 tablespoon lemon juice, garlic and cheese and chill at elast 2 hours. Cut pears in half and remove seeds and skins. Sprinkle with additional lemon juice to prevent browning. Place on lettuce leaves for individual servings, spoon dressing, and serve. Makes 8 salads.

NOTE: This dressing is also delicious on most greens or can be used as a dip for fresh raw vegetables.

JEANNE'S LOW-FAT CREAMY GARLIC DRESSING

This original low-calorie recipe is equally good as a dip or dolloped on crisp hearts of lettuce. *Recipe contest entry: Jeanne Marks, Aptos, CA*

4 large cloves fresh garlic
8 oz. low-fat plain yogurt
1 cup low-fat mayonnaise
¼ cup imitation bacon bits
½ teaspoon prepared mustard

Put garlic through press or mince fine. Combine with remaining ingredients and serve as a dip or salad dressing.

GARLIC FRENCH DRESSING

This is a good basic dressing with subtle but pleasing garlic flavor. For variety add ¾ cup crumbled Roquefort cheese, a chopped hard-cooked egg, or 3 tablespoons chopped onion.

Recipe contest entry: Barbara Van Brunt Halop, Los Angeles, CA

2¼ cups salad oil
1 cup mayonnaise
¾ cup wine *or* cider vinegar
8 cloves fresh garlic, pressed *or* minced
2 teaspoons salt
1½ teaspoons sugar
1½ teaspoons paprika
1½ teaspoons dry mustard
1½ teaspoons Worcestershire sauce
¾ teaspoon coarse ground pepper
¼ teaspoon garlic salt
¼ teaspoon onion salt
¼ teaspoon celery salt
¼ teaspoon seasoned salt
¼ cup catsup *or* chili sauce for color

Combine all ingredients and blend well. Refrigerate in covered container approximately 24 hours before using.

GREEN GODDESS DRESSING

The original Green Goddess dressing was created by the chef of the Palace Hotel in San Francisco for a noted star in the days of the silent films. Without the fresh garlic from Gilroy it would not be such a distinctive concoction! For a really new taste, top shrimp-filled papaya halves with Green Goddess dressing for lunch or a light supper.

1 can (2 oz.) anchovy fillets
3 cups mayonnaise
¼ cup wine vinegar
1 tablespoon chives
1 tablespoon minced green onion
1 tablespoon parsley flakes
1 tablespoon tarragon leaves
¼ teaspoon garlic powder
⅛ teaspoon onion powder
Dash MSG (optional)

Mash anchovies. Add remaining ingredients; mix well. Let stand 30 minutes or longer for flavors to blend. Serve with salad greens. You may toss chicken, shrimp or crab meat with the greens. Makes about 3½ cups.

PARTY-PERFECT GARLIC DRESSING

When it's party time and you're planning a salad, try this flavorful combination. It makes a gallon of tangy dressing to perk up any fresh vegetable combination.

1⅓ teaspoons curry powder
1⅓ teaspoons dry mustard
 2   teaspoons cayenne pepper
 1   tablespoon dehydrated parsley
 1   tablespoon dehydrated chives
 1   teaspoon instant granulated garlic
 ¼   cup salt
 1   tablespoon white pepper
 1   lemon rind, chopped
 ⅓   cup olive oil
 1   cup white wine vinegar
2½   quarts salad oil
1¼   quarts cider vinegar

Moisten instant granulated garlic, parsley and chives with ¼ cup water. To this add curry, mustard, cayenne, salt, pepper and lemon rind. While beating, first add olive oil, then vinegar. Chill well. Shake before serving. Makes about 1 gallon.

GEORGETTE'S FRENCH DRESSING

This is a low-calorie, low-salt salad dressing that is great on any mixed green salad. It was named after the late Georgette Smith, home economics teacher at Gavilan Junior College in Gilroy.

Courtesy of: Louis Bonesio, Jr., Gilroy, CA

 1   cup low-sodium tomato juice
 1   cup red wine vinegar
 1   cup polyunsaturated oil
 ¼   cup honey
 3   to 4 cloves fresh garlic, minced
 ½   teaspoon paprika
 ½   teaspoon coarse pepper
 ¼   teaspoon dry mustard
 ¼   teaspoon curry powder

Combine all ingredients and beat with a rotary beater or shake in a tightly covered jar. Shake well before serving. A little grated Parmesan cheese as a garnish and some sourdough bread for a "backstop" is good.

TART 'N' TANGY ITALIAN DRESSING

It is so simple to make a truly appealing Italian salad dressing and it can be done as close as one hour before serving time. Use as a marinade, too, for steaks and chops.

1 cup olive oil
½ cup wine vinegar
1 teaspoon instant minced onion
1 teaspoon seasoned salt
¾ teaspoon garlic powder
½ teaspoon chives
½ teaspoon parsley flakes
½ teaspoon sugar
¼ teaspoon dry mustard
¼ teaspoon oregano
⅛ teaspoon white pepper
Dash cayenne *or* red pepper

Combine all ingredients in jar; cover and shake vigorously. Chill 1 hour for flavors to blend. Shake well before serving. Makes 1½ cups.

ITALIAN SWEET-SOUR DRESSING

Italians are full of surprises and the sweet-sour flavor captured in this dressing is certainly different. It's especially good over crisp chunks of iceberg lettuce.

1 cup vegetable oil
⅔ cup red wine vinegar
4 tablespoons sugar
1 teaspoon salt
1 teaspoon celery salt
1 teaspoon coarsely ground pepper
1 teaspoon dry mustard
1 teaspoon Worcestershire sauce
½ teaspoon bottled hot pepper sauce
3 cloves fresh garlic, minced

Thoroughly combine all ingredients in a jar or blender. Refrigerate. Makes 2 cups dressing.

Eggs / Cheese

Pesto Quiche	97
Garlic Goddess Cheese Pie	98
Artichoke Pie	99
Mushroom Crust Florentine Pie	100
Artichoke and Carrot Frittata	101
Garlic Frittata	101
Artichoke and Garlic Frittata	102
The Gubsers' Green Bean and Garlic Frittata	103
Sabrina's Garlic Souffle	104

Finalist in 1981 Recipe Contest: ANAHIT LEMON, Berkeley, CA

Calling garlic "a staple of life's" this Cook-off finalist whipped up a classic pesto sauce and combined it with freshly laid duck eggs and cheeses in creating her savory quiche.

PESTO QUICHE

Pesto

- 4 cloves fresh garlic
- 1 cup coarsely chopped fresh basil
- ¼ teaspoon salt
- ¼ teaspoon pepper, freshly ground
- 2 tablespoons pine nuts *or* walnuts
- ¼ cup olive oil
- ½ cup grated Parmesan cheese
- 2 tablespoons melted butter

- 1 deep dish (9-inch) pie shell
- 4 cloves fresh garlic
- 1 large onion
- 3 tablespoons butter
- 3 large eggs
- 1 cup milk
- ½ cup ricotta cheese
- ¼ cup prepared pesto (see recipe above)
- 1½ cups grated Parmesan cheese

Peel and crush garlic. Turn into blender along with basil, salt, pepper and pine nuts *or* walnuts. Blend at high speed. Alternately blend in olive oil and grated Parmesan cheese. Stir in melted butter. Set aside.

Prepare or purchase pie shell. Partially bake shell in a 350-degree oven for 5 minutes. Peel and finely chop garlic and onion. Saute in butter until translucent. Lightly beat eggs. Mix milk with ricotta, then combine with eggs, garlic, onion and ¼ cup of prepared pesto. Turn into crust and sprinkle Parmesan evenly over top. Bake in top of oven at 350 degrees for about 40 minutes, until puffed and lightly browned. Makes one 9-inch quiche.

*Finalist in 1981 Recipe Contest:*JACQUELINE BEARDSLEY, San Francisco, CA

This nutritious filling nestled in a novel potato crust makes a rich, tempting pie which is not only healthy but sooooo good!

GARLIC GODDESS CHEESE PIE

Potato Crust
  2 large raw potatoes
  ½ teaspoon salt
  1 large beaten egg

  3 large cloves fresh garlic
  1 green onion
  2 bunches asparagus
 15 medium-sized
     mushrooms
  3 tablespoons butter
  ½ teaspoon salt
  ½ teaspoon dried basil
     Dash thyme
 2¼ heaping cups grated
     white Cheddar cheese
  2 large eggs
  ¼ cup milk

Preheat oven to hot (400 degrees). Pare and grate potatoes. Combine with salt and turn into a colander. Let drain 10 minutes, then squeeze out excess moisture. Combine with egg. Pat into oiled 9-inch pie pan to make a crust. Bake in preheated oven 40 to 45 minutes. Peel and crush garlic; trim and chop onion. Trim and chop asparagus tips and mushrooms. Saute garlic and onion in butter a few minutes. Add asparagus and mushrooms along with seasonings. Cover and cook 10 minutes stirring occasionally. Spread half the cheese into the baked crust, then the vegetable saute. Cover with remaining cheese. Beat eggs with milk and pour over the pie. Bake in moderately hot oven, 375 degrees, 35 to 40 minutes. Makes one 9-inch pie.

Regional Winner in 1981 Recipe Contest:

MRS. LAWRENCE D'AMICO, Hackensack, NJ

Serve this dish warm or cold, as an hors d'oeuvre or as a main dish for lunch. It's delicious no matter how you serve it.

ARTICHOKE PIE

4 or 5 cloves fresh garlic
1 medium onion
2 tablespoons butter
3 large eggs
1 cup whipping cream
½ cup shredded Mozzarella cheese
¼ cup grated Parmesan cheese
  Salt and pepper to taste
1 can (8½ oz.) artichoke hearts*
1 unbaked (9-inch) pastry shell**

Mince garlic and thinly slice onion. Saute in butter until soft and golden (do not brown). Beat eggs and add cream, cheeses, salt and pepper to taste, and garlic-onion mixture. Drain and cut artichokes in quarters. Add to egg mixture and gently pour into pastry shell. Bake in hot oven (400 degrees) about 45 minutes until set. Serve warm or cold, as entree or appetizer. Makes one 9-inch pie.

* 1 small package frozen artichoke hearts. Parboil and drain well.

** Use your favorite recipe or a frozen, deep 9-inch shell.

Eat leeks in tide and garlic in May, and all the year after physicians may play.

Russian proverb

MUSHROOM CRUST FLORENTINE PIE

Crumb crust with a difference!....sauteed mushrooms! Real garlic devotees will want to add more of their favorite flavoring and yogurt could be substituted for the mayonnaise for a slightly different flavor.

Recipe contest entry: Jamie Schulte, Indianapolis, IN

½ lb. fresh mushrooms, chopped
3 tablespoons margarine
½ cup dry bread crumbs *or* cracker crumbs
1½ cups shredded Swiss cheese
3 tablespoons flour
1 pkg. (10 oz.) frozen chopped spinach, thawed and drained
6 crisp cooked bacon slices, crumbled
3 eggs
3 cloves fresh garlic, minced
3 scallions with tops, chopped
⅔ cup mayonnaise
1 teaspoon parsley
½ teaspoon pepper
Cherry tomatoes and hard-cooked egg slices for garnish
Parmesan cheese

Saute mushrooms in margarine, stir in bread crumbs and press evenly in greased 9-inch pie pan over bottom and sides to form crust. Toss cheese with flour and add remaining ingredients. Mix well and fill crust with mixture. Bake at 350 degrees for about 40 minutes. Garnish as desired and sprinkle lightly with Parmesan. Makes 4 servings.

ARTICHOKE AND CARROT FRITTATA

This vegetable frittata is excellent served as an evening main course or for a brunch. It could be topped with a white sauce and garnished with sliced ripe olives or served on bread as a sandwich filling.

Recipe contest entry: Fanny Cimoli, San Jose, CA

2 cups sliced *or* chopped cooked artichoke hearts
8 eggs, beaten
1 cup grated cheese (Italian *or* American)
1 cup grated carrot
½ cup finely chopped parsley
½ cup chopped onion
⅛ cup chopped celery
5 cloves fresh garlic, minced
1 tablespoon catsup
1 teaspoon salt
¼ teaspoon pepper
   Garlic salt to taste

Combine all ingredients together and blend well. Pour into a 9 x 11-inch baking dish, lightly greased. Bake until golden brown for 20 to 30 minutes at 300 degrees. Do not overbake, as it may become dry. Cut into squares and serve.

GARLIC FRITTATA

For brunch or a light supper, this frittata is a snap to fix and the flavor is superb. Try serving it with steamed artichokes or a green salad and a chilled California white wine, like Chablis.

Recipe contest entry: Anne T. Kahn, Newark

8 eggs
½ cup milk
½ cup grated Parmesan cheese
2 tablespoons butter
4 cloves fresh garlic, minced
½ cup chopped onion
1 to 4 oz. Polish sausage *or* garlic sausage, chopped
4 large potatoes, shredded
4 oz. Cheddar cheese, shredded

Beat together eggs, milk and Parmesan cheese; set aside. In large skillet, over medium-high heat, melt butter and saute garlic, onion, sausage and potatoes for about 5 minutes or until tender. Reduce heat to medium. Pour egg mixture into pan and cook, without stirring, until eggs are almost set. Sprinkle Cheddar cheese over top of frittata. Let cook on top of stove for about 1 more minute. Place pan under broiler and broil about 6 inches from heat until top is bubbly and slightly browned. Cut in wedges to serve.

ARTICHOKE AND GARLIC FRITTATA

A frittata is nothing more than a flat Italian omelet to which, like the omelet, one can add almost any meat, cheese or ingredient, but always it should be topped with a generous sprinkling of freshly grated Parmesan cheese.   *Recipe contest entry: Lisa G. Hanauer, San Francisco, CA*

15 to 20 cloves fresh garlic, peeled and coarsely chopped
1 large Bermuda onion, coarsely chopped
¼ cup olive oil
½ lb. fresh mushrooms, sliced
2 jars (6 oz. *each*) marinated artichoke hearts, drained and halved
8 to 10 eggs
¼ lb. *each* Parmesan, Romano and Mozzarella, freshly grated
⅓ cup Italian bread crumbs
3 tablespoons Italian seasoning
2 tablespoons freshly ground pepper
2 teaspoons salt
Paprika

In large pan, saute garlic and onion in oil until soft. Add mushrooms and saute for 5 minutes more. Add artichoke hearts; let mixture cool. In large mixing bowl, beat eggs. Fold in cheeses, bread crumbs, herbs, pepper and salt. Combine with cooled artichoke and garlic mixture. Pour into two 9-inch cake pans. Sprinkle with paprika and bake at 375 degrees for 40 minutes or until done. Makes 16 servings.

Gilroy is an example of well-managed small-town living that could have remained a secret...., except for a festival it hosts annually called the Gilroy Garlic Festival.

Ford Times

THE GUBSERS' GREEN BEAN AND GARLIC FRITTATA

Joseph Gubser's father began growing garlic in Gilroy in the 1920s and to put it in Joe's words, "I grew up with the industry." This grower / shipper and his wife, Doris, have contributed this unusual and tasty treatment for beans. It can be served as a cold vegetable dish or as an hors d'oeuvre.   *Courtesy of: Joseph and Doris Gubser, Gilroy, CA*

1 green pepper, chopped
1 small onion, chopped
¼ cup plus 3 tablespoons olive oil
3 lbs. canned green beans, drained
¾ cup bread crumbs
½ cup grated Parmesan cheese plus additional cheese for topping
¼ cup sherry
3 eggs, beaten
3 large cloves fresh garlic, minced
1 tablespoon Italian seasoning
¼ teaspoon salt
⅛ teaspoon pepper
Paprika

Saute pepper and onion in 3 tablespoons olive oil. Combine with beans and all other ingredients (except paprika and cheese reserved for topping) into buttered 2-quart baking dish. Sprinkle with additional grated Parmesan and paprika. Bake in 325-degree oven 40 minutes. Serve cold as a vegetable dish or as an hors d'oeuvre. Makes 10 to 12 servings.

SABRINA'S GARLIC SOUFFLE

The youngest entrant in the first Garlic Recipe Contest and Cook-off was a teenager whose recipe for garlic souffle qualified her among the ten finalists. Serve for brunch or as an unusual side dish.

Recipe contest entry: Sabrina Vial, Fresno, CA

¼ cup butter
1 can (10½ oz.) cream of celery soup
½ cup milk
1½ teaspoons salt
¼ teaspoon pepper
2 cups shredded Cheddar cheese
2 teaspoons lemon juice
3 beaten eggs
1 cup minced fresh garlic

In large saucepan, melt butter. Add soup, milk, salt and pepper; blend over medium heat until smooth. Slowly add cheese and lemon juice, blending well. Remove from heat; add well-beaten eggs and garlic. Mix well and pour into a greased 1½-quart casserole. Bake uncovered in 350-degree oven for 50 minutes.

Pasta / Rice

Spinach-Garlic Pasta with
  Garlic-Onion Sauce   107
Hot Brie Pasta ala Diane   108
Nancy and J.R.'s Pasta   108
Eggplant Pasta Fantastico   109
Two Peas-in-a Pasta   109
Pasta Teresa   110
Pasta Verde (Spaghetti with
  Spinach and Almond Sauce)   111
Pasta con Pesto alla Melone   112
Spaghettaccini Carolini   113
Gagootza   114
Spaghetti Josephine   115
Patchwork Calico Pasta   115
Fettuccelle al Limone   116
Fettuccine Roberto   117
Fettuccine Garli-Mari   118
Fettuccine Gloriosa   119
Mary Ann's Fettuccine Zucchini   120
Fettuccine Fragale   120
Spinach Fettuccine with
  Artichoke Sauce   121
Pesto Lasagna Firenza   121
Fusilli con Aglio, Olio,
  Peperoncino e Zucchini   122
Handmade Garlic-Cheese Ravioli
  with Garlic Bechamel Sauce
  and Shrimp   123
Garlic Ravioli   124
Green Ravioli with Garlic Filling   125
Baked Manicotti with Meat Sauce   126
Garlic-Cheese Mostaccioli   127
Linguine Contessa   127
Family Favorite Linguine and
  Clam Sauce   128
Garlic in the Straw and Hay   129
Linguine with White Clam Sauce   130
Glorioso for One Person   130

Manti   131
Walnut Sauce from Garlic Country   131
Italian Meatballs and Sauce
    for Spaghetti   132
Super Meat Sauce for Pasta   133
Noodles Romanoff   134
Mahony's Rice   134
California Pilaf   135
Sausage and Rice, Swiss Style   135
Hollister Hot Rice   136
Garlic Dill Rice   136

Finalist in 1986 Recipe Contest: IRA J. JACOBSON, Oakland, CA

Vidalia onions may be hard to come by (genuine Vidalias come from Vidalia, Georgia, and, according to Ira, are as sweet as apples). Spanish onions make a good substitute.

SPINACH-GARLIC PASTA WITH GARLIC-ONION SAUCE

Spinach-Garlic Pasta

- 1½ cups all-purpose flour
- 2 eggs plus 4 yolks
- 1 tablespoon olive oil
- ½ lb. fresh spinach, blanched, squeezed dry and finely chopped
- 6 large cloves fresh garlic, crushed and finely chopped
- ½ teaspoon salt

Place 1 cup flour in large stainless steel bowl. Make a well in the center. Break eggs into well and add yolks and olive oil. Add spinach and garlic to which salt has been added. Mix. Work in more flour as needed. Knead until dough is smooth. Let rest. With pasta machine, roll dough to desired thickness. Cut to desired width and cook fresh, approximately 2 minutes. Drain. Toss with sauce.

Garlic-Onion Sauce

- ½ cup butter
- 1 tablespoon olive oil
- ⅓ cup chopped fresh garlic (about 12 large cloves)
- 1 lb. Vidalia or other sweet onions, peeled and sliced
- 1 tablespoon honey
- ¼ cup Marsala wine Parmesan cheese

Melt butter with oil in skillet; add garlic and onion. Cover and cook at medium heat until soft and clear. Remove lid, add honey and lower heat. Cook gently about 30 minutes. Add wine and cook 5 to 10 minutes longer. Toss with pasta and top with cheese. Makes 2 to 4 servings.

Finalist in 1983 Recipe Contest: DIANE TARANGO, Hacienda Heights, CA

A very simple dish but very, very good. Might need more garlic for some. Be sure the Brie is well ripened, so that it will have good flavor.

HOT BRIE PASTA ALA DIANE

1 lb. ripe French Brie
½ cup olive oil
1 cup fresh basil, cut into strips
4 large cloves fresh garlic, minced
4 tomatoes, seeded and cubed
½ teaspoon salt
¾ teaspoon freshly ground pepper
1 lb. linguine *or* capelli d'angelo (angel hair) pasta
6 oz. Parmesan, freshly grated

Remove rind from cheese and cut into irregular pieces. Combine with next 6 ingredients in large bowl and let stand for 2 hours at room temperature. Cook pasta *al dente* and drain. Toss hot pasta with Brie mixture. Top with Parmesan cheese and serve at once. Delicious! Makes 4 to 6 servings.

NANCY AND J.R.'S PASTA

A crowd-pleasing pasta recipe that can be made with mild or super hot Italian sausage as your taste dictates.

Recipe contest entry: Nancy Mertesdorf and Jeanette Renouf, San Jose, CA

1 lb. hot Italian sausage
2 tablespoons oil
¾ lb. fresh mushrooms, sliced
8 to 10 large cloves fresh garlic, minced
2 medium green bell peppers, julienned
1 bunch green onions, chopped
¼ cup dry white wine
4 tablespoons butter, softened
¾ lb. fresh, thin, coiled spaghetti
6 oz. Parmesan cheese, freshly grated

Remove casing from sausage. Crumble and fry in small skillet. Drain off excess fat and set aside. Heat oil in large skillet or wok. Add mushrooms, half the garlic, peppers, onions and wine. Stir fry until crisp-tender. Meanwhile add remaining minced garlic to butter and set aside. Cook pasta for 4 to 5 minutes or until tender. Drain well. Toss with garlic butter and Parmesan cheese, saving some for garnish. Add sausage and vegetable mixture to pasta and toss well. Makes 12 servings.

EGGPLANT PASTA FANTASTICO

Eggplant and herbs, gently simmered, make a richly satisfying sauce for pasta. An extra sprinkling of Parmesan cheese adds zip.

Recipe contest entry: Leatrice Resnick, Los Angeles, CA

½ cup olive oil
8 cloves fresh garlic, slivered
2 tablespoons minced onion
1 medium eggplant
1 tablespoon parsley flakes
1 tablespoon oregano flakes
1 teaspoon basil
1 teaspoon salt
½ teaspoon ground pepper
½ to 1 cup water
Juice of ½ lemon
8 oz. spaghetti or linguine
½ cup pasta liquid
1 tablespoon grated Parmesan cheese plus additional cheese, if desired

In large skillet, heat olive oil. Add garlic and onion and slowly saute until lightly browned. While garlic is cooking, peel and dice eggplant into ½-inch cubes. Add eggplant, parsley, oregano, basil, salt and pepper to garlic mixture. Stir all ingredients well. Cover and cook over medium-low heat for 30 minutes, stirring occasionally. Add ½ cup water and lemon juice. Stir and continue cooking until eggplant is soft, adding more water as needed if mixture gets dry. (Mixture should be very moist.) Cook pasta *al dente* (just until tender; do not overcook). Drain pasta, reserve ½ cup liquid. Add pasta and liquid to eggplant mixture. Add Parmesan cheese. Toss well and heat through for 1 minute. Serve immediately with additional cheese, if desired. Makes 2 servings.

TWO PEAS-IN-A-PASTA

A very tasty combination. Try it also with small egg noodles or macaroni.

Recipe contest entry: Mrs. J. Rhodes, Prescott, AZ

5 cloves fresh garlic, minced
6 tablespoons olive oil
1 pkg. (10 oz.) frozen peas
1 can (16 oz.) chick peas (garbanzos), drained, reserving liquid
1 teaspoon *each* dried basil and salt
1 lb. fettuccine *or* linguine
½ cup half-and-half
½ cup grated Parmesan cheese
¼ lb. Mozzarella cheese, grated

In 10-inch skillet, cook garlic in olive oil until golden but not brown. Add frozen peas and chick peas, basil and salt. Lower heat; cover and simmer for 10 minutes. Meanwhile, cook pasta according to package directions. Drain. In large serving dish, gently mix cooked pasta with half-and-half, Parmesan and Mozzarella. Pour cooked mixture over all, gently mixing through. Add reserved liquid if moister pasta is desired. Makes 4 to 6 servings.

PASTA TERESA

This tasty combination of artichoke hearts, tomatoes, garlic and thin spaghetti makes a great meal-in-a-hurry.

Recipe contest entry: Geoff Berkin, Los Angeles, CA

1 whole head garlic, peeled
3 tablespoons *each* chopped fresh basil and oregano
4 medium tomatoes
¾ cup olive oil
2 thick slices of onion
2 pkg. (9 oz. *each*) frozen artichoke hearts, thawed and drained
¾ lb. spaghettini
4 oz. grated Parmesan cheese
Salt and pepper to taste

In blender or food processor, puree garlic, basil and oregano. Slice each tomato into 8 or 10 thin wedges, then slice wedges in half. Heat oil in large skillet, add garlic puree and onion slices and saute over medium heat for about 2 to 3 minutes. Remove onion and discard. Add tomatoes and artichoke hearts to pan and gently mix. Lower heat and stir occasionally while pasta cooks. Cook pasta according to package directions until *al dente*. Drain. With slotted spoon, remove tomatoes and artichoke hearts from skillet to bowl. Add drained pasta to skillet and toss to coat with oil. Add Parmesan cheese and toss, then salt and pepper. Divide pasta onto 4 plates, then top with equal portions of tomatoes and artichoke hearts. Makes 4 servings.

PASTA VERDE (SPAGHETTI WITH SPINACH AND ALMOND SAUCE)

Serve this pasta as a side dish with grilled or barbecued meats.

Recipe contest entry: Carole L. Rutter, Hayward, CA

1 bunch spinach *or* 1 pkg. (10 oz.) frozen spinach
¼ cup coarsely chopped fresh parsley
¼ cup *each* grated Romano and Parmesan cheese
¼ cup vegetable oil
2 tablespoons butter *or* margarine
1 oz. blanched almonds
4 or more cloves fresh garlic
¼ cup boiling water, plus extra on hand
1 lb. spaghetti *or* macaroni
Parmesan cheese and chopped parsley for garnish

Wash spinach, remove white stems and chop leaves coarsely. Cook in small quantity of boiling salted water until tender or cook frozen spinach according to package directions. Drain, then place in blender with all remaining ingredients except hot water. Blend to smooth paste. Add boiling water, blend again for a few seconds. Extra water may be added to achieve desired consistency. Cook spaghetti according to package directions. Drain and pour sauce over; toss well. Garnish with extra Parmesan cheese and / or parsley if desired. Makes 4 to 6 servings.

NOTE: Sauce is best when served immediately, so time the cooking of the spaghetti to be ready when sauce is finished.

Community leaders agreed that the time had come for garlic to come storming out of the pantry closet.
MIKE DUNNE
Sacramento *Bee*

PASTA CON PESTO ALLA MELONE

Take a man of Italian descent who loves to cook, make him president of a community college which just happens to be in the center of a 90-mile radius of 90 percent of the nation's production of garlic and stand back! The Gilroy Garlic Festival could not have "happened" without the inspiration and creative mind of Dr. Rudy Melone and his foresight to know it was possible.

In this recipe from Dr. Melone's private collection, he suggests a light, fine pasta to go with his gloriously garlicky pesto creation.

Courtesy of: Dr. Rudy Melone, President, Gavilan Gollege;
Chairman, Gilroy Garlic Festival

1 cup grated fresh Parmesan cheese
2 cups fresh basil leaves
½ cup melted butter
10 to 20 cloves fresh garlic (depending on their size and your taste)
1 tablespoon pine nuts
¾ cup olive oil
Pasta (preferably capellini *or* vermicelli)

Using blender or food processor, grate enough Parmesan cheese to make 1 cup; add basil. Then add melted butter, followed by garlic, pine nuts and finally the oil. Allow each added ingredient to blend smoothly with the preceding ones, and let stand at least 1 hour. This is the pesto sauce. Prepare pasta according to package directions. Mix pesto with pasta fresh from the boiling water. Do not add too much pesto, but allow each person a chance to adjust flavor to taste, by adding more pesto if desired. Leftover pesto will last for quite a long while if refrigerated in a plastic container, but do not freeze.

A light salad with oil and vinegar dressing and a veal dish go great with this. Pasta Con Pesto is also a versatile accompaniment to a variety of dishes—meat, fish, poultry, etc.

The soul of pesto may be basil, but its heart is garlic.

Pittsburgh Press

Third Prize Winner 1984 Recipe Contest: ROBERT J. DYER, Gilroy, CA

"If you live in the Garlic Capital of the World, it's only fitting that you should be a good garlic cook," claims Bob Dyer, Gilroy businessman, who was also chairman of the very first Garlic Festival in 1979. Bob's colorful spaghetti dish attracted the judges with its stir-fried vegetables, succulent prawns and plenty of garlic—24 cloves in all.

SPAGHETTACCINI CAROLINI

1 lb. spaghetti noodles	
4 tablespoons oil	
¼ lb. butter	
24 cloves fresh garlic, peeled and chopped	
1 lb. fresh jumbo shrimp, peeled and butterflied	
1 red bell pepper, thinly sliced	
1 bunch broccoli, cut into serving-size spears	
2 cups chopped fresh mushrooms	
1 cup chopped fresh parsley	
1 cup chopped green onions	
1 tablespoon dried red pepper	
2 tablespoons flour	
½ cup dry white wine	
1 pint heavy cream	
1 small wedge (about 3 oz.) Parmesan cheese, grated	
Salt to taste	

Cook noodles according to package directions in boiling water with 2 tablespoons oil. Meanwhile, melt butter in large skillet over medium, high heat. Add chopped garlic and shrimp; cook until shrimp turn pink, but do not allow garlic to brown. Set aside. In another skillet, over medium-high heat, stir-fry red bell pepper and broccoli in remaining 2 tablespoons oil. Cook until crisp-tender. Drain and set aside. Add mushrooms, half the parsley, onions and red pepper to garlic and shrimp; saute for 1 minute. Add flour, mix thoroughly, and add wine. Simmer for about 30 seconds, then add cream and heat through, stirring. Drain noodles and add to sauce with half the grated cheese. Toss gently until noodles are well coated and cheese is melted. Salt lightly. If sauce is too thin, continue heating until sauce reduces to a creamy consistency. If sauce is too thick, add cream. Gently toss in the stir-fried vegetables. Garnish with remaining chopped parsley and grated cheese and serve immediately. Makes 8 servings.

GAGOOTZA

For your next party, try a different kind of pasta—spicy-hot with green chili salsa, California style.

Recipe contest entry: Carl Stockdale, Pasadena, CA

Olive oil
3 large sweet white onions
2 to 3 heads fresh garlic, pressed
3 bunches minced parsley (just tops)
14 medium-sized zucchini, unpeeled, sliced ¼-inch thick
3 cans (7 oz. *each*) green chili salsa
3 lbs. Italian sausage, hot *or* mild
2 lbs. spaghetti
Garlic salt
Mozzarella cheese (about 2½ lbs.), grated
1 can (about 7 oz.) ripe pitted olives, halved
1 can (about 8 oz.) button mushrooms

Cover bottom of electric skillet with ⅛ to ¼-inch olive oil. Slice onions ⅛-inch thick, separate into rings and saute in oil. Add garlic, parsley, zucchini and salsa; stir lightly and let simmer until zucchini becomes tender. Brown sausage in separate skillet and drain. Cook spaghetti 8 minutes in salted water and rinse with cool water. Grease six 8x10x2 pans with olive oil. Cover bottom of pans with ¾-inch layer of spaghetti; sprinkle lightly with garlic salt and add layer of sausage. Cover generously with zucchini mixture. Sprinkle grated cheese over top to thickness desired. Garnish with olives and mushrooms. Bake for 30 minutes at 350 degrees and serve immediately, or freeze without baking for future use; it keeps indefinitely. When ready to use, remove from freezer and bake for 45 minutes at 350 degrees. Serve with garlic toast, tossed green salad and beer or wine. Serves a bunch!

SPAGHETTI JOSEPHINE

This recipe is a tribute to a lovely little Italian aunt-by-marriage who taught a North Carolina girl not to fear garlic. Aunt Jo hasn't been so well lately, and doesn't cook as often as she used to, but her style of cuisine lives on in a niece-in-law who turned to her husband one night and said, "How can I cook dinner—we're out of garlic!"

Recipe contest entry: Kathleen Kenney, Sausalito, CA

1 medium head cauliflower, separated into florets
1 lb. spaghetti
5 cloves fresh garlic, finely minced
2 tablespoons olive oil
¼ cup minced parsley
½ cup butter
½ cup freshly grated Parmesan cheese plus additional cheese
Freshly ground pepper

Cook cauliflower in a large amount of boiling, salted water. When almost tender (about 10 to 12 minutes), add spaghetti and cook until spaghetti is *al dente*. While cauliflower is cooking, saute garlic in olive oil for about 1 minute. Add parsley and butter and cook over low heat until hot and bubbly. Drain spaghetti and cauliflower; add garlic butter and toss gently. Add grated cheese and toss again. Serve with additional grated cheese and freshly ground pepper.

PATCHWORK CALICO PASTA

An excellent pasta dish which combines zucchini, broccoli, tomatoes and toasted pine nuts for unusual flavor and texture.

Recipe contest entry: Cynthia Kannenberg, Brown Deer, WI

4 zucchini (about ¾ lb.), cut into diagonal slices
2 cups broccoli florets
½ cup pine nuts
3 fresh tomatoes
1 lb. spaghetti
¼ cup olive oil
1 tablespoon minced fresh garlic,
1 chile pepper (optional)
Salt and pepper to taste
½ cup half-and-half *or* heavy cream
¼ cup butter
½ cup grated fresh Parmesan cheese

Blanch zucchini in boiling water for 1 minute, remove. Blanch broccoli for 3 to 4 minutes in boiling water. Drain. Peel and chop tomatoes. Toast pine nuts in 350-degree oven for 5 to 10 minutes, being certain not to burn. Cook spaghetti as package directs until *al dente*. Drain. Heat oil in skillet; add garlic, zucchini, broccoli, tomatoes, chile peppers, and salt and pepper. Cook briefly, stirring. Add drained spaghetti, cream, butter, cheese and nuts. Discard chile pepper. Toss and serve immediately. Garnish with additional cheese if desired. Makes 6 to 8 servings.

Finalist in 1985 Recipe Contest: DAWN D. CARDELLIO, Agoura, CA

If you're looking for a pasta dish that's a little out of the ordinary, try this one with its piquant lemon sauce.

FETTUCCELLE AL LIMONE
Fettuccelle Pasta with Lemon Sauce

½ cup (1 stick) butter
½ cup olive oil, extra virgin preferred
12 large cloves fresh garlic, finely chopped
1 teaspoon dry sweet basil leaves, finely crushed by hand
1 whole small fresh lemon, including rinds, finely chopped in blender or food processor
½ cup beef broth, regular strength
1 tablespoon (overflowing) wild honey, or more to taste
¼ teaspoon (rounded) crushed red pepper flakes
12 oz. fettuccelle (*or* other) pasta
8 oz. sliced cooked ham, cut into ¼-inch pieces
⅔ cup grated Parmesan cheese

In large skillet, melt butter over medium heat, add oil, stir to mix with butter, then add garlic and basil. Cook uncovered just until garlic begins to brown, stirring frequently. Do not burn! Reduce heat to low and add lemon, including juice, and simmer, uncovered, for 5 minutes, stirring frequently. Stir in broth, honey and red pepper. Simmer 5 minutes longer, then remove from heat. Puree mixture in blender or food processor and set aside. In 5-quart cooking pot, cook pasta in rapidly boiling salted water (about 1 rounded teaspoon salt) until *al dente* (still slightly chewy). Drain and return to cooking pot. Add pureed sauce and ham; toss to blend. Cook uncovered over medium heat until well heated through, about 2 to 3 minutes. Stir often. Remove from heat and add Parmesan cheese. Toss gently with two large wooden forks or similar utensils until pasta is well coated and cheese well blended. Makes about 4 servings.

Honorable Mention 1983 Recipe Contest: ROBERT J. DYER, Gilroy, CA

This Honorable Mention winner went on the next year to win third prize with another pasta recipe. This dish will serve 6 or more as a small appetizer or starter course.

FETTUCCINE ROBERTO

  1 lb. fettuccine noodles
 ½ cup oil
 ¼ lb. butter
24 cloves fresh garlic, chopped
  1 lb. fresh jumbo shrimp, butterflied
  1 cup chopped fresh parsley
  2 cups chopped fresh mushrooms
  1 cup chopped green onions
  1 tablespoon red pepper
  2 tablespoons flour
 ½ cup dry white wine
  1 pint heavy cream
  1 small wedge (about 5 oz.) Parmesan cheese, grated
     Salt to taste

Cook noodles according to package directions in boiling water with oil. While noodles are cooking, melt butter in large skillet over medium-high heat. Add chopped garlic and shrimp; cook until shrimp turn pink, but do not allow garlic to turn brown. Add parsley, mushrooms, onions and red pepper; saute for 1 minute. Add flour, mix thoroughly and add wine. Simmer for about 30 seconds, then add cream and heat through. Drain noodles and add to sauce with half the grated cheese. Fold in gently until noodles are well coated and cheese is melted. Salt lightly. If sauce is too thin, continue heating until sauce reduces to a creamy consistency. If sauce is too thick, add cream. Garnish with chopped parsley and additional grated cheese and serve immediately. Makes 4 servings.

Second Place Winner 1982 Recipe Contest:

BYRON RUDY, Livermore, CA

A zesty calamari sauce using two heads of fresh garlic tops off this rich creamy fettuccine concoction. It was good enough to win second place for the chef who created it in the third annual Gilroy Garlic Recipe Contest.

FETTUCCINE GARLI-MARI

2 heads fresh garlic, about 30 cloves
2 lbs. calamari
4½ tablespoons butter
1 tablespoon olive oil
¼ cup packed finely chopped parsley
2 tablespoons dry white table wine
12 oz. fettuccine
½ cup heavy cream
2½ oz. freshly grated Parmesan cheese

Put garlic cloves through press. Clean calamari, filet and cut into ¼-inch strips. Saute garlic in 1½ tablespoons butter and olive oil, stirring often, until soft and golden. Add calamari and cook over medium-low heat, turning often, until strips curl. Reduce heat, add wine and parsley, and cook 2 minutes longer. Meanwhile, cook fettuccine as package directs (coordinate cooking time with calamari, so both are done at once); drain. Melt remaining 3 tablespoons butter in a hot serving bowl, combine butter, heavy cream and Parmesan cheese, and mix together. Add fettuccine and calamari, and mix together with pasta forks. Serve immediately on warm serving plates. Makes 6 servings.

FETTUCCINE GLORIOSA

Guaranteed to please the gourmet palate, this 1981 first place winner was created when Rudy Melone was preparing calamari one evening and his wife, Gloria, came home with fresh mussels. They adapted, blended both sauces together and improvised this fabulous seafood fettuccine. Worth every minute it takes! It helps to have two cooks in the kitchen, one who prepares the Moules and the second who prepares the Calamari.

Recipe contest entry: 1981 Recipe contest and Cook-off first place winner:
Rudy Melone, Gilroy, CA

Moules (Mussels)
- ¾ cube butter
- 3 to 4 cloves fresh garlic, peeled and diced
- 1 medium size onion or 5 to 6 shallots, diced
- 8 sprigs parsley, chopped fine
- 18 to 24 fresh mussels or clams (or combination), scrubbed clean
- 1 cup dry white wine

Calamari (Squid)
- ⅓ cup olive oil
- 6 to 12 cloves fresh garlic peeled and crushed
- 2 lbs. calamari, cleaned and cut into 2-inch strips
- 2 tablespoons oregano
- 1 cup dry white wine
- 1 lemon, halved
- 1 can (8 oz.) tomato sauce
- 2 shakes tabasco sauce, to taste

Fettuccine
- 2 teaspoons salt
  Water
- 2 tablespoons olive oil
- 1 lb. white or green fettuccine (preferably home made)
  Parmesan cheese

In pan with lid, melt butter and add garlic, onions and parsley. When onions are translucent, add mussels. Cover and when mussels start to open, add the wine. Stir and remove from stove when mussels have opened. If any do not open they should be removed and discarded.

Heat olive oil in skillet; add garlic and cook until garlic is golden brown. Add calamari, cook for about 1 minute, add oregano, and then the wine. Cook about ½ minute longer, squeeze juice of both lemon halves over the mixture and, for good measure, throw in the lemon halves. Add the tomato sauce and tabasco, and simmer for about 1 minute.

In large pot, bring salted water to a rapid boil. Add olive oil and then the fettucine. While fettuccine is cooking, combine the mussels and calamari to create the sauce. When the fettuccine is cooked *al dente*, strain fettuccine and place on a large pasta platter. Mix with the combined sauce. Arrange the mussels around the platter, decorate with sprigs of parsley, sprinkle liberally with freshly grated Parmesan cheese and serve. Serves 4 to 6.

MARY ANN'S FETTUCCINE ZUCCHINI

Zucchini, tomatoes, garlic, herbs and spices make a savory sauce for fettuccine.   *Recipe contest entry: Mary Ann Rohm, Simi Valley, CA*

3 tablespoons margarine
3 tablespoons olive oil
1 medium-sized sweet red onion, chopped
4 cloves fresh garlic, sliced
1 lb. sliced zucchini
1 tablespoon parsley
¼ teaspoon oregano
¼ teaspoon sweet basil
¼ teaspoon thyme
⅛ teaspoon marjoram
⅛ teaspoon coarsely ground black pepper
⅛ teaspoon ground red pepper
1 teaspoon lemon juice
2 fresh tomatoes, chopped
1 lb. fettuccine
¼ cup Parmesan cheese

Melt margarine with olive oil in heavy saucepan over medium heat. Add onion and garlic and saute for 5 minutes. Add zucchini and saute 10 minutes. Add herbs and spices and saute until zucchini is almost tender. Then add lemon juice and tomatoes. Simmer. Cook fettuccine in salted boiling water until *al dente* and drain. Toss with zucchini mixture and top with Parmesan cheese. Serve at once.

FETTUCCINE FRAGALE

Garlic-buttered fettuccine, served with a creamy ricotta sauce, makes a superb pasta course or a hearty main dish. Louise Fragale sent her favorite recipe all the way from West Virginia for this cookbook.
Courtesy of: Louise Fragale, Clarksburg, W.Va.

¾ cup soft butter *or* margarine
2 tablespoons parsley flakes
1 teaspoon crushed basil
1 carton (about 8 oz.) ricotta
¼ teaspoon salt
½ teaspoon pepper
⅔ cup warm milk
1 lb. fettuccine, thin noodles or spaghetti
3 cloves fresh garlic, minced
1 cup shredded or grated Romano or Parmesan cheese

Combine ¼ cup butter, parsley flakes and basil; blend in ricotta, salt and pepper. Stir in milk and blend well; keep warm. Cook noodles in large amount of boiling salted water until just tender; drain. Cook garlic in ½ cup butter for 1 to 2 minutes. Pour over noodles; toss lightly and quickly to coat well. Sprinkle with ½ cup cheese; toss again. Pile noodles on warm serving platter, and spoon the warm ricotta sauce over; sprinkle with the remaining cheese. Garnish with additional parsley, if desired. Makes 6 to 8 servings.

SPINACH FETTUCCINE WITH ARTICHOKE SAUCE

A great pasta dish to serve with Thirty Clove Chicken (see page 241).

Recipe contest entry: Karen Harmatiuk, San Francisco, CA

2 jars (6 oz. *each*) marinated artichoke hearts,
  drained, reserving
  marinade
3 tablespoons butter
1 cup sliced mushrooms
¾ cup chopped walnuts
4 cloves fresh garlic,
  minced
3 tablespoons minced fresh
  basil *or* 1 tablespoon
  dried
1 cup ricotta cheese
¾ cup Parmesan cheese
½ cup heavy cream
1 pkg. (10 oz.) spinach
  fettuccine *or* equivalent
  homemade pasta

Coarsely chop artichoke hearts. Melt butter with reserved marinade in skillet. Saute artichokes, mushrooms, walnuts, garlic and basil just until tender. In blender, puree cheeses and cream. Mix well with artichoke mixture. Cook fettuccine according to package directions until *al dente*. Pour sauce over, toss to mix well and serve at once. Makes 6 servings.

PESTO LASAGNA FIRENZA

Pasta and pesto are natural go-togethers and especially good when combined in this delightfully different lasagna. For a good pesto recipe, see Pesto Mushrooms (page 34).

Recipe contest entry: Florence Oefinger, Novato, CA

6 or 7 lasagna noodles
2 cups pesto, freshly made
  or frozen
½ cup half-and-half
4 large cloves fresh garlic,
  minced
2 tablespoons olive oil
1 tablespoon softened
  butter
1 lb. Monterey Jack cheese,
  grated
3 tablespoons grated
  Parmesan cheese

Boil noodles as package directs. Rinse in cold water and drain. Mix pesto, half-and-half, garlic, oil and butter in small bowl. Grease a loaf pan and spread several spoonsful of pesto mixture over bottom. Cut noodles to fit pan and place in single layer over pesto. Spread ⅓ of pesto on top and sprinkle with ⅓ of Jack cheese. Repeat twice, ending with cheese. Sprinkle with Parmesan and bake at 350 degrees for 45 minutes. Makes 2 or 3 servings.

FUSILLI CON AGLIO, OLIO, PEPERONCINO E ZUCCHINI

This spicy pasta dish is also good chilled and served as a pasta salad.

Recipe contest entry: Laurie P. Farber, Sacramento, CA

1 zucchini, ends trimmed and coarsely chopped
⅔ cup olive oil
4 cloves fresh garlic
1 fresh jalapeno pepper, stem and seeds removed
1 tablespoon *each* fresh basil, thyme and oregano *or* 1 teaspoon dried
Dash *each* black and cayenne pepper, salt
1 can (16 oz.) cannellini beans, drained and rinsed
1 lb. fusilli (curly noodles)
Grated Parmesan, Romano, asiago or pecorino cheese (optional)
Garlic powder (optional)

In food processor or blender, combine zucchini, oil, garlic, jalapeno pepper, basil, thyme, oregano, black and red peppers and salt. Process with on-off motion until chopped but *not* pureed. Pour into small saucepan and simmer over low heat for about 5 minutes, stirring occasionally. Add drained and rinsed beans; simmer another 5 minutes until beans lose a bit of moisture. Meanwhile cook pasta according to package directions. Drain and pour sauce over, topping with grated cheese and a sprinkling of garlic powder, if desired. Makes 4 servings.

Finalist in 1986 Recipe Contest: BOB SALYERS, Monterey, CA

The 1986 Cook-off winner is a delicious blend of garlic, ricotta and Parmesan cheese. The ravioli can be made ahead of time and frozen until you're ready for it. If you have no time to make ravioli (and have none in the freezer), try the shrimp sauce on plain linguini. The effect, of course, will not be the same, but will still be delicious.

HANDMADE GARLIC-CHEESE RAVIOLI WITH GARLIC BECHAMEL SAUCE AND SHRIMP

Pasta

- 3 cups flour
- 3 eggs, beaten
- 1 tablespoon olive oil
- 1 to 2 tablespoons water

Mix flour, eggs and olive oil. Add water to proper consistency.

Filling

- 24 large cloves fresh garlic, chopped
- 1 teaspoon Italian spices
- ½ teaspoon coarse black pepper
  Olive oil
- 1½ lb. whole milk ricotta cheese
- 1 cup grated fresh Parmesan cheese
- ¼ cup chives (fresh *or* frozen), chopped
- 2 eggs, beaten

Saute garlic, Italian spices and black pepper in olive oil until garlic browns. Drain oil. In large bowl mix ricotta, Parmesan cheese, garlic mixture, chives and eggs.

Roll out oblong sheets of pasta to fit ravioli form. Lay out first sheet, fill with garlic and cheese mixture. Moisten between fillings, add second sheet of pasta and roll. May be used immediately or frozen for later use. Boil approximately 15 minutes for fresh or 22 minutes if frozen.

Sauce

- 6 cloves fresh garlic, chopped
  Olive oil
- 3 tablespoons butter
- 3 tablespoons flour
- 2 cups milk
- ½ teaspoon salt
- ¼ teaspoon white pepper
- 1 lb. medium shrimp
- 1 cup grated fresh Parmesan cheese

Saute garlic, set aside. Melt butter over low heat (or in double boiler); stir in flour until smooth; gradually add milk. Stirring constantly, cook until sauce is thick. Stir in salt, pepper and garlic. Use as needed, refrigerate remainder.

To Serve: With slotted spoon gently place hot ravioli on plate. Top with handful of shrimp, cover with sauce and top with fresh Parmesan cheese. Makes 6 to 8 servings.

Winner of Prize for Best Recipe Using Most Garlic 1983 Recipe Contest:

KELLEE KATZMAN, North Hollywood, CA

For those who like to make their own pasta and who love garlic, here is an irresistible recipe for ravioli.

GARLIC RAVIOLI

5 large heads fresh garlic
2 cups chicken broth (preferably homemade)
11 tablespoons unsalted butter
1½ cups ricotta cheese
1 cup grated Parmesan cheese
1 teaspoon garlic salt
2 sheets homemade pasta (about 5x24 inches *each*)
1 egg, slightly beaten
⅓ cup heavy cream
½ cup grated Romano cheese

Put heads of garlic in shallow baking pan; pour chicken broth over and dot each head with 1 tablespoon butter. Cover and bake for 45 minutes, or until tender. Strain and reserve ⅓ cup liquid. Allow garlic to cool; then squeeze each clove into a bowl. Discard skins. Add ricotta, ½ cup Parmesan and garlic salt and mix thoroughly. Brush 1 sheet of pasta with egg and place garlic-cheese mixture on pasta in mounds (1 teaspoon each) about 2 inches apart. Place second sheet of pasta over the first and press with fingers around each mound. With fluted pastry wheel, cut up into 2-inch square ravioli. Refrigerate for 30 minutes. Bring large pot of water to boil. Just before water boils, start sauce. In frying pan, melt remaining 6 tablespoons butter, add cream and reduce slightly. Add reserved ⅓ cup liquid and reduce to good sauce consistency. When water reaches a rapid boil, drop ravioli in and boil for 3 to 5 minutes. Remove with slotted spoon and put directly into reduced sauce. Sprinkle with remaining Parmesan and Romano cheeses. Serves 4 to 6 as an appetizer.

GREEN RAVIOLI WITH GARLIC FILLING

What could be more appealing than homemade ravioli. Serve these with an "Alfredo" (cream) sauce, or make a sauce of melted butter, chopped parsley and minced garlic.

Recipe contest entry: James F. Benson, San Carlos, CA

Filling
   12 oz. Monterey Jack cheese
    3 cloves fresh garlic
   12 oz. grated Parmesan
       cheese
   12 oz. dry bread crumbs
       Freshly ground pepper
    1 cup dry white wine
    3 eggs

Process Jack cheese through food processor with grating blade. Remove cheese to bowl. With steel blade, process garlic. Add remaining dry ingredients and return Jack cheese to food processor container. Pulse until well mixed. Add wine to moisten, then eggs and pulse until mixed.

Ravioli Pasta
    1 pkg. (10 oz.) frozen
       chopped spinach
    2 cups unbleached white
       flour
    1 tablespoon salt
    1 tablespoon olive oil
    2 eggs
       Water as needed

Cook spinach according to package directions. Drain. When cool, press water out of spinach. Chop with steel blade until finely chopped. Add flour and salt and mix. Add oil and mix. Add eggs and mix. Add water until a ball of dough is formed. Place on floured board. Knead until smooth and velvety. Place mixture in plastic bag for 1 hour. At this point, if you have a pasta machine, proceed to make dough. If not, roll only as much dough as you can handle at one time out on floured board until thin. On half the dough spread some of the filling and cover with other half of dough. With ravioli rolling pin or ⅛-inch board form ravioli, pressing rows of squares. Cut rows with pastry cutter or knife. In large pot of boiling water, cook ravioli until just done *al dente*. Drain and serve with sauce of your choice. Makes about 220 ravioli.

BAKED MANICOTTI WITH MEAT SAUCE

An excellent pasta dish, this recipe makes enough filling to stuff 14 manicotti with some left over.

Recipe contest entry: Vicki Hilton, Santa Barbara, CA

Sauce
- 1 lb. lean ground beef
- 1 lb. hot Italian sausage, casings removed
- ½ cup Italian bread crumbs
- ½ cup virgin olive oil
- 3 cups chopped onion
- 8 to 10 cloves fresh garlic, chopped
- 2½ cups water
- 2 cans (1 lb. 12 oz. *each*) Italian tomatoes, undrained
- 9 oz. tomato paste
- 4 tablespoons chopped parsley
- 2 teaspoons *each* dried basil leaves and dried oregano leaves
- 1½ tablespoons *each* sugar and salt
- ½ teaspoon pepper

Filling
- 2 lb. ricotta cheese
- 8 oz. Mozzarella cheese, chopped
- ⅓ cup grated Parmesan cheese
- 1 tablespoon chopped parsley
- 2 eggs
- 1 teaspoon salt
- ½ teaspoon Italian seasoning
- ¼ teaspoon pepper
  Freshly grated Parmesan cheese for garnish

Place beef and sausage in skillet and brown thoroughly. Drain off grease; add bread crumbs and blend with meat. Set aside. In hot oil in 8 quart pot, saute onion and garlic 3 to 5 minutes. Mix in rest of sauce ingredients. Chop tomatoes into smaller pieces as they cook. Bring to boil, reduce heat and add meat mixture to sauce. Simmer, covered, stirring occasionally 1½ hours. Cook manicotti according to package directions; *parboil only*. Drain and set aside. Meanwhile combine all ingredients for filling and mix well with wooden spoon. After manicotti has cooled and dried, stuff them with spoon, being careful not to split them open. Set aside. In large casserole dish (8 to 10 quart) spread a thick layer of suace. Neatly place stuffed manicotti close together on top of sauce. Add remainder of sauce until casserole is nearly full. Sprinkle with about ¼ cup Parmesan cheese. Bake, covered, at 350 degrees for 45 minutes or until bubbly; uncover and continue baking for another 10 to 15 minutes. Makes 10 to 12 servings.

GARLIC-CHEESE MOSTACCIOLI

Great dish for a potluck originated by a finalist in the 1982 Recipe Contest who recommends serving it with his recipe for "Tomatoes a la William," also in this book.

Recipe contest entry: Bill Scales, Gilroy, CA

1 pkg. (12 oz.) mostaccioli
20 cloves fresh garlic, minced
1 large yellow onion, minced
4 tablespoons butter
Freshly ground black pepper
1½ lb. Colby cheese, grated
½ cup dry white wine
¼ lb. Mozzarella cheese, grated
¼ cup chopped fresh parsley

Prepare mostaccioli according to package directions, using a little olive oil in water. Drain. Keep warm in shallow ovenproof baking dish. Saute garlic and onion in 2 tablespoons butter. Add pepper and set aside. Melt remaining 2 tablespoons butter in top of double boiler, add grated Colby cheese and stir in wine. When cheese has melted, combine with garlic-onion mixture and pour over mostaccioli. Sprinkle grated Mozzarella and parsley over; place on middle shelf of oven and broil for 1 to 2 minutes. Makes 10 servings.

LINGUINE CONTESSA

Served as a main course or side dish, this pasta is superb!

Recipe contest entry: Donna Richard, Bala Cynwyd, PA

3 chicken bouillon cubes
1½ cups water
¼ cup olive oil
1 lb. fresh mushrooms, sliced
¼ to ½ lb. prosciutto (thin-sliced Italian ham), chopped
1 medium onion, chopped fine
4 cloves fresh garlic, minced
½ teaspoon black pepper
½ cup dry sherry
1 lb. linguine
1 teaspoon salt
Freshly grated Parmesan cheese and parsley sprigs for garnish

Combine bouillon cubes and water and boil for a few seconds, mixing thoroughly. Set aside. Heat oil in large, deep pot and saute mushrooms, prosciutto, onion, and garlic until onions and garlic are light golden brown. Add pepper, bouillon and sherry. Bring to boil, reduce heat and simmer for 10 minutes. Meanwhile, cook pasta in salted water until just done (*al dente*). Drain pasta and combine with sauce. Serve hot with Parmesan cheese, granished with small parsley sprigs. Makes 6 servings.

FAMILY FAVORITE LINGUINE AND CLAM SAUCE

This recipe, which originated in west central Italy, has been in the Robinson family for over 100 years. For variation, add 3 cups drained, canned Italian tomatoes to the sauce and simmer for 30 minutes before adding clams.

Recipe contest entry: John M. Robinson, Granada Hills, CA

8 cloves fresh garlic
½ teaspoon salt
½ teaspoon white pepper
3 egg yolks
1 cup plus 4 tablespoons olive oil
2 tablespoons butter
3 tablespoons finely chopped shallots
3 tablespoons flour
2 to 2½ cups clam juice
3 to 4 cups coarsely chopped clams
1 cup chopped parsley
½ cup chopped basil
1 lb. linguine
Grated Romano cheese

Crush garlic in a mortar until it becomes a paste. Add salt, white pepper and egg yolks. Beat with a whisk until lemon colored. Continue to beat, adding olive oil a few drops at a time until 2 tablespoons have been added. Continue to beat, adding 1 cup olive oil in a thin stream until finished. Set sauce aside. In frying pan, heat remaining 2 tablespoons olive oil and butter; add shallots and saute over low heat until shallots are light golden. Add flour and continue cooking for 5 minutes, stirring constantly. Slowly add clam juice, stirring constantly, until well blended; then cook 5 to 8 minutes more, stirring occasionally. Slowly add clam sauce to garlic sauce, stirring with a whisk to keep well blended. Heat over low flame, stirring occasionally, until hot.

Add clams and continue to heat until hot again. Add parsley and basil. Heat until steaming and serve with freshly cooked linguine, prepared according to package instructions. Top with grated Romano cheese.

GARLIC IN THE STRAW AND HAY

The "straw" and "hay" refer to the white and green linguine that are combined to make this unique and colorful pasta presentation. Laced with sliced, fresh mushrooms, and minced prosciutto and topped with a creamy cheese sauce, it's delightful!

Recipe contest entry: Phyllis Gaddis, Venice, CA

6 tablespoons butter
8 cloves fresh garlic, minced
1 lb. fresh mushrooms, sliced thin with stems included
Dash salt (optional)
¼ lb. minced prosciutto, (¼ lb. crumbled cooked bacon may be substituted)
8 oz. white linguine
8 oz. green (spinach) linguine
1 cup light cream
¼ cup chicken broth
¼ cup grated Parmesan cheese, plus additional cheese for topping

Melt half the butter in large frying pan. Add garlic and saute until slightly browned. Add sliced mushrooms, sprinkle with a dash of salt and saute for 3 minutes, tossing occasionally, or until mushrooms are lightly browned. Remove from heat. In another pan saute prosciutto in remaining butter until browned. Remove from heat. Using two pots, prepare noodles according to package directions. The green pasta will take about 1 minute longer to cook than the white. If you drain the white noodles first, the green should be done and ready for draining when you are finished with the white. Combine both noodles in one bowl. Reheat skillet with garlic and mushrooms; add cream and chicken broth. When sauce simmers, add Parmesan cheese and stir to mix. Add both straw and hay noodles and toss to mix. Add prosciutto and toss again. Heat carefully, because high heat will change texture of Parmesan cheese. Just before serving, sprinkle with additional cheese.

LINGUINE WITH WHITE CLAM SAUCE

Make a meal in minutes with this linguine topped with white clam sauce. Add a tossed green salad to round out this quickie dinner.

Recipe contest entry: Paul Dana, Sunnyvale, CA

¾ cup olive oil
4 to 6 cloves fresh garlic
3 cans (6 to 7 oz. *each*) chopped clams
¼ teaspoon *each* salt, pepper, and thyme
1 lb. linguine
¼ cup chopped parsley

Heat oil in pan. Press garlic and cook until golden. Add clam juice from cans, salt, pepper and thyme. Let simmer very slowly. Add clams. Cook linguine. Add parsley to sauce 5 minutes before linguine is cooked.

GLORIOSO FOR ONE PERSON

Although this recipe serves but one, it can be doubled, tripled or increased to fit any number you wish.

Courtesy of: Jon Seeger

5 oz. shell pasta
2 tablespoons *each* butter and olive oil
¼ teaspoon crushed red pepper flakes
Salt and pepper
1½ large mushrooms, sliced
1 heaping tablespoon fresh garlic, minced
1 tablespoon minced parsley
½ cup grated Romano cheese

Cook pasta according to package directions. Meanwhile, heat butter and oil in saute pan until very hot, but do not brown. Add red pepper, pinch of salt and pepper and mushrooms and toss thoroughly. Add garlic, being careful not to burn garlic, reduce heat. When pasta is done, raise heat and add drained pasta to saute pan. Toss, add cheese and parsley and toss again. Makes 1 "glorioso" serving.

MANTI

An easy-to-fix casserole with surprising flavor and rich sauce.

Recipe contest entry: Cindy Mayron, Gilroy, CA

1 pkg. (12 oz.) large shell pasta
¾ lb. ground lamb
1 tablespoon oil or butter
1 or 2 bunches green onions, minced
¼ cup chopped fresh parsley
4 cloves fresh garlic, minced
4 tablespoons butter
1 can (10¾ oz.) beef broth
1 can (8 oz.) tomato sauce

Cook pasta according to package directions. Drain and cool. Saute lamb lightly in oil or butter; combine with onions, parsley and garlic; mix well. Stuff shells with meat mixture. Butter bottom of 3-quart baking dish with cover. Place shells in baking dish and dot with butter. Cover and bake in 350-degree oven for 20 minutes. Combine broth and tomato sauce in small pan and bring to boil. Pour over manti and bake 15 to 20 minutes longer until lamb is cooked and sauce thickens slightly. Makes 4 to 6 servings.

WALNUT SAUCE FROM GARLIC COUNTRY

A rich mixture of nuts, olive oil, garlic and cheese makes a uniquely different topping for pasta.

Recipe contest entry: Mrs. Bernarr Wilson, Gilroy, CA

12 oz. egg tagliarini
2 cups walnut meats
3 cloves fresh garlic
¼ cup butter
¼ cup olive oil
½ cup grated Parmesan cheese plus additional cheese, if desired

Cook tagliarini as directed for about 9 minutes or until *al dente*. While tagliarini is cooking, mix walnut meats in blender with enough hot tagliarini water to make a paste. Add garlic, butter, olive oil and Parmesan cheese; blend, adding enough hot water to form desired consistency. Pour sauce over drained tagliarini; toss until well coated and serve hot. Sprinkle on additional Parmesan cheese, if desired. Makes 4 to 6 servings.

ITALIAN MEATBALLS AND SAUCE FOR SPAGHETTI

This recipe is intended to serve 10 or more hungry people. You'll need a very large cooking pot (or use two smaller Dutch ovens) and be sure to watch it while cooking to prevent scorching.

Recipe contest entry: Teresa Traversone, Tucson, AZ

Meatballs
- 2 lb. lean ground beef
- 4 eggs, slightly beaten
- 1½ cups grated Parmesan and Romano cheese combined
- 1½ cups dry bread crumbs
- 1 cup milk
- 2 tablespoons chopped parsley
- 2 teaspoons salt
- ½ teaspoon garlic powder

Mix first 8 ingredients and shape into meatballs. Spray flat baking dish or pan with Pam and place meatballs in pan. Bake at 350 degrees for 30 minutes or until lightly browned. Meanwhile prepare sauce.

Sauce
- 1 onion, chopped
- ½ cup olive oil
- 2 teaspoons instant minced garlic
- 3 cans (12 oz. *each*) tomato paste
- 3 cans (15 oz. *each*) tomato sauce
- 3 cans (29 oz. *each*) whole tomatoes, chopped
- 2 teaspoons *each* oregano, garlic salt and Italian seasoning

In large heavy pot, brown onion in oil. Add minced garlic. Cook 1 minute longer. Add remaining ingredients including meatballs and simmer very gently for about 3 hours or until sauce is proper thickness. Serve over cooked spaghetti. Sprinkle with additional grated Italian cheese, if desired. Makes sauce for 10 or more servings.

Nothing beats the versatility of garlic, the great international seasoning.

Betsy Balsley in the
Los Angeles Times

SUPER MEAT SAUCE FOR PASTA

Sliced meat rolls add a new dimension to traditional pasta sauce. Use leftover sauce to make a delicious pizza.

Recipe contest entry: Becley Hill, Malibu, CA

1 whole round steak, sliced ¼ inch thick
12 cloves fresh garlic, peeled and minced
2 cups chopped parsley
4 tablespoons oil
3 cans (8 oz. *each*) tomato sauce
2 teaspoons sweet basil
1 teaspoon oregano
1 teaspoon salt
½ teaspoon crushed red pepper
8 oz. spaghetti *or* other pasta
½ cup grated Parmesan cheese, *or* a mixture of Parmesan and Romano

Remove bone from steak and save. Cut steak into 4 pieces. Brush pieces with oil, top with garlic and parsley, dividing evenly. Roll up each piece of meat and secure by wrapping with sewing thread. Heat 4 tablespoons oil in heavy Dutch oven. Brown rolls of meat thoroughly. For added flavor, add the bone to the pan while meat is browning. Add the rest of the ingredients except pasta and cheese and cook over medium-low heat, stirring often, until tomato sauce has a slightly brown color. Cover and simmer 2 hours or until meat is very tender. Cook spaghetti according to package directions and drain. In a large, warmed serving bowl toss spaghetti with 1 cup sauce and ¼ cup cheese. Keep warm. Remove thread from meat rolls and slice. Top the spaghetti with meat and more sauce. Pass extra cheese. Makes 6 to 8 servings.

NOODLES ROMANOFF

Transform ordinary noodles into party fare in an instant using seasonings from your spice shelf.

2½ cups noodles
1 cup cottage cheese
1 cup sour cream
1½ teaspoons seasoned salt
1 teaspoon instant minced onion
1 teaspoon Worcestershire sauce
½ teaspoon instant minced garlic
Dash cayenne *or* red pepper
⅓ cup grated Cheddar cheese

Cook noodles as directed on package and drain. Combine noodles with remaining ingredients except grated cheese. Put in buttered 1½-quart casserole; sprinkle top with grated cheese. Bake in 350-degree oven 30 minutes or until cheese has melted. Makes 6 servings.

MAHONY'S RICE

This colorful rice dish is the inspiration of the creator of Mahony's Bruschetta which won the 1983 Recipe Contest. Neil suggests serving it with barbecued meats "and a good Gewurztraminer." He also advises that it can be made in the morning, refrigerated and reheated just before serving.   *Recipe contest entry: Neil Mahony, Ventura, CA*

5 strips lean bacon, diced
1 medium onion, diced
1 medium green bell pepper, diced
8 cloves fresh garlic, chopped
1 cup long grain white rice, rinsed in cold water
⅓ cup plus 2 tablespoons soy sauce
1⅔ cups water
1 can (8 oz.) button mushrooms, drained
⅓ lb. cooked cocktail shrimp, fresh not canned
1 jar (4 oz.) diced pimentos, drained
6 tablespoons finely chopped fresh parsley

Fry bacon until crisp. Drain *thoroughly* and set aside. Fry onion, pepper and garlic in bacon grease until onions are translucent. Drain *thoroughly* and add to bacon. In saucepan combine rice with soy sauce and water and bring to a boil. Cover tightly, reduce heat and simmer for about 20 minutes or until all liquid is absorbed. Remove lid and leave pan on very low heat to drive off any remaining moisture. After about 10 minutes, stir in bacon mixture, add half the parsley and almost all of the mushrooms, shrimp and pimentos, saving some of each for garnish. Mix and transfer to shallow serving dish and garnish as desired. Serve at once. Makes 6 to 8 servings.

CALIFORNIA PILAF

Although this recipe calls for the use of a Crockpot, it can be made by using a Dutch oven or casserole and baking at 350 degrees for about 1 hour or until rice is tender and all liquid has been absorbed.

Recipe contest entry: E. Saavedra, Denver, CO

2 lb. ground beef	Brown beef in skillet; drain off fat. Place beef and all remaining ingredients in 4-quart Crockpot. Stir well. Cover and cook on low for 5 to 6 hours or on high for 3 hours. Makes 6 servings.

2 lb. ground beef
2½ cups water
2 cans (8 oz. *each*) tomato sauce
1⅓ cups long grain rice
⅔ cup sliced ripe olives
1 green bell pepper, seeded and chopped
1 small onion, chopped
3 cloves fresh garlic, minced
2½ teaspoons salt
¼ teaspoon pepper

Brown beef in skillet; drain off fat. Place beef and all remaining ingredients in 4-quart Crockpot. Stir well. Cover and cook on low for 5 to 6 hours or on high for 3 hours. Makes 6 servings.

SAUSAGE AND RICE, SWISS STYLE

An excellent "quickie" meal. The caraway seed, frequently used in European cooking, adds a distinctive flavor to the dish. To serve 6, use 1½ lb. sausage, 1 cup rice and 2 cups stock.

Recipe contest entry: Christine Ammer, Lexington, MA

2 tablespoons margarine *or* vegetable oil
1 cup chopped onion
3 or more cloves fresh garlic, minced
1 lb. Polish sausage (Kielbasa), cut in 1-inch pieces
1½ cups chicken stock *or* broth
¾ cup rice
1 teaspoon caraway seed
Salt and pepper to taste

In large skillet, heat margarine and cook onion and garlic until onion is soft. Add sausage and cook, stirring, for 2 minutes. Stir in remaining ingredients. Bring to a boil, reduce heat and cover. Simmer for about 30 minutes or until rice is done and liquid has been absorbed. Makes 4 servings.

HOLLISTER HOT RICE

This recipe is a family favorite which is often prepared in double quantities since it is so popular.   *Recipe contest entry: Christy Funk, Hollister, CA*

2 cups long grain rice
6 or more cloves fresh garlic, minced
½ cup butter
2 cans (7 oz. *each*) whole green chiles
¼ lb. Jack *or* Cheddar cheese
2 cans (10½ oz. *each*) beef consomme (gelatin added) plus 2 consomme cans hot water

Saute rice and garlic in butter in skillet over medium heat for about 3 minutes. Divide rice mixture in half, spreading half on bottom of 13x9x2-inch baking dish. Wash chiles in cool water. Cut cheese in strips and insert into whole chiles. Lay stuffed chiles on rice mixture and spread remaining rice over. In a bowl mix soup and hot water thoroughly; then pour over rice and chiles. Cover tightly with foil to keep rice from drying out. Bake at 375 degrees for 40 to 50 minutes. Makes 8 servings.

GARLIC DILL RICE

Garlic and herbs flavor this rice dish, an excellent accompaniment for roasted or broiled meats.

Recipe contest entry: Charles Valdes, Sacramento, CA

3 to 4 cloves fresh garlic, minced
2 tablespoons olive oil
1 cup rice
1 can (14½ oz.) chicken broth
1 teaspoon *each* dried dill and cilantro (coriander)
1 teaspoon salt
½ teaspoon onion powder

Saute garlic in hot oil until golden. Add rice and saute for 4 to 5 minutes over high heat. Add broth and seasonings. Bring back to boil, cover and simmer over low heat for 30 minutes. Fluff and mix rice and allow to stand uncovered for 5 minutes. Makes 4 to 6 servings.

Vegetables

Artichokes alla Rosina   140
Stuffed Artichokes Castroville   141
Very Garlic Artichokes   142
Italian Broccoli   142
Best Broccoli   143
Eileen's Greens   143
Garlic-Cheese Filled Carrots   144
Ali Baba's Carrots   145
Transylvanian Carrots   146
Capered Carrots and Zucchini   146
Cauliflower with Garlic Oil   147
Epicurean Eggplant Bake   147
Marinated Eggplant   148
Eggplant Delight   149
Light 'n' Lovely Eggplant
  Casserole   149
Garlic Eggplant   150
Eggplant Parmigiana   151
Basque-Style Eggplant Casserole   151
Nina's Ratatouille   152
Gilroy Ratatouille   153
Green Beans au Garlic   153
Garlic Green Beans   154
Queen's Beans   154
Green Beans Asadoor   155
Dilled Green Beans   155
Val and Elsie's Julienne Beans   156
Greek Beans   156
Garlic Mushroom Casserole   157
Garlicky Mushrooms Supreme   157
Onions Stuffed with Garlic
  and Chestnuts   158
Baked Garlic Potatoes   158
Garlic Potatoes with Cheese Sauce   159
Delicious Potatoes   160
Garlic Jalapeno Potatoes   160
Roasted Garlic Potatoes   161
S.O.S. (Super Omnipotent Spuds)   161

138   *The Complete Garlic Lovers' Cookbook*

Potato-Garlic Puree   162
Garlic Pie   162
Spinach Casserole   163
Cheesy Spinach   163
Big Daddy's Big-on-Flavor
  Spinach Treats   164
Red Bellies   165
Tomatoes a la William   166
Tomatoes a la Clare   166
Garlic Butter Crumb Tomatoes   167
Pureed Turnips with Garlic   167
Zesty Zucchini Saute   168
Myrna's Stuffed Zucchini   168
Zucchini Zap!   169
Zucchini Leaves   169
Zippy Zucchini Fritters   170
Zucchini alla Pelliccione   170
Mock Oyster Stir-Fry   171
Hollister Vegetable Casserole   171
Vegetables Veracruz   172
Mediterranean Rainbow   173
China Camp Stir-Fried
  Vegetables   173
Snow Peas Canton   174
Heaven Scent   175
Sweet and Sour Garlic
  Vegetables   175

QUICK AND EASY RECIPE IDEAS

Perk up frozen spinach with garlic. Simply cook spinach in a little water until thawed, then add pressed fresh garlic cloves and butter. Heat just until done.

Cook green beans in wine for real flavor enhancement. Partially steam the beans, then cook in white wine, fresh minced garlic and butter.

Give Quiche Lorraine a sassy twist by adding fresh minced garlic to the filling.

Potatoes go from ordinary to extra-delicious when fried with minced fresh garlic cloves. Season with garlic salt and sprinkle with grated cheese.

When cooking vegetables, add some sliced fresh garlic cloves to the cooking water to impart subtle flavor.

Winner of 1982 Recipe Contest: ROSINA WILSON, Albany, CA

This winning recipe from a very talented lady combines steamed artichokes and whole cloves of garlic which are dipped in a tantalizing basil-laced aioli sauce, then drawn between the teeth to extract the pulp and sauce simultaneously. Thoroughly delightful! The name for the sauce, "Baioli," came from her daughter. It's a contraction of basil and aioli. Substitute fresh tarragon for "Taioli," fresh dill for "Daioli," or parsley for "Paioli."

ARTICHOKES ALLA ROSINA

6 medium artichokes
6 large heads fresh garlic
1 large lemon, halved
½ teaspoon salt
½ cup olive oil

Clean artichokes and place in a large kettle. Peel off outer papery skin from garlic, leaving heads intact. Nestle garlic heads among artichokes. Add water to cover artichokes halfway, squeeze in juice from lemons, and tuck in the lemon peels. Add salt, and pour olive oil over. Bring to a boil, and simmer 45 to 60 minutes, until tender, depending on size of artichokes. Drain well. Serve warm or cold, with Baioli Sauce. The garlic heads will be soft enough to eat like the artichokes, picking off cloves, pulling out pulp between the teeth, and discarding skin. Makes 6 servings.

Baioli Sauce
4 to 6 cloves fresh garlic, peeled
2 egg yolks
3 tablespoons lemon juice
1 tablespoon Dijon-style mustard
½ teaspoon salt
1 cup olive oil
½ cup fresh basil leaves

In blender jar, place 4 to 6 cloves fresh garlic, peeled, 2 egg yolks, 3 tablespoons lemon juice, 1 tablespoon mustard and ½ teaspoon salt. Cover and blend smooth. With blender running, remove cover and very slowly pour in 1 cup olive oil in a very thin stream. Cover blender, turn off and scrape down sides. Adjust seasoning. Add ½ cup fresh sweet basil leaves and blend briefly, until coarsely chopped.

STUFFED ARTICHOKES CASTROVILLE

The garlic and Parmesan cheese, classic flavor mates, make these stuffed artichokes a very special dish and one very popular, not only in Gilroy, but throughout the West.

Recipe contest entry: Nikki DeDominic, Guerneville, CA

6 or 8 small artichokes
½ cup bread crumbs
½ cup grated Parmesan cheese
5 cloves fresh garlic
2 tablespoons parsley
Salt and pepper to taste
Olive oil

Clean outer leaves of artichokes and cut the tops and bottoms so they are flat. Scoop out choke, if desired. Mix bread crumbs, cheese, 3 cloves of garlic (minced), parsley, salt and pepper. Spread the leaves of artichokes and fill in every leaf with the bread mixture, including the center of the artichoke. In a low saucepan large enough to hold the artichokes, heat 1 tablespoon of oil and saute remaining 2 cloves of garlic (minced) until the garlic is slightly brown. Stand artichokes in the pan and fill pan with water to about 1 inch deep. (Water level depends on the size of the artichokes—do not allow water to reach bread crumb stuffing.) Cover pan with aluminum foil to allow artichokes to steam. Cook until tender. If water evaporates before artichokes are ready, add more water.

VERY GARLIC ARTICHOKES

Artichokes are wonderful cooked only with fresh garlic for seasoning, but this recipe includes oregano and sherry for an intriguing flavor boost. When she serves them prepared this way, there's nary a leaf left, claims Ms. Van Dam.   *Recipe contest entry: Caroline Van Dam, Tarzana, CA*

4 medium to large artichokes
1 head fresh garlic
¼ lb. margarine
½ to ¾ cup dry sherry
1 teaspoon oregano

Steam or boil artichokes until tender; drain and arrange in serving dish, opening leaves slightly. Peel garlic and chop coarsely or cut in thin slices. Saute lightly in margarine, add wine and oregano and bring to a boil. Spoon sauce over artichokes, drizzling down through the leaves. Serve hot or cold as an appetizer or a vegetable course. Makes 4 servings.

ITALIAN BROCCOLI

This is an old family recipe which has been enjoyed by the Kovatches for many years. It's an excellent company dish which can be made ahead and heated just before serving. Try it with cauliflower or cabbage, too.

Recipe contest entry: Mrs. A. Kovatch, Sr., River Ridge, LA

1 large bunch broccoli
1 small onion, chopped
8 cloves fresh garlic, peeled and chopped
½ cup olive oil
1 cup Italian bread crumbs
¾ cup grated Parmesan cheese
1 egg, beaten lightly
   Salt, pepper and garlic powder to taste

Steam or boil broccoli until tender. Drain and mash as you would potatoes, leaving small bits of broccoli. In large skillet, saute onion and garlic in oil. When onion begins to brown, add broccoli and stir to mix. Add bread crumbs and cheese and stir until well blended. Remove from heat and add egg. Stir again to blend; add seasonings and stir again. Place in casserole and, when ready to serve, warm in 350-degree oven for about 15 minutes. Makes 6 servings.

BEST BROCCOLI

Prepare this dish well ahead so that broccoli can refrigerate long enough to permit the flavors to penetrate. Then serve cold, preferably with a homemade garlic mayonnaise such as Marie's Aioli (page 315).

Recipe contest entry: Sara Janene Evans, San Luis Obispo, CA

1½ lb. fresh broccoli
10 large cloves fresh garlic, unpeeled
⅓ cup red wine vinegar
3 tablespoons olive oil
2 teaspoons salt

Separate broccoli into florets with small stems, then peel main trunk and slice into strips. Crush garlic partially, using the flat side of a knife. Fill large pot with water, add all ingredients being sure that broccoli stems are submerged, and cook, covered, until tender. Drain and refrigerate for several hours or overnight. Makes 4 servings.

EILEEN'S GREENS

Napa cabbage, also called Chinese cabbage, looks somewhat like a combination of Romaine lettuce and celery, but the individual leaves are pale green at the top and blanched white at the bottom. It is excellent in salads or cooked as a vegetable.

Recipe contest entry: Eileen Hu, Monterey, CA

1 tablespoon sesame oil
3 cloves fresh garlic, minced
7 large leaves Napa cabbage, washed and cut in bite-size pieces
¼ onion, chopped
1 tomato, washed and sliced
2 tablespoons soy sauce
1 tablespoon sugar

Heat sesame oil in skillet to 475 degrees. Saute garlic, being careful not to burn. Add cabbage and onion. Stir fry for 1 minute. Add tomato, soy sauce and sugar. Cook for 2 minutes. Makes 4 servings.

Regional Winner in 1982 Recipe Contest: JIMMY HOBBS, Palacios, TX

Rarely does anyone do anything quite so special with carrots. Prepare them ahead, if you wish, and bake about 20 minutes before serving. The sweetness of the cooked carrot and garlic makes a very happy blend.

GARLIC-CHEESE FILLED CARROTS

1   lb. carrots (6 to 8 large)
1   teaspoon salt
½   teaspoon sugar
3   cloves fresh garlic
1½   cups grated mild Cheddar cheese
1   tablespoon milk
1   teaspoon finely chopped onion
⅛   teaspoon black pepper

Scrub carrots and scrape lightly. Cut in halves crosswise. Barely cover with boiling water, add ½ teaspoon salt and sugar, cover and cook slowly until tender, 10 to 20 minutes, depending on size of carrots. Do not overcook. Drain and cool slightly. Simmer garlic in small amount of boiling water 1 minute. Drain, peel and chop or mash to a pulp. Split each carrot half lengthwise down center. Gently lift out core and mash to fine pulp (or process 3 to 4 seconds in food processor). Add ½ cup cheese, mashed garlic, milk, onion, remaining ½ teaspoon salt and pepper and continue mashing or processing to a paste. Mound the mixture into half the carrot pieces and press the corresponding half over filled one. Place sections close together in buttered 8-inch square pan or a decorative shallow casserole. Sprinkle remaining cheese over tops of carrots. Bake at 400 degrees 10 to 15 minutes, until tops are lightly toasted. Makes 4 servings.

ALI BABA'S CARROTS

This cold vegetable side dish is perfect with a summer meal of barbecued meat, beans and potato salad. It can be made a day or two ahead, which even improves its flavor.

Recipe contest entry: Phyllis Gaddis, Venice, CA

2 lb. carrots
  Boiling water
6 tablespoons water *or*
  chicken broth
6 tablespoons olive oil
7 cloves fresh garlic
  Salt and pepper
3 tablespoons tarragon or
  white wine vinegar
½ teaspoon dill weed
¼ teaspoon cayenne pepper
¼ teaspoon paprika
¼ teaspoon cumin
2 tablespoons chopped
  parsley

Peel carrots and cut into 2-inch pieces. Blanch in boiling water for 1 minute, then plunge into bowl of cold water. After 2 minutes, remove from cold water and drain. Meanwhile, in saucepan, heat water *or* chicken broth with olive oil, 2 whole cloves garlic, and salt and pepper to taste. Bring to a boil, then add carrots. Lower heat and simmer until tender but firm. Drain carrots, reserving liquid and whole cloves garlic. In a glass or plastic bowl large enough to hold carrots, mix marinade by combining vinegar, dill weed, cayenne pepper, paprika, cumin, 5 garlic cloves (minced) and salt and pepper to taste. Add whole cloves garlic and reserved liquid. Cover and chill in refrigerator at least 6 hours (or as long as a day or two). To serve, drain carrots from marinade and place in dish. Sprinkle with chopped parsley. Makes 6 servings.

Three nickles will get you on the subway, but garlic will get you a seat.

New York Yiddish saying

TRANSYLVANIAN CARROTS

This dish is absolutely great! It's the garlic that does the trick!

Recipe contest entry: Tracy King, Glendale, CA

1 lb. carrots
6 to 8 cloves fresh garlic
4 *or* more tablespoons butter
½ teaspoon pepper
Salt and pepper to taste
Chopped fresh parsley

Peel carrots and slice diagonally into 1-inch lengths. Peel garlic and slice thinly lengthwise. Place carrots and garlic in 1½-quart saucepan with enough water to barely cover. Add butter and pepper and cook, covered, over medium heat until carrots are tender. Remove cover and cook over high heat until water has boiled away and carrots are glazed with the butter, about 5 minutes. Salt to taste and garnish with chopped parsley. Makes 4 servings.

CAPERED CARROTS AND ZUCCHINI

Two ordinary vegetables become special when sauteed with garlic and rosemary. Capers add an elegant touch and a spicy flavor.

Recipe contest entry: Angie Herrera, Norwalk, CA

5 medium-sized carrots
3 small zucchini
2 tablespoons butter
3 cloves fresh garlic, minced
Pinch rosemary
Salt and pepper
Water
1 tablespoon capers

Slice carrots and zucchini about ¼ inch thick. Melt butter in a frying pan over medium heat; lightly saute garlic, then stir in carrots and cook 2 minutes. Stir in zucchini, rosemary, salt and pepper to taste. Stir until zucchini is heated through, then add 1 or 2 tablespoons water and cover pan. Cook over medium heat until carrots are barely fork tender, shaking pan and stirring occasionally. Don't overcook. Stir in capers and serve.

CAULIFLOWER WITH GARLIC OIL

This unusual treatment gives cauliflower a delightfully different flavor.

1 head cauliflower *or*
  broccoli
1 cup olive oil
½ teaspoon salt
4 cloves fresh garlic,
  minced
2 tablespoons chopped
  parsley
3 hard-cooked eggs,
  chopped

Separate cauliflower into florets and steam in a small amount of water or in steamer basket until crisp-tender. Drain and set aside in warmed serving dish. Heat oil and salt in small pan and cook garlic and parsley until garlic is lightly browned. Pour oil mixture over cauliflower and garnish with chopped egg. Makes 4 servings.

Finalist in 1986 Recipe Contest: ROXANNE CHAN, Albany, CA

Roxanne Chan is one of the contest's most creative cooks (she's been a finalist three years in a row). Her latest invention is a colorful concoction—meringue-topped eggplant slices surrounded by a creamy red pepper sauce.

EPICUREAN EGGPLANT BAKE

6 large eggplant slices, ½
  inch thick
2 tablespoons olive oil
½ teaspoon garlic powder

Brush eggplant slices with oil on both sides. Sprinkle with garlic powder. Place slices on baking sheet and bake at 350 degrees for 30 minutes or until fork tender.

Filling
1 lb. Italian sausage, casings removed, crumbled
2 tablespoons butter
1 small onion, chopped
1 small head fresh garlic,
  cloves separated, peeled
  and minced
½ cup white wine
¼ cup chopped green
  pepper
¼ cup chopped yellow
  pepper
1 tomato, peeled, and
  seeded and diced
1 teaspoon dried oregano

Combine the sausage and butter in skillet. Add onion and minced garlic. Saute 5 minutes. Add wine, cover and simmer 10 minutes. Add peppers, tomato and oregano. Cook uncovered 2 minutes. Cool slightly.

Meringue
1 large head fresh garlic, separated into cloves
¼ teaspoon garlic salt
4 egg whites
Pinch of cream of tartar

Cook the separated garlic cloves in boiling water until soft. Peel and mash. Stir in garlic salt. Beat egg whites with cream of tartar until stiff peaks form. Fold in garlic. Remove eggplant from oven. Top with some of the filling, then cover the filling with meringue. Return to the oven and bake until the meringue is golden, about 15 minutes.

Cream
1 large red pepper, seeded and cut into strips
½ cup cream
2 large cloves fresh garlic, peeled
⅛ teaspoon seasoned pepper
Parsley sprigs for garnish

Cook red pepper strips in boiling water for 5 minutes. Drain. Place in a blender with cream, garlic and seasoned pepper. Blend until smooth. Place in a saucepan and heat through. Place eggplant slices on a serving platter. Surround with pepper cream and garnish with parsley sprigs. Makes 6 servings.

Finalist in 1986 Recipe Contest: BETTY WENGER, Gilroy, CA

Keep a batch in the refrigerator and you'll always be ready when unexpected guests drop by.

MARINATED EGGPLANT

2 eggplants
Salt
5 cups wine vinegar
30 cloves fresh garlic, chopped
3 tablespoons oregano
1½ cups oil

Peel and slice eggplants. Lay slices on board and sprinkle generously with salt. Put another board on top and leave overnight. In large pot, bring wine vinegar to a boil. Put 4 to 5 pieces of eggplant in deep fry basket: submerge in vinegar and boil 3 to 4 minutes. Remove and pat dry on towel. In baking dish with lid, layer eggplant slices, garlic, oregano and oil in several layers until all ingredients are used. Marinate for 1 week. Will keep for months in covered dish.

EGGPLANT DELIGHT

Originated in 1900 by Elizabeth Powell's grandmother, Elizabeth Shallow Bowden, this highly acclaimed dish has been updated somewhat over the years. It qualifies as a vegetarian dinner and can be doubled to feed a large crowd.   *Recipe contest entry: Elizabeth Powell, Media, PA*

4 eggplants
4 cloves fresh garlic, peeled
½ lb. *each* shredded Cheddar and Swiss cheeses
3 to 4 tablespoons butter

Lightly spray two 12x9x2-inch ovenproof casseroles with Pam. Peel and slice eggplants lengthwise about ¼ inch thick. Slice garlic lengthwise in paper thin slices. Arrange layers of eggplant and garlic in casseroles with cheeses and dots of butter separating each, ending with a top layer of garlic and butter. Bake at 375 degrees for about 45 minutes or until deep brown in color, bubbly and crusted. Makes 10 ample servings.

LIGHT 'N' LOVELY EGGPLANT CASSEROLE

A different kind of eggplant dish, this recipe requires no cheese and no preliminary frying of the eggplant. It's great for controlled fat diets.   *Recipe contest entry: Joseph Noury, Sunnyvale, CA*

4 large eggplants
3 large onions, diced
1 cup diced celery
5 cloves fresh garlic, minced
2 lb. ground chuck
2 cans (16 oz.) tomatoes
1 can (6 oz.) tomato paste
1½ teaspoons allspice

Cut eggplants in slices about ⅜ inch thick. Salt each slice and place in colander to drain. Combine onion, celery, garlic and ground meat in large pan. Brown all together, drain off fat and let cool. Crush tomatoes and combine with tomato paste and allspice. Bring to a slow boil for 15 minutes and then simmer for thirty minutes. Let cool before using. Rinse off eggplant. Cover the bottom of a 10x13x2 baking pan with 1 cup tomato sauce mixture. Layer pan with eggplant, meat, and tomato mixture. You should be able to make three layers. Add meat and sauce on top layer. Cover with foil and bake at 350 degrees for 30 minutes. Reduce heat to 300 degrees for 30 minutes; remove foil and bake another 15 minutes. Serve over steamed rice.

Regional Winner 1982 Recipe Contest: ILENE HELLMAN, Kennet, MO

An Oriental-style dish very good served over rice.

GARLIC EGGPLANT

½ lb. ground pork
2 tablespoons soy sauce
1½ lb. eggplant, peeled and cut into ½-inch squares
1 large onion, chopped
⅓ cup sherry
3 tablespoons oyster sauce
2 teaspoons sesame oil
1 teaspoon sugar
3 tablespoons peanut oil
10 cloves fresh garlic, minced
1 tablespoon chili paste with garlic
½ teaspoon ginger, minced

Mix pork with 1 tablespoon soy sauce in small bowl and set aside. Combine eggplant and onion in another bowl. Mix sherry, oyster sauce, remaining soy sauce, sesame oil and sugar in small bowl and set aside. Heat wok or electric skillet until hot; pour in peanut oil and add minced garlic, chili paste and ginger. Cook for a few seconds, stirring constantly. Add pork mixture and stir fry, stirring constantly, until pork loses pink color. Add eggplant and onion mixture. Stir in sauce, adding more sherry if necessary for liquid to be about halfway up mixture in wok. Cover and cook on high heat for about 7 minutes. If sauce evaporates before eggplant is tender, add more sherry as needed. When eggplant is tender, uncover and cook until most of remaining sauce has evaporated. Serve immediately. Makes 4 servings.

EGGPLANT PARMIGIANA

This famous Italian dish takes full advantage of the wonderful flavor combination of garlic, tomatoes and Parmesan cheese.

2 medium eggplants
Oil for frying
2 cups canned tomatoes
1 can (6 oz.) tomato paste
¾ teaspoon garlic powder
1½ teaspoons seasoned salt
⅛ teaspoon black pepper
1 tablespoon parsley flakes
1 bay leaf
½ cup grated Parmesan cheese
2 cups soft bread crumbs
½ lb. sliced Mozzarella cheese

Peel eggplants and cut into ½-inch slices. Saute in oil 5 minutes or until tender and lightly browned. Remove and keep warm. In skillet combine tomatoes, tomato paste, garlic powder, seasoned salt, pepper, parsley flakes and bay leaf. Cover and simmer 15 minutes. Remove bay leaf; add Parmesan cheese and bread crumbs, mixing well. Place a layer of eggplant in buttered, shallow 2-quart baking dish. Cover with half the tomato sauce then with half the Mozzarella cheese. Repeat layers. Bake in 350-degree oven 20 minutes or until cheese melts and is lightly browned. Serve at once. You will find this dish excellent for Lent. Makes 5 to 6 servings.

BASQUE-STYLE EGGPLANT CASSEROLE

Basques, people from northern Spain and southwestern France, are noted for serving foods with robust flavor. They love their garlic, too!

6 tablespoons oil
1 onion, sliced into rings
2 green peppers, cut into strips
5 large mushrooms, sliced
1 celery stalk, sliced diagonally
5 cloves fresh garlic, minced
6 tomatoes, peeled and diced
Salt to taste
1 tablespoon fines herbes
1 large eggplant
2 eggs, beaten with 1 tablespoon water and pinch of salt
½ cup freshly grated Parmesan cheese
1 cup grated Swiss cheese

Heat 3 tablespoons oil in large skillet; add onion, green peppers, mushrooms, celery and garlic. Saute until tender. Add tomatoes. Bring to a boil. Add salt and fines herbes. Turn heat to low and simmer sauce for 30 minutes. Peel eggplant and slice into ½-inch slices. Dip in egg mixture and fry eggplant in skillet with remaining oil until tender. Arrange eggplant slices in large baking dish. Sprinkle with Parmesan cheese. Pour tomato sauce over the top and sprinkle with Swiss cheese. Heat in 350-degree oven until cheese is melted. Makes 4 servings.

NINA'S RATATOUILLE

A delicious, healthful and satisfying dish. Try filling crepes with this mixture and serving as a main dish. If rocambole (a relative of both garlic and shallots) is not available, increase the amount of garlic used.   *Recipe contest entry: Nina Landy, Pacific Palisades, CA*

1 medium eggplant, peeled and diced
2 to 3 tablespoons sesame oil
2 onions, peeled and sliced
3 shallots, peeled and sliced
3 cloves fresh garlic, minced
3 rocambole, squeezed in garlic press
2 zucchini, sliced
2 medium ripe tomatoes *or* 1 can (16 oz.) drained stewed tomatoes
1 green bell pepper, sliced
1 can (8 oz.) tomato sauce
½ cup dry white wine (optional)
½ teaspoon *each* dried basil and thyme
1 bay leaf
Salt, pepper and garlic powder to taste
Chopped fresh parsley
Freshly grated Parmesan cheese

Salt eggplant lightly and let stand 15 minutes. Dry in paper towel. Heat oil in skillet and saute onions, shallots, garlic and rocambole for 3 minutes until all are soft and onion is transparent. Add eggplant and zucchini and saute for 5 minutes until both are soft and lightly browned. Add all remaining ingredients except parsley and cheese. Cover and continue cooking for about 20 minutes until all vegetables are soft and tender. Garnish with parsley and sprinkle with cheese. Makes 4 servings.

GILROY RATATOUILLE

Enhanced by sausage and cheese, this ratatouille makes a complete meal. For vegetarians, just omit the sausage.

Recipe contest entry: Mrs. Gene Stecyk, Los Angeles, CA

3 cloves fresh garlic, minced
2 thinly sliced onions
⅓ cup olive oil
1 green pepper, cut into thin rounds
2 medium eggplants, diced, unpeeled
2 medium zucchini, sliced ¼ inch thick
1 can (20 oz.) whole Italian tomatoes
1½ teaspoons basil
1½ teaspoons parsley
1½ teaspoons salt
Fresh ground pepper to taste
1½ lb. sliced Italian sausage
½ lb. whole mushrooms
1 cup grated Swiss cheese

Saute garlic and onions in oil until soft. Add green pepper, eggplants and zucchini and cook 5 minutes over medium heat, tossing well. Add tomatoes with liquid and seasonings. Simmer uncovered 15 minutes, then cover and simmer 15 minutes more. Meanwhile, cook sausage in frying pan until done and drain well. Add mushrooms to vegetables during last 10 minutes of cooking time. Add sausage to vegetables. Sprinkle with grated cheese. Cover and simmer until cheese melts. Makes 8 servings.

GREEN BEANS AU GARLIC

Served as an antipasto, these good and garlicky beans will get the tastebuds working. *Recipe contest entry: John Proynoff, Phoenix, AZ*

2½ lb. young fresh green beans
1 large onion, chopped
½ cup salad *or* olive oil
1 teaspoon paprika
2 tomatoes, chopped
1 head fresh garlic, peeled and crushed
2 tablespoons chopped parsley
1 teaspoon salt

Wash beans, trim and cut in half if too long. Cook, uncovered, in boiling water, or steam, about 15 minutes until crisp-tender. Do not overcook. Drain and set aside. Meanwhile in separate pan, saute onion in oil until soft, add paprika and cook 1 minute more before adding tomatoes, garlic, parsley and salt. Simmer on low heat for 8 to 10 minutes, stirring occasionally. Add beans and mix well. Refrigerate until ready to serve. Makes 6 to 8 servings.

GARLIC GREEN BEANS

This spicy side dish would be appropriate served with any grilled or roasted meat or fish.   *Recipe contest entry: Kathy Borges, Morgan Hill, CA*

2 lb. fresh green beans
¼ lb. bacon, diced
1 small onion, chopped
3 cloves fresh garlic, minced
½ green bell pepper, seeded and chopped
1 can (8 oz.) tomato sauce
¾ teaspoon Italian seasoning
½ teaspoon salt
¼ teaspoon pepper

Wash beans, trim and cut into 2-inch pieces. Steam until crisp-tender, approximately 7 to 10 minutes. Set aside. Meanwhile, in large saucepan, fry bacon until crisp. Remove from pan with slotted spoon and set aside. Discard all but 3 tablespoons of bacon drippings. Add onion, garlic and green pepper and cook over medium heat until soft, about 5 minutes. Add tomato sauce, seasonings and reserved bacon. Simmer together for about 10 minutes to blend flavors. Add cooked beans and heat through. Makes 6 to 8 servings.

QUEEN'S BEANS

This easy-to-fix vegetable dish can be a hearty meal-in-one with the addition of ham, ham hocks or hamburger.
Recipe contest entry: Mrs. Gil (Queen) Murphy, San Diego, CA

1 cup small white beans
7 cups cold water
1 teaspoon salt
¼ teaspoon paprika
2 large onions, quartered
½ cup tomato sauce
10 large cloves fresh garlic, halved
½ cup parsley sprigs
¼ cup olive oil

Cook beans in water for 1 hour. Add salt, paprika and onions. Cover and cook 1 more hour. Add tomato sauce, garlic, parsley and olive oil. Cook 30 minutes longer. Serve with lemon juice.

GREEN BEANS ASADOOR

There must be a thousand ways to serve green beans. This one has a wonderful Italian flavor.

Recipe contest entry: Virginia Asadoor, Pasadena, CA

1 cup chopped onions
4 cloves fresh garlic
4 oz. butter *or* margarine
4 tablespoons tomato sauce
1 teaspoon sweet basil
1 lb. fresh green beans, strings and ends removed

Saute onions and garlic in butter; add tomato sauce and basil. Place green beans over onions and garlic; cover and simmer until cooked (approximately 15 to 20 minutes).

DILLED GREEN BEANS

It is always nice to have something homemade on the shelf to bring out to complete a party meal, sharpen your family's appetite or take as a house gift next time you visit friends. These dill- and garlic-flavored green beans would be welcome anytime.

2 lb. green beans (young and tender)
1 teaspoon powdered alum
1 gallon water
4 teaspoons dill seed
2 teaspoons mustard seed
1 teaspoon crushed red pepper
½ teaspoon dehydrated minced garlic
2 cups water
2 cups vinegar
¼ cup salt

Wash beans and trim ends; place in stone crock or glass container. Dissolve alum in the 1 gallon water; pour over beans and let stand 24 hours. Drain and wash. Put beans in saucepan and add about 1 cup water. Cover and boil 5 minutes, then drain. Pack beans lengthwise into 4 sterilized canning jars. To each jar add 1 teaspoon dill seed, ½ teaspoon mustard seed, ¼ teaspoon crushed red pepper and ⅛ teaspoon dehydrated garlic. Combine remaining ingredients and bring to a boil. Pour over beans, leaving ¼-inch head space. Seal at once. Makes 4 jars beans.

VAL AND ELSIE'S JULIENNE BEANS

Val Filice, garlic grower and head chef of Gourmet Alley, and his wife Elsie even glamorize canned green beans when cooking at home!

Courtesy of: Val and Elsie Filice, Gilroy, CA

4 cloves fresh garlic, crushed
1 bacon strip, cut crosswise into ¼-inch strips
4 tablespoons olive oil
3 cans (1 lb. *each*) julienne-style green beans
¼ cup liquid reserved after draining beans
1 teaspoon dry oregano
1 teaspoon dry basil (*or* fresh)
Salt and pepper to taste

Saute garlic and bacon in olive oil until garlic turns amber in color. Remove pan from heat and add beans, liquid, herbs, and salt and pepper and cook over medium heat until beans are warmed through.

GREEK BEANS

The Greeks also know how to season food well with garlic. This dish is particularly easy to prepare, but good enough for company!

Recipe contest entry: Barbara Flory, South Laguna, CA

1 lb. fresh green beans
1 cup tomato juice
¼ cup olive oil
3 cloves fresh garlic, pressed
3 tomatoes, cut in quarters
1 chopped onion
½ cup chopped parsley
½ teaspoon crushed oregano leaves
½ teaspoon paprika
1 teaspoon garlic salt
Salt and pepper to taste

Cut beans into thirds. Cook in tomato juice until tender. Meanwhile, in olive oil, saute garlic, tomatoes, onion, parsley and oregano until tender but still crisp. When beans are tender, add sauteed ingredients, paprika, garlic salt and salt and pepper to taste. Simmer 5 more minutes, then serve.

Finalist in 1980 Recipe Contest: R.J. HARRIS, Gilroy, CA

Plump, fresh mushrooms are stuffed with a hardy filling that includes plenty of garlic and a surprise ingredient: chopped almonds. For a vegetarian meal it is also quite palatable prepared with soy paste as a substitute for the beef.

GARLIC MUSHROOM CASSEROLE

16 large fresh mushrooms for stuffing
½ lb. small mushrooms
1 cup finely diced fresh garlic
1 cup chopped almonds
½ lb. butter
1 lb. ground beef
2 cups seasoned bread crumbs
1 cup grated Swiss *or* Mozzarella cheese
½ cup grated Parmesan cheese

Trim large mushrooms; discard ends. Remove stems and chop together with small mushrooms. Saute garlic, chopped mushrooms and almonds in half the butter until well done. Add beef and cook until done. Add 1½ cups bread crumbs and mix thoroughly. Line bottom of greased casserole with 8 large mushrooms (open side up). Press sauteed mixture firmly over mushrooms. Use remaining 8 large mushrooms to cover sauteed mixture (place open side down). Sprinkle with grated Swiss or Mozzarella cheese, remaining bread crumbs and Parmesan cheese. Dot with remaining half of the butter and bake at 350 degrees for 35 minutes or until mushrooms are tender. Serves 8.

NOTE: Can use soy paste instead of ground meat. Add extra ½ lb. butter for moisture.

GARLICKY MUSHROOMS SUPREME

This great mushroom dish can substitute for one of the vegetables at your next dinner party.

Recipe contest entry: Carrie Cohen, Woodland Hills, CA

1 lb. sliced mushrooms
4 tablespoons olive oil
7 cloves fresh garlic, sliced
3 tablespoons chopped parsley
Salt and pepper to taste

Saute mushrooms in olive oil, covered, about 15 minutes. Uncover; add garlic, parsley, salt and pepper. Simmer until liquid evaporates. Do not let garlic brown. Serve and enjoy.

Regional Winner 1984 Recipe Contest:

DR. JOYCE M. JOHNSON, Altanta, GA

Onions and garlic are "kissin' cousins" in the plant kingdom with quite different individual flavors which blend together beautifully in this elegant baked vegetable dish.

ONIONS STUFFED WITH GARLIC AND CHESTNUTS

4 large Spanish onions
4 slices bacon, chopped
1 tablespoon butter
1 whole head fresh garlic, peeled and chopped
1 can (8 oz.) water chestnuts, drained and chopped
¼ cup bread crumbs
½ teaspoon salt
¼ teaspoon black pepper
1 cup apple cider

Put the unskinned onions in boiling water for about 5 minutes. Remove and cool. Cut off tops, peel and scoop out the insides. Chop the insides of onions. Set aside. In frying pan cook bacon until crisp. Drain off fat, add butter and saute the bacon bits, chopped onion, and the chopped cloves of garlic until just lightly brown. Add the water chestnuts and bread crumbs and continue to brown for another 3 minutes. Add salt and pepper. Fill each onion with the mixture. Place in casserole. Pour apple cider over and bake at 375 degrees for 45 to 50 minutes. Makes 4 servings.

BAKED GARLIC POTATOES

The goodness of garlic and the popular appeal of potatoes make this dish a winning combination. Small unpeeled potatoes are baked whole in a casserole and drizzled with garlic-flavored oil.

1 lb. small white potatoes (about 1½ inches in diameter)
4 cloves fresh garlic, minced
4 tablespoons olive oil
¼ cup chopped parsley
2 teaspoons coarse salt
¼ teaspoon freshly ground pepper
Butter *or* margarine

Wash and dry potatoes; arrange in a casserole in two layers. Combine garlic, oil, parsley, salt and pepper. Pour over potatoes and toss to coat with oil mixture. Cover and bake in a 450-degree oven for 20 minutes. Turn potatoes to recoat in oil, then bake another 25 minutes. Cut potatoes open and squeeze ends to fluff them up. Serve with butter or margarine. Makes 6 servings.

Regional Winner 1981 Recipe Contest:

HARRIETT MACHT, Santa Rosa, CA

Bread may be the staff of life, but potatoes run a close second. You can never have too many good recipes for serving potatoes. This regional contest winner kept her recipe simple, but it is simply delicious.

GARLIC POTATOES WITH CHEESE SAUCE

3 large potatoes
1 medium onion
6 or more large cloves fresh garlic
2 tablespoons butter
½ cup grated Cheddar cheese

Pare and *thinly* slice potatoes; peel and mince onion; peel garlic. Grease a 10-inch baking dish or equivalent-size casserole. Cover bottom with one layer potatoes. Sprinkle with minced onion. Using a garlic press, press 2 cloves garlic and sprinkle over potatoes. Dot with a portion of the butter. Repeat until all potatoes are used, making 3 or 4 layers. Pour Cheese Sauce over potatoes. Sprinkle ½ cup grated cheese over top. Cover and bake in moderate oven (350 degrees) 30 minutes. Uncover and bake 30 minutes longer until potatoes are done. Makes 6 generous servings.

Cheese Sauce
2 tablespoons butter
2 tablespoons flour
½ teaspoon *each* salt and dry mustard
Dash of paprika
¾ cup grated Cheddar cheese
½ cup milk

Melt butter in a saucepan. Blend in flour. Slowly stir in milk. Cook and stir over moderate heat until sauce is smooth and slightly thickened. Blend in salt and dry mustard, a generous dash paprika, and ¾ cup grated Cheddar cheese. Heat, stirring, until cheese melts.

DELICIOUS POTATOES

Another wonderful old family recipe to be shared among garlic lovers.

Recipe contest entry: Pearl Bruce, Winamac, IN

5 cups cooked, diced potatoes
2 cups cottage cheese
1 cup shredded Cheddar cheese
2 teaspoons garlic salt
1 cup sour cream

Mix all ingredients together in order given. Bake at 350 degrees for 1 hour in buttered casserole. Makes 3 servings.

GARLIC JALAPENO POTATOES

Great for a potluck! The jalapeno cheese adds zesty flavor to "au gratin" potatoes

Recipe contest entry: Mrs. Milton E. Falk, Onaga, KS

8 medium red potatoes, cooked until tender
1 green bell pepper, slivered
1 jar (4 oz.) pimentos, drained
Salt and pepper to taste
¼ lb. butter
2 tablespoons flour
3 cloves fresh garlic, minced
2 cups milk
2 cups jalapeno cheese, cubed
1½ cups crushed Rice Chex cereal

Peel and slice potatoes. Layer in buttered casserole with bell pepper and pimentos. Salt and pepper each layer to taste. Melt butter in saucepan, add flour and minced garlic and stir until well blended. Gradually add milk, stirring constantly. Add cheese. Stir until cheese melts. Pour over potatoes and top with crushed cereal. Bake for 45 minutes at 350 degrees. Makes 8 to 10 servings.

ROASTED GARLIC POTATOES

A very simple dish with only a few ingredients but lots of good flavor.

Recipe contest entry: Angela Rainero, Oakland, CA

4 large baking potatoes, peeled
4 cloves fresh garlic
6 tablespoons butter
¾ cup grated Parmesan cheese
Salt and pepper to taste

Cut potatoes in half lengthwise, then slice medium thin and place in large bowl. Mince garlic or put through press. Melt butter in a small saucepan and add garlic. Cook on medium heat for 1 minute. Add to potatoes with half the cheese and salt and pepper. Stir until potatoes are well coated. Pour into a greased shallow baking dish. Top with remaining cheese and bake at 400 degrees uncovered until golden brown, about 30 minutes. Do not stir or turn during cooking. Makes 6 servings.

S.O.S. (SUPER OMNIPOTENT SPUDS)

The onion and garlic flavor are surprisingly mild in this light and fluffy potato dish.

Recipe contest entry: Christina Lee, Laguna Hills, CA

8 baking potatoes, peeled and quartered
1 teaspoon salt
1 large onion, peeled and sliced
6 cloves fresh garlic, peeled
½ cup cream *or* condensed milk
4 tablespoons sweet butter
½ cup grated Cheddar cheese
½ cup buttered bread crumbs

Boil potatoes, onion and garlic in salted water for 15 minutes, or until soft. Drain well. Mash potatoes, onion and garlic until smooth. Add cream and butter and beat well. Place in buttered casserole, sprinkle with mixture of cheese and bread crumbs and bake at 350 degrees for 25 to 30 minutes, until bubbly. Makes 4 to 6 servings.

POTATO-GARLIC PUREE

An excellent accompaniment to roast beef. To prepare garlic puree, place garlic in boiling water and simmer until tender, about 25 minutes. Remove cloves from water and cool. Remove skins and mash with fork to form smooth paste.

Recipe contest entry: Joella Prause Enna, Dallas, TX

4 medium baking potatoes
20 cloves fresh garlic, pureed
3 tablespoons butter
½ to ¾ cup hot milk *or* cream
½ teaspoon salt
¼ teaspoon white pepper

Peel potatoes and cut into ½-inch cubes. Place in 3-quart saucepan and add water to cover. Simmer until tender, about 25 minutes. Drain well. Mash potatoes until smooth. Add garlic puree, butter and enough hot milk or cream to form a smooth mixture. Whip until fluffy. Add salt and pepper and serve immediately. Makes 4 servings.

GARLIC PIE

An attractive, well seasoned and hearty dish which can be made ahead and baked just before serving.

Recipe contest entry: Kenneth Poppa, Gilroy, CA

8 medium red potatoes, cooked
3 medium white onions, chopped
15 cloves fresh garlic, minced
3 to 4 tablespoons butter
½ teaspoon garlic salt
1 lb. Italian sausage, removed from casings
1½ tablespoons oregano
1 tablespoon cumin
Salt and pepper to taste
2 eggs
1 cup milk
6 oz. Mozzarella cheese, sliced
Paprika

Peel potatoes, reserving skins, and slice. Over low heat in covered pan, cook onion and garlic in 2 to 3 tablespoons butter for about 20 minutes. In a buttered 11-inch pie pan make a crust out of the potato skins by pressing skins firmly into pan. Sprinkle with garlic salt and dot with butter. Add sausage to onion-garlic mixture and brown. Add oregano, cumin and salt and pepper and pour into pie crust. Beat eggs and milk together lightly and pour over sausage. Top with cheese and then arrange sliced potatoes on top to form top crust. Dot with butter, sprinkle with paprika and bake in 450-degree oven for 20 to 30 minutes until heated through and top is browned. Makes 6 to 8 servings.

SPINACH CASSEROLE

The flavor of fresh garlic comes through loud and clear in this vegetable casserole. Look for "Vegeroni" in health food stores if your local supermarket doesn't handle it.

Recipe contest entry: Lila Daoud, Monterey, CA

1 pkg. (8 or 12 oz.) Vegeroni (vegetable macaroni)
1 pkg. (10 oz.) frozen chopped spinach, defrosted
1 container (16 oz.) creamed *or* Farmer style cottage cheese
1½ to 2 lb. Monterey Jack cheese, shredded
8 large cloves fresh garlic, minced *or* pressed
½ to ¾ cup milk

Cook macaroni as package directs, drain and cool. Combine with spinach, cottage cheese and Jack cheese and garlic; mix well. Pour into baking pan. Smooth surface with spoon and pour milk over. Bake at 350 degrees for 35 to 40 minutes. Halfway through baking, mix casserole slightly so the top does not get too hard or crisp. Smooth surface and continue baking. Makes 6 to 8 servings.

CHEESY SPINACH

Easy, economical and very good.

Recipe contest entry: Patricia Lentz, Sunland, CA

1 large bunch spinach *or* other leafy greens
2 onions, peeled and chopped
3 cloves fresh garlic, peeled and chopped *or* ½ teaspoon powdered garlic
1 cup cooked brown rice
⅓ cup *or* more grated cheese
2 tablespoons soy sauce *or* to taste

Clean spinach leaves well, remove stems and chop leaves and stems separately. In wok or skillet, saute stems, onion and garlic until onions are translucent. Stir in cooked rice well. Lay spinach leaves on top of rice mixture. Cover pan and cook until spinach is wilted. Stir leaves into the rice mixture. Add the cheese and season to taste with soy sauce. Stir until the cheese melts and holds mixture together. Makes about 3 servings.

BIG DADDY'S BIG-ON-FLAVOR SPINACH TREATS

An unusual treatment for spinach. Good for company as it can be made ahead and not cooked until about 30 minutes before serving.

Recipe contest entry: Thomas O. Davis, Waynesboro, MS

2 pkg. (10 oz. *each*) frozen chopped spinach, cooked, drained
10 cloves fresh garlic, finely chopped
3 cups commercial herb stuffing mix
6 eggs
½ cup melted butter *or* margarine
½ cup grated Parmesan-Romano cheese mixture
1¼ teaspoons salt
¼ teaspoon Tabasco
1 can (10¾ oz.) condensed cream of celery soup

Mix together all ingredients except soup. Shape into small balls. Place in large, ungreased baking pan. Bake, uncovered, at 325 degrees for 20 to 25 minutes. Remove to serving dish. Heat soup to boiling and pour over. Serve hot. Makes 8 to 10 servings.

Finalist in 1980 Recipe Contest: BOB DIXON, Santa Cruz, CA

These little tomato red bellies are chock-full with a delightful filling of bulgur wheat, crunchy nuts and fresh seasonings. Spoon on the Green Walnut and Garlic Butter for the final treat.

RED BELLIES

1 cup chicken stock
½ cup bulgur wheat
4 firm, large, fresh tomatoes
8 large cloves fresh garlic
½ cup chopped walnuts
3 tablespoons olive oil
¼ cup fresh parsley, chopped
3 tablespoons fresh basil, minced (*or* ½ teaspoon dried)
2 tablespoons minced watercress (optional)
1 tablespoon Worcestershire sauce
Juice of 1 lemon
Salt to taste
Green Walnut and Garlic Butter (recipe below)

Pour heated chicken stock over bulgur. Cover and let stand 1 hour. Slice top off each tomato. Remove pulp and reserve. Place tomatoes upside down on paper towel to drain. Saute garlic and walnuts in 2 tablespoons of olive oil over low heat for 2 to 3 minutes. In a medium bowl combine bulgur, walnuts, garlic, parsley, basil, watercress, Worcestershire sauce, lemon juice, salt and reserved tomato pulp. Fill tomato shells with mixture and sprinkle with remaining olive oil. Place in an oiled dish and bake at 350 degrees for 15 to 20 minutes. Add a generous tablespoon of the Green Walnut and Garlic Butter on top of each tomato and return to oven for 2 or 3 minutes.

Green Walnut and Garlic Butter
4 cloves fresh garlic, minced and mashed
6 walnut halves, minced
1 tablespoon olive oil
½ cup butter (creamed)
4 large spinach leaves, minced
2 tablespoons minced basil
Dash of Tabasco

Saute garlic and walnuts for 2 minutes in olive oil. Mash well. Combine butter with all ingredients and chill until needed.

Finalist in 1982 Recipe Contest: BILL SCALES, Gilroy, CA

Fresh whole tomatoes are scooped out and filled with a savory mixture of onion, sausage, garlic and bread crumbs, then baked with their caps on until juicy and tender.

TOMATOES A LA WILLIAM

6 medium to large tomatoes
   Salt
   Garlic powder
2 lb. ground sausage meat
2 tablespoons butter
3 onions, diced
4 cloves fresh garlic, minced
1/3 bunch fresh parsley, finely chopped
1/4 cup bread crumbs

Cut tops from tomatoes and set aside. Scoop out insides of tomatoes and reserve for another use. Sprinkle insides of tomatoes with salt and garlic powder and turn upside down on paper towels to drain. Brown sausage in buttered skillet. Drain and discard fat. Saute onions and garlic in butter until soft. Combine with sausage, parsley and bread crumbs. Cook gently over medium heat 5 minutes. Spoon into tomato shells and set tops back in place. Sprinkle lightly with additional bread crumbs. Bake uncovered at 325 degrees 45 minutes. Makes 6 servings.

TOMATOES A LA CLARE

"Delicious and pretty" says the woman who entered this recipe in the 1979 Great Garlic Recipe Contest. We have to agree.

Recipe contest entry: Clara M. Lutz, Redondo Beach, CA

6 medium to large tomatoes, sliced
3 cloves fresh garlic, minced
1 bunch green onions, chopped fine (include some green tops)
1/3 cup finely chopped parsley
1/2 teaspoon salt
   Coarse black pepper to taste
1/3 cup corn oil
1/4 cup brown cider vinegar
1 tablespoon Dijon mustard

Arrange tomatoes in a shallow dish or platter. Mix garlic, onions, parsley, salt and pepper; sprinkle over tomatoes. Cover with plastic wrap and refrigerate for 3 to 4 hours. Prepare dressing by combining oil, vinegar and mustard. At serving time, shake well and pour over tomatoes.

GARLIC BUTTER CRUMB TOMATOES *Excellent*

Karen Christopher says, "I'm not a person who enjoys long hours in the kitchen, but I always serve dishes laced with fresh garlic. This recipe for crumb-topped tomatoes makes up fast and easy." They are attractive to serve and a happy blend of flavors which make them a good choice for the second vegetable.

Courtesy of: Karen Christopher, Gilroy, CA

4 fresh tomatoes
½ cup seasoned dressing mix, crushed into crumbs
4 tablespoons melted butter
2 large cloves fresh garlic, minced
½ teaspoon basil
Salt and pepper to taste
Fresh parsley, minced

Cut tomatoes into halves. Moisten crumbs with mixture of butter, garlic, basil and seasonings. Place crumb mixture on tomato halves and broil in preheated broiler 10 inches from heat source until browned and heated. Garnish with minced parsley and serve.

PUREED TURNIPS WITH GARLIC

An excellent flavor combination and especially good with poultry or pork. This dish may be reheated in the top of double boiler.

Recipe contest entry: Kelly Hendleman, Palo Alto, CA

2 lb. turnips, peeled and quartered
12 tablespoons butter *or* margarine
12 cloves fresh garlic, peeled
Salt and pepper, both red and black, to taste

Parboil turnips 7 minutes in salted water. Drain. Cook turnips and garlic gently in 8 tablespoons butter until both are soft. Puree in food processor or by hand, adding the remaining 4 tablespoons of butter during process. Season to taste with salt and pepper. Makes 5 to 6 servings.

ZESTY ZUCCHINI SAUTE

A quick and tasty way to serve zucchini, this dish goes well with any meat.

4 medium-sized zucchini
2 teaspoons seasoned salt
2 teaspoons parsley flakes
1 teaspoon instant minced onion
½ teaspoon ground oregano
¼ teaspoon garlic powder
¼ teaspoon pepper
¼ cup olive oil

Wash zucchini but do not peel. Slice in rounds about ¼ inch thick. Mix together remaining ingredients except olive oil. Sprinkle over zucchini and toss until seasoning is well distributed. Heat oil in skillet; add zucchini and saute until browned on both sides, about 10 minutes. Drain on absorbent paper. Makes 4 servings.

MYRNA'S STUFFED ZUCCHINI

An unusual stuffing for this popular vegetable, it includes both white and garbanzo beans. . . . and garlic, of course. If you cook the beans yourself, be sure to add a bay leaf to the water.

Recipe contest entry: Myrna Slade, San Francisco, CA

6 medium zucchini
1 bay leaf
6 cloves fresh garlic
½ cup chopped onion
¼ cup chopped parsley
2 tablespoons butter *or* olive oil
1 large tomato, chopped
½ teaspoon *each* thyme, cumin and oregano
Dash of cayenne pepper
Salt and pepper to taste
2 cups cooked white beans, drained
1 cup cooked garbanzo beans, drained
2 tablespoons olive oil

Slice zucchini in half lengthwise and simmer in ½ inch water with the bay leaf until tender, about 5 minutes. Cool slightly and scoop out insides, leaving a ½-inch thick shell. Chop insides. Chop 4 cloves garlic coarsely and saute with onion and parsley in butter *or* oil until golden and soft, about 5 minutes. Stir in tomato and cook 1 minute more. Season with thyme, cumin, oregano, cayenne pepper, salt and pepper. Add chopped zucchini. Mash beans until semi-smooth. Stir into vegetable mixture. Stuff into zucchini shells and place in buttered baking dish. Mince remaining 2 cloves garlic and mix with bread crumbs and olive oil and sprinkle evenly over stuffed zucchini. Bake at 350 degrees for 10 to 15 minutes, until crumbs are golden and crisp and all is heated through. Makes 6 servings.

ZUCCHINI ZAP!

Another delicious approach to preparing the prolific squash, this would be very pleasant served as a light lunch or as a side dish with grilled meats.   *Recipe contest entry: Cynthia Kannenberg, Brown Deer, WI*

3   lb. fresh zucchini, sliced
½   cup chopped onion
6   tablespoons butter, softened
3   cloves fresh garlic, minced
18 saltine crackers (with salt), crushed
1   cup grated sharp Cheddar cheese
2   eggs, beaten
    Seasoned salt and freshly ground pepper to taste
    Italian seasoned dry bread crumbs
    Paprika and fresh parsley sprigs for garnish

Boil zucchini for 20 minutes. Drain and mash. Saute onion in 2 tablespoons butter and add to zucchini with garlic, crackers, cheese, remaining 4 tablespoons butter, eggs and seasonings. Mix well. Pour into greased 9x13-inch casserole and sprinkle with bread crumbs. Bake at 350 degrees for 30 minutes. Garnish with paprika and sprigs of parsley. Makes 6 servings.

ZUCCHINI LEAVES

Attractive appearance and excellent flavor are two good reasons to prepare this stuffed zucchini recipe.

Recipe contest entry: Rose Montgomery, Redding, CA

8   fresh zucchini, about 7 inches long
2   cups cottage cheese
2   eggs, well beaten
¼   cup minced parsley
3   cloves fresh garlic, minced
    Salt and white pepper to taste
    Dash nutmeg
¼   cup grated sharp Cheddar cheese

Cut zucchini in half lengthwise and parboil in boiling salted water for 10 minutes until just tender but not soft. Drain, scoop out centers and discard, turning shells over on paper towels to drain and cool. When cool, place shells in oblong buttered baking dish. Mix remaining ingredients and fill zucchini shells, dividing mixture evenly. Sprinkle each shell with cheese, being careful not to allow cheese to fall between zucchini shells as it will burn. Bake at 350 degrees for 15 to 20 minutes. Makes 8 servings.

ZIPPY ZUCCHINI FRITTERS

Not low in calories, perhaps, but this recipe is another very good way to use the ever-abundant zucchini and who can resist when it's paired with garlic and chiles?   *Recipe contest entry: Nancy Bruce, Fair Oaks, CA*

2½ cups shredded zucchini
4 eggs
1 can (4 oz.) diced green chiles
¾ cup dry bread crumbs
⅓ cup grated Parmesan cheese plus more for garnish
4 cloves fresh garlic, minced
1 teaspoon chicken-flavored soup base
¼ teaspoon pepper
Oil for frying

Squeeze as much water as possible from grated zucchini (leaving about 1 cup of zucchini). Place all ingredients, except oil, in a bowl and mix well. Pour oil in skillet to ⅛-inch depth and heat over medium heat. Drop batter into hot oil 1 heaping tablespoon at a time to make 8 fritters. Fry about 5 minutes on one side, turn and fry until golden brown on the other. Sprinkle lightly with additional Parmesan cheese, if desired. Serve immediately. Makes 4 servings.

ZUCCHINI ALLA PELLICCIONE

Served as a cold side dish or salad, this minty marinated zucchini dish from a Gourmet Alley chef is an unusual accompaniment for almost any meal.   *Courtesy of: Paul Pelliccione, Gilroy*

7 to 8 zucchini (not over 2½-inch diameter)
Salt
2 cups flour
2 cups vegetable oil
3 cups dry bread crumbs
30 slices fresh garlic (6 to 8 cloves)
30 fresh mint leaves
Wine vinegar

Wash zucchini and trim ends. Slice uniformly to ³⁄₁₆-inch thickness. Arrange 1 layer in colander and sprinkle with salt. Continue with layers, sprinkling each with salt until all slices have been used. Let stand for 1 hour. Roll slices in flour and set aside. Heat oil to 300 degrees in large skillet. Fry slices on both sides until they barely begin to brown. Set aside on cookie sheet to cool completely. Place layer of sliced zucchini in large bowl. Sprinkle generously with bread crumbs. Arrange some of the garlic slices and mint leaves over the crumbs. Sprinkle generously with wine vinegar. Continue to layer zucchini and other ingredients in this order until all ingredients are used. Cover bowl and refrigerate.

Finalist in 1980 Recipe Contest: LEONARD BRILL, San Francisco, CA

An imaginative combination of ingredients transforms this inexpensive, quick-to-prepare dish into a delectable treat. You won't even miss the oysters.

MOCK OYSTER STIR-FRY

3 tablespoons oil
(½ vegetable, ½ sesame)
3 to 4 cloves fresh garlic, chopped
2 cups sliced zucchini
½ cup sliced fresh mushrooms
2 cups tofu, cut in ½-inch cubes
1 tablespoon soy sauce
⅓ cup oyster sauce
Sesame seeds

Heat oil in wok or frying pan over medium-high heat. Add garlic, zucchini and mushrooms. Stir-fry until zucchini starts to brown (about 2 minutes). Add tofu and toss. Reduce heat to low-medium. Mix soy sauce and oyster sauce and pour over. Toss and cook, covered, 2 to 3 minutes. Remove cover and cook another minute or so until sauce thickens. Sprinkle with sesame seeds. Serves 4.

Finalist in 1979 Recipe Contest: LENA LICO, Hollister, CA

A finalist in the Garlic Recipe Contest and Cook-off, Lena says this entry is a favorite with her family and some of the Gavilan College staff where she is manager of the cafeteria. "This dish is particularly good for vegetarians," says Lena. It would also be a good choice as a side dish to serve with barbecued meats.

HOLLISTER VEGETABLE CASSEROLE

6 zucchini, sliced
6 potatoes, peeled and sliced
3 bell peppers, cut in strips
2 large onions, sliced
1 large eggplant, sliced
½ cup Romano or Parmesan cheese
Salt and pepper to taste
5 cloves fresh garlic, pressed
1 teaspoon oregano
8 large tomatoes, sliced or 2 lb. canned tomatoes, broken up
½ cup oil

Place layers of vegetables in greased baking pan alternating with 4 tablespoons grated cheese, salt and pepper. Combine garlic and oregano with tomatoes. Top the casserole with tomatoes and 4 tablespoons cheese. Drizzle oil over top. Cover and bake at 350 degrees for 1½ hours. Uncover and bake at 375 degrees for another 1½ hours.

VEGETABLES VERACRUZ

Inspired by the classic Mexican sauce for red snapper, this vegetable dish has a flavor all its own.

Recipe contest entry: Norman Simmons, Los Angeles, CA

1 whole head fresh garlic
1 medium eggplant
  (approx. 1½ lb.)
2 small zucchini
1½ teaspoons salt
½ teaspoon ascorbic acid
  (*or* fruit canning mix)
1 medium onion
¼ cup olive oil
2 tablespoons butter
1 teaspoon oregano
1 teaspoon sweet basil
¼ teaspoon pepper
1 can (28 oz.) firm whole
  peeled tomatoes
1 teaspoon cornstarch
  mixed with 1 tablespoon
  water

Separate the garlic cloves and remove skins. Peel and cut eggplant into ¾-inch cubes. Cut zucchini into ¾-inch rounds and then into quarters. Place zucchini and eggplant in a bowl and cover with water in which 1 teaspoon salt and the ascorbic acid have been dissolved. Weight down and let stand while preparing remaining ingredients. Cut onion in half, then quarters and slice thinly. Reserve 4 garlic cloves and gently saute the remainder with onions in oil and butter on low heat for 10 minutes. Add oregano, basil, ½ teaspoon salt, pepper and the drained liquid from the tomatoes. Reduce heat to simmer. Seed the drained tomatoes, cut them into ¾-inch pieces, and set aside. Steam zucchini and eggplant for 10 minutes. When done, add to the onion and garlic mixture along with the tomatoes. Add reserved garlic cloves which have been minced fine. Raise heat and add the cornstarch in water, stirring until thickened and glazed. Simmer 5 minutes more and remove. *Do not overcook.* Let stand to blend flavors. This is delicious served hot or cold, and even better the next day. Makes 6 servings.

MEDITERRANEAN RAINBOW

This dish is best served lukewarm with buttered French bread to sop up the sauce. It can be a light lunch, an antipasto or a vegetable accompaniment to a simple (but garlicky) meat or chicken main course. Slightly chilled Beaujolais or a light and fruity Zinfandel would complete the meal.   *Recipe contest entry: Rosina Wilson, Albany, CA*

1 cup peeled fresh garlic cloves (2 to 4 heads)
½ lb. *each* green and yellow zucchini
2 *each* red and green bell peppers
1 bunch baby carrots
½ cup olive oil
3 small hot chile peppers
1 large onion, thinly sliced
12 wrinkled black olives
4 anchovies, mashed
2 tablespoons lemon peel, cut in strips
   Salt and pepper to taste
½ cup chopped parsley
   Freshly grated Parmesan cheese

Cut garlic in slivers. Slice zucchini and bell peppers in long, thin strips. Cut larger carrots into quarters or leave whole if really small. In skillet, saute garlic in oil slowly, along with chile peppers, for about 5 minutes. Add onion and bell peppers and saute 5 minutes more. Add zucchini and carrots, stir gently to coat with boil. Cover and steam for 5 minutes, then remove cover, add anchovies, olives and lemon peel. Continue stirring until vegetables are cooked, but still crunchy. Add salt and pepper; stir in parsley and transfer all to serving platter. Top with Parmesan cheese. Makes 6 servings.

CHINA CAMP STIR-FRIED VEGETABLES

Without fresh garlic, stir-fry vegetables might be good but not great. This combination is the greatest!

2 tablespoons oil
4 cloves fresh garlic
2 lb. vegetables cut into ½-inch diagonal slices (asparagus, broccoli, green beans, etc.)
1 can (8 oz.) water chestnuts, drained and sliced
2 tablespoons soy sauce
   Salt and pepper to taste
¼ cup toasted nuts, if desired (peanuts, almonds, cashews, etc.)

Heat in oil in large skillet or wok. Smash garlic by whacking cloves with butt end of a knife handle. Remove peel. Add garlic to oil. When garlic begins to give off aroma, remove and discard. Add vegetables and stir-fry over high heat until crisp-tender. Add water chestnuts, soy sauce, salt and pepper. Stir-fry another minute to heat through. Sprinkle with nuts and serve at once. Makes 4 to 6 servings.

SNOW PEAS CANTON

The Chinese have had a strong influence on California's history as well as its cuisine, and who knows better than the Chinese how to combine vegetables and garlic into mouth-watering dishes like this one!

1 tablespoon peanut oil
4 to 5 cloves fresh garlic, minced
½ lb. Chinese pea pods, ends trimmed, strings removed
1 can (5 oz.) sliced bamboo shoots, drained
1 can (8 oz.) water chestnuts, drained and sliced
¼ cup canned *or* fresh chicken broth
2 teaspoons soy sauce
1 teaspoon cornstarch
2 teaspoons water

Heat oil in a large skillet or wok. Saute garlic until light brown. Add peas, bamboo shoots and water chestnuts. Stir-fry 1 minute. Add chicken broth and soy sauce. Cover and cook another minute. Combine cornstarch and water. Stir into skillet. Cook over high heat until sauce thickens and appears glossy, about 1 minute. Makes 4 servings.

Cooking with garlic works magic with fresh vegetables.

Nashville Banner

HEAVEN SCENT

Uncomplicated, but uncommonly good. Zucchini, mushrooms and garlic make this vegetable dish very tasty indeed.

Recipe contest entry: Janice Smith, Delano, CA

2 tablespoons butter *or* margarine
1 tablespoon olive oil
4 cloves fresh garlic, sliced
1 cup fresh mushrooms, sliced
4 *or* 5 zucchini, sliced thin
1 teaspoon minced parsley
½ teaspoon thyme
Salt and lemon pepper to taste

In large skillet or wok, melt butter over high heat. Add olive oil and garlic and stir for 1 minute. Add mushrooms and stir-fry for 3 minutes. Next add zucchini and stir-cook for 4 minutes. Sprinkle in parsley, thyme, salt and pepper, stir and serve immediately. Makes 4 or 5 servings.

SWEET AND SOUR GARLIC VEGETABLES

So easy and tastes just great!

Recipe contest entry: Nancy Stamatis, Union City, CA

2 lb. fresh sliced vegetables (carrots, broccoli, mushrooms, cauliflower, etc.)
4 tablespoons white vinegar
4 tablespoons sugar
1½ teaspoons salt
4 tablespoons vegetable oil
3 cloves fresh garlic, peeled and sliced

Pare, trim and slice vegetables. Combine vinegar, sugar and salt in large jar. Add vegetables and shake to mix well. Cover and refrigerate overnight, shaking occasionally. In another small jar, mix oil and garlic (no need to refrigerate). When ready to serve, drain vegetables and place on a serving platter. Pour garlic oil over and serve with toothpicks. Makes about 4 cups.

Meats

Flank Steak Ole   179
Roast with Garlic/Dill Sauce   180
Roast Tenderloin San Benito   181
Spit-Roasted Rolled Rib   181
Pot Roast a la Gilroy   182
Herbed Pot Roast with Eggplant
    and Tomatoes   183
Pacific Pot Roast   184
Steak and Mushrooms San Juan   184
Pajaro Peppered Tenderloin   185
Charcoal Grilled Steak   185
Larry's Favorite Beef in Beer   186
Angela's Milanese   187
Herbed Minute Steaks   187
Quickie Cube Steaks   188
John's Neapolitan Beef Entree   188
Beef Stew Bonesio   189
Chili Verde (Mexican Stew)   190
Tortilla Loaf   190
Garlic Beef Enchiladas   191
Caballero Casserole   192
Green Garlic Chili   192
Tamale Party Pie   193
Tijuana Jail Chili   193
Gilroy Chili   194
Flautas al Bau   194
Wayne's Bulgogi   195
Beef Teriyaki   195
Chow Yuk   196
Gilroy Meat-Potatoes Quiche   197
Veal Garlic Chop   198
Scaloppine al Limone   198
Veal Shanks with Garlic   199
Veal Cutlet Parmigiana   200
Veal Parmigiana   201
Veal Fricassee with Garlic   202
Dr. Jensen's Uncensored 7-Clove
    Hash   203

Lena's Meatballs   204
Buffet Meat Loaf   204
Limas and Sausage Italiano   205
Spareribs a la Gilroy   205
Garlic Spareribs   206
Tenth Anniversary Ribs   206
Sumptuous Spareribs   207
Orange-Garlic Pork Chops   207
Pork and Chicken Los Arcos   208
Spicy Chops and Cabbage   209
Pork and Green Chiles   209
Annabelle's Portuguese Pork in
    Orange Juice   210
Annabelle's Pork in Vinegar   210
Adobo   210
Lamb Shanks with Barley and Garlic   211
Garlic-Stuffed Leg of Lamb with
    Cabernet Sauce   212
Lamb Shanks a la Basque   213
Rack of Lamb Breadbin   214
Chad's Garlic Lamb   215
Garlicious Lamb Roll-Ups   216
Marinated Grilled Leg of Lamb   217
Crusty Lamb con Ajo   217
Lamb Shanks Divine   218
Good 'n Garlicky Kebabs   218
Diane's Barbecued Mexican
    Lamb Chops   219
Mrs. Joseph Gubser's Barbecued
    Lamb   219
Ragout of Lamb   220
Curried Lamb Chops   220
Mighty Good Moussaka   221
Gloria's Lamb Stew   222
Rabbit with Lentils   223
Sherried Oxtails   224
Conejo a la Chilindron   225
Tripe a la Louis   226

Finalist in 1982 Recipe Contest: SANDY HOILES, Sunnyvale, CA

This recipe was named by the happy group who first sampled it and exclaimed "Ole!" Don't worry about small chunks of tamale which might fall out of the steak rolls; they add an interesting texture to the sauce.

FLANK STEAK OLE

1 flank steak (2 to 2½ lb.), tenderized
10 cloves fresh garlic (about 1 head)
½ teaspoon salt
¼ teaspoon pepper
1 teaspoon chili powder
1 can (15 oz.) tamales, papers discarded and sauce reserved
¼ cup flour
2 to 3 tablespoons olive oil
1 can (8 oz.) tomato sauce
1 cup red table wine
⅓ cup grated Parmesan cheese

Stretch steak gently without tearing to a rectangular shape. Press 3 cloves garlic over meat, sprinkle with salt, pepper and chili powder. Crumble tamales over steak, spreading to within 1 inch of edges. Roll up, making a firm roll but not too tight and tie with string at intervals or secure with skewers. Dust with flour, shaking off excess. Heat oil in Dutch oven or heavy pan with cover and brown roll on all sides over medium-high heat. Reduce heat to low. Pour tomato sauce over roll. Measure wine into tomato sauce can and pour into tamale can with its reserved sauce. Press remaining 7 cloves garlic into this sauce, stir, and pour *around* roll not over it. Cover and simmer until tender, about 2 to 2½ hours. Remove from heat and remove string or skewers, disturbing topping as little as possible. Sprinkle with cheese and return to low heat. Cover and cook until cheese melts, about 20 minutes. Place roll on serving platter and cut into 1-inch slices. Pass sauce separately in gravy boat or bowl. Makes 4 servings.

ROAST WITH GARLIC / DILL SAUCE

Dill pickle is one ingredient that gives this pot roast its piquant flavor. The addition of sour cream at the last minute helps to blend all the flavors into a delicious sauce.

Recipe contest entry: Alexis Ann Smith, Bowie, MD

4 lb. boneless rolled beef rump roast
1 teaspoon *each* salt and white pepper
½ teaspoon ginger
2 tablespoons bacon grease
½ cup dry white wine
Water
2 cups sliced mushrooms
4 cloves fresh garlic, minced
2 tablespoons *each* chopped dill pickle and chopped pimento
1 tablespoon chopped fresh parsley
¾ teaspoon caraway seed
2 tablespoons cornstarch
2 tablespoons dill pickle juice
¾ cup sour cream, at room temperature

Sprinkle roast with salt, pepper and ginger. In Dutch oven, brown roast on all sides in hot grease. Add wine, cover and simmer for 2½ hours. Remove roast and keep warm. Skim fat from drippings, add enough water to make 1½ cups broth in pan. Add mushrooms, garlic, pickle, pimento, parsley and caraway seed. Blend cornstarch with pickle juice and 2 tablespoons water. Add to pan. Cook, stirring, for 5 minutes. Gradually blend in the sour cream. Heat through. Slice meat and serve with sauce. Makes 6 to 8 servings.

ROAST TENDERLOIN SAN BENITO

The technique of marinating this roast in lemon juice and oil a half hour or so before cooking helps to ensure that the meat will be juicy and tender when served.

1 4-lb. beef tenderloin
¼ cup lemon juice
¼ cup oil
1 teaspoon MSG *or* ½ tea-spoon salt
1 teaspoon coarse black pepper
1 teaspoon herb seasoning
1 teaspoon powdered horseradish
½ teaspoon garlic powder
¼ teaspoon mace

Marinate roast in mixture of lemon juice and oil 30 minutes to 1 hour, turning once or twice. Remove meat from marinade. Combine season-ings and rub over meat. Roast in 450-degree oven approximately 45 minutes for rare, or until meat ther-mometer registers desired degree of doneness.

SPIT-ROASTED ROLLED RIB

This rolled rib roast is seasoned with a delicious combination of seasonings which can be varied by adding either 1 teaspoon crushed rosemary leaves or ½ teaspoon crushed thyme leaves.

1 4- to 5-lb. rolled rib roast
2 teaspoons seasoned salt
1 teaspoon salt
¾ teaspoon garlic powder
½ teaspoon onion salt
½ teaspoon coarse black pepper
¼ teaspoon ginger
¼ teaspoon dry mustard

Trim off most of the outside fat from roast. Combine seasonings and rub into all surfaces of the roast. Place on spit, 5 to 6 inches from coals, and cook 1½ hours or until desired degree of doneness is reached. Makes 6 to 8 servings.

POT ROAST A LA GILROY

Red wine and coffee help to create an abundance of rich brown gravy to serve with this pot roast over noodles, potatoes or rice.

Recipe contest entry: Sylvia Barber, Danville, CA

8 or more cloves fresh
  garlic
1 large onion
1 4- to 5-lb. lean chuck
  roast
1 cup dry red wine, preferably Burgundy
3 tablespoons oil
2 cups strong black coffee
1 bay leaf
  Water
  Salt and pepper to taste
  (*or* part seasoned salt)
2 tablespoons cornstarch

Peel garlic and onion and slice into lengthwise strips. Pierce roast all the way through in several places with a sharp knife. Stuff 2 or 3 slivers of garlic and 1 or 2 slices of onion into each slit. Place in enamel, glass or stainless steel pan and pour wine over. Cover and refrigerate 24 to 48 hours, turning occasionally. Drain wine and reserve. Pat roast dry and brown in hot oil in large pot until very well browned. Drain off excess fat and discard. Add coffee, bay leaf and enough water mixed with the reserved red wine to make 2 cups. Bring to a boil, then simmer for 2 to 3 hours. Add salt and pepper during last half hour of cooking. Remove meat and bay leaf from pot. Mix cornstarch and water to make a thin paste. Add to simmering liquid and stir until thickened. Return meat to gravy or slice and pour gravy over. Serve with mashed potatoes, noodles or rice. Makes 6 to 8 servings.

HERBED POT ROAST WITH EGGPLANT AND TOMATOES

This pot roast marinates in a garlic-herb mixture for extra flavor for eight hours before being baked in the oven. Eggplant is a surprise ingredient.

Recipe contest entry: Anonymous

1 4- to 5-lb. chuck *or* other well-marbled beef roast
12 cloves fresh garlic, finely chopped
1 cup plus 2 tablespoons olive oil
¼ cup red wine vinegar
2 tablespoons lemon juice
2 tablespoons dried basil
1 onion, chopped
1 medium eggplant, cubed
1 cup Italian plum tomatoes
2 tablespoons tomato paste

Marinate beef in a garlic marinade made by combining 8 cloves finely chopped garlic, ¾ cup olive oil, wine vinegar, lemon juice and dried basil, for 8 hours, turning often. Remove from marinade and pat meat dry. Reserve marinade. Heat remaining 6 tablespoons oil in skillet; add onions and remaining 4 cloves finely chopped garlic and cook until transparent. Add beef and brown on all sides. Transfer meat and onion-garlic mixture to large Dutch oven. Add reserved marinade, eggplant and tomatoes. Cover and bake at 350 degrees for about 2 hours or until meat thermometer inserted into the center of the roast registers "rare." Remove meat to platter and keep hot. Skim fat from mixture in pot and spoon remaining juices over sliced beef. Makes 6 servings.

PACIFIC POT ROAST

There is no question but that garlic improves the flavor of a simple pot roast, and tomato juice enriches the gravy which tastes very good served over rice.

Recipe contest entry: Elaine R. Muse, San Diego, CA

1 boneless rolled chuck roast
8 cloves fresh garlic
1½ teaspoons salt
½ teaspoon black pepper
¼ teaspoon red pepper
Oil for browning
1½ cups water
1 large onion, chopped
Flour
Water
1 tablespoon Worcestershire sauce
¼ cup tomato juice
Salt to taste

Make 8 slits in roast at random intervals. Into each slit insert 1 whole clove garlic and rub roast with a mixture of salt and pepper. Lightly coat bottom of a Dutch oven with oil. Brown meat well on all sides. Add water and onion; cover and simmer 2 hours or until tender. When roast is done, remove to platter and thicken gravy with flour mixed with water. Season gravy with 3 remaining ingredients. Slice roast and serve with gravy over cooked rice.

STEAK AND MUSHROOMS SAN JUAN

A lesser-priced cut of meat can be tender and delicious if prepared properly. This recipe for round steak capitalizes on the tenderizing effect of the wine and calls for a variety of seasonings to create a superb dish to serve over rice or noodles.

Courtesy of: Betty Angelino, Gilroy, CA

2 lb. top round steak
½ cup flour
Salt and pepper to taste
3 tablespoons olive oil
3 cloves fresh garlic, minced
2 teaspoons oregano
1 teaspoon rosemary
1 teaspoon garlic salt
½ teaspoon onion powder
½ teaspoon thyme
1 cup water
½ cup red wine
1 cup sliced fresh mushrooms

Preheat electric frying pan to 420 degrees. Cut round steak into 2-inch strips. Roll in flour, salt and pepper. Add olive oil to frying pan; brown meat on both sides. Reduce heat to 220 degrees; add herbs and ½ cup water and steam for 20 minutes. Add remaining water, wine and mushrooms and cook 20 minutes more, or until tender. Check periodically, adding more water if needed. Remove meat from pan and add 1 to 2 tablespoons flour if necessary to thicken gravy. Serve with rice.

PAJARO PEPPERED TENDERLOIN

A gourmet steak, peppery, pungent, with a zesty sauce. Excellent served with wild rice and sauteed mushrooms.

6 slices beef tenderloin, cut 1 inch thick
¾ teaspoon garlic salt
½ teaspoon salt
¼ teaspoon MSG (optional)
Coarse black pepper
3 tablespoons butter
1 teaspoon flour
½ teaspoon beef flavor base
¼ cup hot water
2 tablespoons Sauterne
¼ teaspoon shredded green onions

Trim off most of the outside fat, and slash remaining fat every inch or so to prevent curling. Season steak with a mixture of garlic salt, salt and MSG. Sprinkle pepper generously over each side and press down with knife. Saute in butter about 4 minutes on each side. Remove meat to heated serving platter. To essence in skillet add flour and beef flavor base, stirring to mix well; then add hot water, Sauterne and shredded green onions. Bring to a boil and spoon sauce over steak. Serve immediately. Makes 6 servings.

CHARCOAL GRILLED STEAK

For best flavor, most barbecue chefs recommend marinating steaks for several hours before cooking.

4 club steaks, cut 1 inch thick
½ cup salad oil
2 tablespoons lemon juice
1 teaspoon onion salt
1 teaspoon Worcestershire sauce
¾ teaspoon garlic powder
½ teaspoon seasoned salt
¼ teaspoon black pepper

Place steaks in shallow baking dish. Combine remaining ingredients and pour over steaks, coating all sides. Marinate several hours in refrigerator, turning once. Place on grill and sear on both sides. Raise grill to about 5 inches from coals. Cook 15 minutes, turning once, or until desired degree of doneness is reached.

LARRY'S FAVORITE BEEF IN BEER

"When Larry comes to town, he always shows up with a six-pack of beer, a juicy round steak and pleads with me to fix this dish," explains Phyllis Gaddis about her recipe contribution. "Whether or not it's my recipe or the rest of the six-pack that makes his eyes shine when I serve it, I'll never know, but he can count on my having the rest of the ingredients!"   *Recipe contest entry: Phyllis Gaddis, Venice, CA*

1 round steak, fat trimmed
   away
½ cup chopped parsley
1 bay leaf, crumbled
½ teaspoon thyme
¼ teaspoon celery seed
   Pinch of sage
2 tablespoons vegetable oil
3 tablespoons prepared
   mustard
2 large onions, chopped
   Salt and pepper to taste
5 cloves fresh garlic,
   minced
12 oz. beer
1 cup sour cream

Cut steak into 4 portions, or slice across the grain into ¼-inch slices. Mix parsley, bay leaf, thyme, celery seed and sage together and place in cheesecloth bag, tied with string. Cut tail of string short after knotting. In large skillet, heat oil and saute steak portions or slices on one side, spreading mustard on top side. Turn and saute mustard-topped side. Only sear the meat on high heat. Quickly add onions; stir-fry 1 minute and lower heat. Add salt and pepper to taste, then add garlic, Pour in beer slowly, and add spice bag. Return heat to simmer, cover and reduce heat to low. Cook for 1 hour for 4 steak portions, and about 30 minutes if steak is sliced, adding additional beer if needed. When the beer has reduced considerably, about 5 minutes before the end of the cooking time, stir in sour cream, mixing well. Raise heat slightly and serve when sauce is hot. Needless to say, we serve beer with Larry's Favorite Beef, and a large salad of greens, cut tomatoes and Bermuda onions sliced very thin with a simple oil and vinegar dressing, and sesame seeds sprinkled on top.

ANGELA'S MILANESE

An inexpensive version of a classic recipe substituting thinly sliced round steak for veal. *Recipe contest entry: Angela Vannucci, Fremont, CA*

¾ lb. lean round steak, sliced thin (slice steak once through horizontally)
1 egg
¼ cup water
1 cup plain bread crumbs
¼ cup olive oil (approx.)
5 to 6 cloves fresh garlic
  Pinch of salt
2 dried hot chile peppers, finely chopped
  Peel of ½ lemon, cut into thin strips
2 sprigs fresh rosemary without stems
2 cans (8 oz. *each*) tomato sauce

Dip steak in egg which has been beaten with water. Dredge meat in crumbs. Pour olive oil into large skillet to ⅛ inch and heat until very hot. Brown steak quickly in oil turning once, until golden, adding more oil if needed. Remove from skillet and drain on paper towel. Wipe out skillet and pour about 1⁄16 inch oil. Heat to very hot. Chop garlic with salt and add with chile peppers, lemon peel and rosemary to hot oil; saute briefly then add tomato sauce and meat. Gently cover meat with sauce and simmer over low heat for at least 30 minutes. Makes 3 to 4 servings.

HERBED MINUTE STEAKS

Marinating in a wine and herb sauce before grilling does wonders for minute steaks, and the topping of sour cream and paprika dresses up what otherwise might be considered a plain cut of meat.

1 cup salad oil
½ cup red wine
¾ teaspoon garlic powder
½ teaspoon onion powder
½ teaspoon celery salt
½ teaspoon salt
½ teaspoon oregano
½ teaspoon basil
¼ teaspoon black pepper
¼ teaspoon MSG (optional)
  Dash nutmeg
6 minute *or* cube steaks
½ cup sour cream
  Paprika

Combine all ingredients, except steaks, sour cream and paprika, in glass or enameled flat pan; mix well. Add steaks and marinate 1 hour, turning several times. Remove from marinade; pan-fry in hot skillet, or broil just until browned on each side. Top each steak with a spoon of sour cream and sprinkle with paprika. Makes 6 servings.

QUICKIE CUBE STEAKS

Fast and easy and, best of all, "delicioso."

Recipe contest entry: Ann Laramee, Los Angeles, CA

4 cube steaks
4 slices American *or*
   Monterey Jack cheese
4 cloves fresh garlic,
   minced
1 can (4 oz.) diced green
   chiles
   Salt and pepper to taste
2 tablespoons oil *or* butter,
   or combination

On each cube steak, place 1 slice of cheese and top with garlic, chiles and salt and pepper. Roll up and fasten with toothpicks. In a skillet fry steaks in oil until meat is browned and cooked to your liking. Makes 4 servings.

JOHN'S NEAPOLITAN BEEF ENTREE

An everyday casserole that bakes with a crusty cheese topping and plenty of good garlic flavor.

Recipe contest entry: Vicki Leffler, Independence, KY

⅓ cup chopped onion
4 or more cloves fresh
   garlic, crushed
1 cup diced carrots
½ cup diced celery
¼ cup salad oil
1½ lb. ground chuck
1 can (16 oz.) tomatoes
1 can (6 oz.) mushrooms,
   drained
1 can (6 oz.) tomato paste
½ cup sherry
1 teaspoon salt
½ teaspoon *each* pepper,
   dried oregano and basil

8 oz. shell macaroni,
   cooked
1 pkg. (9 *or* 10 oz.) frozen
   spinach, drained
1 cup grated sharp
   Cheddar cheese
½ cup buttered bread
   crumbs
   Parmesan cheese

Saute onion, garlic, carrots and celery in oil for 5 minutes. Add meat; cook and stir until lightly browned. Add next 8 ingredients. Simmer, uncovered, for 1½ hours. Add macaroni and spinach; mix well. Turn into 2-quart casserole. Top with Cheddar cheese and bread crumbs. Bake uncovered at 325 degrees for about 30 minutes or until hot. Serve with Parmesan cheese. Makes about 8 servings.

BEEF STEW BONESIO

Nearly everyone has a favorite beef stew recipe. This one produces a gravy rich with the combined flavors of wine and herbs, which is equally good with both the meat and the vegetables.

Courtesy of: Louis Bonesio, Jr., Gilroy, CA

1½ lb. lean beef stew meat, cut into 1½-inch cubes
 3 tablespoons flour
 3 tablespoons polyunsaturated oil
 ½ cup dry red wine
1½ cups boiling water
2½ medium onions, sliced
 3 medium carrots, cut into ½-inch slices
 3 cups potatoes, peeled and cut into 1-inch cubes
 ½ stalk celery, sliced into ½-inch slices
 3 medium cloves fresh garlic
 ⅛ teaspoon marjoram
 ⅛ teaspoon dry crushed oregano
 ⅛ teaspoon ground sage
 1 teaspoon thyme
 2 tablespoons chopped parsley
 1 teaspoon freshly ground pepper
 ½ lb. whole small mushrooms

Remove visible fat from meat. Dredge well in flour; brown lightly in oil in a 4-quart Dutch oven. Gradually add wine and enough boiling water just to cover meat. Reduce heat and simmer, covered, for 1 hour. Add onions, carrots, potatoes, celery and garlic, marjoram, oregano, sage, thyme and parsley. Continue to simmer 30 minutes. Remove from heat and let stand 15 minutes. Skim fat off top. Add pepper and mushrooms and bring to boil; reduce heat and simmer 10 more minutes. Garnish with additional chopped parsley. Makes 4 to 6 servings.

CHILI VERDE (MEXICAN STEW)

This dish is quite different from the classic Mexican dish of the same name, but it is a very delicious adaptation. And it can be made ahead and held in the refrigerator for serving the next day.

Recipe contest entry: Jeannine Johnson, Guerneville, CA

1 lb. beef stew meat (boneless chuck, preferably)
½ lb. pork stew meat
2 large onions, chopped
6 cloves fresh garlic, minced *or* pressed
1 teaspoon *each* salt and powdered garlic
2 tablespoons olive oil
1 can (4 oz.) diced green chiles
3 cans (8 oz. *each*) tomato sauce

Cut meat into 1-inch cubes. Combine meat in pot, cover with water and add half the onion and half the garlic, salt and powdered garlic. Cover and simmer gently until meat is almost fork tender. Remove cover and continue cooking until meat is tender and liquid has boiled away. Meanwhile in separate saucepan, combine olive oil, remaining onion and garlic, chiles and tomato sauce. Simmer for about 10 minutes. Pour over meat and bake for 1 hour at 350 degrees.

TORTILLA LOAF

Gilroy's Spanish/Mexican heritage can be seen, not only in the names of streets, ranches and public buildings, but in the types of food prepared by its citizens. Dishes like this tortilla loaf, for example, utilize ingredients native to Mexico and combine them into a wonderful supper dish.

Courtesy of: Rose Emma Pelliccione, Gilroy, CA

1 large onion, chopped
3 cloves fresh garlic, minced
¼ cup oil
1½ to 2 lb. ground beef
2 cans (8 oz. *each*) hot sauce
1 can (10½ oz.) beef consomme
1 can (7½ oz.) pitted ripe olives, sliced
2 tablespoons wine vinegar
2 tablespoons chili powder
1½ cups grated sharp Cheddar cheese
1 dozen corn tortillas

Saute onion and garlic in oil; add ground beef and saute until redness disappears and meat is crumbled. Add other ingredients, except cheese and tortillas. Cook for a few minutes to blend flavors. If sauce is too thick, thin with a little water. Place tortillas, sauce and cheese in layers, ending with sauce and cheese on top. Bake for 45 minutes at 350 degrees.

GARLIC BEEF ENCHILADAS

Although at first glance this recipe may seem complicated, it is actually easy to prepare. The sauce and meat filling can even be made ahead and refrigerated. Reheat slightly when ready to use.

Courtesy of: Julie Gutierrez, Gilroy, CA

Sauce
- 4 cloves fresh garlic, minced
- 3 tablespoons shortening
- 1 can (28 oz.) red chili sauce
- 3 tablespoons flour
- 1 can (8 oz.) tomato sauce

To prepare sauce: Saute garlic until golden in hot shortening in large saucepan. Add can of chili sauce and lower heat. Put flour in separate bowl and stir in can of tomato sauce until smooth. Pour into chili sauce mixture and stir over medium heat until slightly thickened. Set aside; let cool.

Filling
- 1 lb. ground chuck
- 2 cloves fresh garlic, minced
- Salt and pepper to taste

To prepare meat filling: In medium skillet over low heat, saute chuck with garlic, salt and pepper until chuck is browned. Set aside.

Enchiladas
- 1 cup shortening
- 2 cloves fresh garlic, minced
- 1 medium-sized onion, finely chopped
- 4 cups grated Cheddar cheese
- 2 cans (6 oz. *each*) medium pitted ripe olives
- 2 dozen fresh corn tortillas

To prepare enchiladas: Heat shortening in large skillet over medium-high heat. Carefully dip 1 tortilla at a time into hot shortening, frying each side for 5 seconds. Dip fried tortilla into cooled enchilada sauce and place on flat plate. After you have prepared 6 tortillas, fill center of each with meat, garlic, onion, cheese and olives (reserving some cheese and olives to sprinkle on top). Roll up tortillas.

Pour half the sauce in a large baking dish. Then arrange filled tortillas seam side down in sauce. Repeat, 6 tortillas at a time, until all have been cooked and assembled. Pour remaining sauce over tortillas. Sprinkle with cheese and garnish with olives. Bake 15 to 20 minutes at 350 degrees until cheese is melted. Makes 2 dozen.

CABALLERO CASSEROLE

Tex-Mex cuisine is all the rage. Try this southwestern version of lasagna. It's appealing as well as good eating.

Recipe contest entry: Micky Kolar, Fountain Hills, AZ

2 tablespoons cooking oil
2 cups chopped onion
1 red bell pepper, seeded and chopped
1 green bell pepper, seeded and chopped
3 cloves fresh garlic, minced
2 lb. lean ground beef
1 can (16 oz.) ready-cut tomatoes, drained
1 can (4 oz.) chopped jalapeno peppers, drained
2 tablespoons chili powder
2 teaspoons salt
½ teaspoon *each* ground cumin and oregano
¼ teaspoon ground coriander
3 corn tortillas (10-inch diameter)
½ cup shredded Longhorn Cheddar cheese
1 ripe avocado, peeled and cut into 6 slices
1 cup sour cream
2 teaspoons minced parsley

Heat oil in large, heavy skillet. Saute onion and peppers until tender. Add garlic and saute 2 minutes. Add meat and brown, breaking it up until crumbly. Add tomatoes, jalapenos and spices, mixing well, and cook over medium heat until mixture is slightly thickened, about 5 minutes. Remove from heat. Oil a round 10x1½-inch baking dish. Place 1 tortilla in bottom of dish, trimming to fit, if necessary. Spread ⅓ of meat mixture over tortilla. Repeat layers, ending with meat. Bake in preheated 400-degree oven 15 minutes. Sprinkle with cheese and return to oven for 5 minutes. Arrange avocado slices in sunburst pattern in center of casserole. Place spoonful of sour cream in center, sprinkle with parsley and serve with additional sour cream, if desired. Makes 6 servings.

GREEN GARLIC CHILI

Much like a chile verde, this recipe for Green Garlic Chili is easy to prepare and quite good. *Recipe contest entry: Wesley L. Minor, Seal Beach*

2 lb. beef (use any desired cut)
½ cup olive oil
3 heads fresh garlic
6 fresh green chiles
½ teaspoon salt
½ teaspoon white pepper
1 large onion
3 large green tomatoes

Cut beef into slices or ½-inch cubes. Heat oil in skillet and cook beef until well done and tender. Separate heads into cloves and peel. Place whole cloves in skillet and cook until tender. Add green chiles and onions. Dice green tomatoes and add to skillet. Add the remainder of the seasonings and cook, covered, to retain as much juice as possible.

TAMALE PARTY PIE

Tamale pie has wide popular appeal. This recipe goes together easily and will serve about 20 people. If you prepare it for your family and have some left over, freeze it for use another time or in small individual portions for family members to prepare for themselves on the cook's night out!

Courtesy of: Florence Sillano, Gilroy, CA

1 can (1 lb.) creamed corn
2 cans (8 oz. *each*) hot sauce
2 large onions, finely chopped
1 cup salad oil
2 tablespoons chili powder
4 cloves fresh garlic, minced
2 cups polenta (cornmeal)
1 pint milk
3 eggs, beaten
1 can pitted ripe olives, including juice
Salt and pepper to taste
1½ lb. lean ground beef

Mix all ingredients and place in a 16x11x2½ baking dish. Bake 30 minutes at 350 degrees. Reduce heat to 300 degrees and continue to bake 45 minutes longer.

TIJUANA JAIL CHILI

Like all border towns, Tijuana, Mexico, just across the line from San Diego, has a colorful, if somewhat shady, reputation. It's hard to believe such delightful fare would be served in any of the prisons there, but regardless of how this dish got its name, it's worth preparing. Serve it with a tossed salad and plenty of cold beer.

Courtesy of: Louis Bonesio, Jr., Gilroy, CA

⅛ lb. suet, finely chopped
3 lb. round steak, coarsely cubed
3 cloves fresh garlic, minced
6 tablespoons chili powder
1 tablespoon ground oregano
1 tablespoon crushed cumin seed
1 tablespoon salt
½ to 1 tablespoon cayenne pepper
1 teaspoon Tabasco sauce
1½ quarts water
½ cup white cornmeal

In Dutch oven fry suet until crisp; add steak cubes and brown. Add seasonings and water; heat to boil. Then cover and simmer 1½ hours. Skim off fat; stir in cornmeal and continue to simmer, uncovered, for 30 minutes. Stir occasionally. Serve in bowls with either beans and tortillas or cornbread.

GILROY CHILI

When this recipe for chili was served at a Gilroy barbecue to accompany grilled steaks, everyone declared it outstanding and many had second and third helpings.

Recipe contest entry: David B. Swope, Redondo Beach, CA

3 cloves fresh garlic, minced
2 large onions, finely chopped
2 tablespoons olive oil
2 lb. ground beef
1 can (4 oz.) green chiles
1 cup canned stewed tomatoes
2 cups beef stock
1 tablespoon chili powder
1 tablespoon ground cumin
1½ teaspoons MSG (optional)
1 teaspoon salt
¼ teaspoon pepper

In large skillet slowly brown garlic and onions in olive oil; stir and cook until tender. Heat skillet to hot, add meat and cook until done. Add all other ingredients. Cover and reduce heat. Cook about 45 minutes more. Either remove grease or add a small amount cornstarch to absorb it.

FLAUTAS AL BAU

Californians have so long enjoyed Mexican food like tacos, enchiladas, tamales and tostadas, it is sometimes difficult to realize that much of the rest of the U.S. population is just discovering these fine dishes. This recipe, for example, is quite easy to prepare and could serve as an appetizer or first course as well as an entree.

Recipe contest entry: Baudelia Leaderman, San Diego, CA

Butter as needed
1½ lb. ground beef
½ lb. chorizo (Mexican sausage, beef or pork)
2 large yellow onions, minced
3 large semi-hot Jalapeno chiles, finely diced
4 medium tomatoes, cut into 1-inch cubes
1 tablespoon paprika
Salt and pepper to taste
Juice of 1 lemon
2 tablespoons sour cream
16 corn tortillas

Melt enough butter in a large skillet to cook the beef, chorizo, onions and chiles (chorizo should be mashed into mixture); cook until beef has browned and chorizo separates. Add tomatoes, paprika, salt, pepper and garlic; mix together. Turn heat to low and let simmer about 10 minutes. Remove from heat and drain off half of liquid. Mix in lemon juice; fold in sour cream. Let mixture stand 5 minutes to blend flavors. Divide mixture evenly into tortillas and roll tightly, using toothpick to hold each together. Fry tortillas in butter until semi-brown. Remove and serve hot.

WAYNE'S BULGOGI   *Korean Barbecue Meat*

In the Vessey household, five or six of these Korean-style marinated flank steaks, fragrant with fresh ginger and garlic, only seem to serve six to eight people. Wayne is a grower and shipper of fresh garlic and his family really knows good flavor and good food.

Courtesy of: Wayne Vessey, Hollister, CA

1½ cups sugar
1½ cups soy sauce
 ½ cup sesame *or* vegetable oil
20 green onions, minced
20 cloves fresh garlic, crushed
10 fine slices fresh ginger, chopped
 ½ cup sesame seeds
 3 tablespoons pepper
 5 *or* 6 flank steaks
    Hot cooked rice

Combine all ingredients except steak and rice and marinate steaks in the sauce for 6 to 8 hours (do not refrigerate). Cook over barbecue to desired doneness. Heat remaining marinade and pour over meat and rice when serving.

BEEF TERIYAKI

No garlic cookbook would be complete without a beef teriyaki recipe because garlic is so important to the flavor of this Oriental marinade. Alternate the meat with pineapple chunks for an eye-appealing presentation.

1   lb. sirloin beef, cut 1 inch thick
¾   cup soy sauce
¼   cup dark brown sugar, packed
2   tablespoons lemon juice
1   teaspoon ground ginger
½   teaspoon garlic powder
½   teaspoon onion salt

Cut meat into bite-sized cubes. Combine remaining ingredients; pour over beef cubes and let stand at room temperature 1 hour or in refrigerator several hours. Thread cubes of meat onto a skewer. (Pineapple chunks may be alternated with the beef cubes.) Broil about 3 inches from heat 10 to 12 minutes, turning once, or cook over grill or hibachi. Serve hot as an appetizer or with rice as a main course.

CHOW YUK

In Chinese restaurants, this dish usually contains a wide variety of vegetables, and this recipe is no exception. It also calls for "fresh Chinese noodles." If not available, substitute dried noodles or rice.

Recipe contest entry: Barbara Towe, Gilroy, CA

1½ lb. flank steak
½ cup soy sauce
6 cloves fresh garlic, peeled
3 tablespoons peanut oil
3 slices fresh ginger
½ lb. fresh mushrooms, sliced
¼ lb. fresh bean sprouts
¼ lb. fresh sugar peas, blanched (optional)
1 can (5 oz.) water chestnuts, drained and sliced
1 green bell pepper, seeded and cut into slivers
1 medium tomato, cut into eighths
   Fresh Chinese noodles, cooked and fried

Cut flank steak in half lengthwise; slice each half diagonally into thin slices. Marinate in ¼ cup soy sauce with 3 sliced garlic cloves for 2 to 3 hours. Heat oil in a wok or large skillet. Stir-fry ginger and 3 whole garlic cloves, discarding both when lightly browned. Stir-fry meat quickly until brown and add remaining ¼ cup soy sauce. Cover and steam meat for 45 seconds. Transfer meat to a platter and keep warm. To the liquid in the pan add all the vegetables except the tomato. Stir-fry for about 1 minute. Return meat to wok and mix thoroughly with the vegetables. Add tomato wedges on top, cover and cook for 1 minute. Serve meat and vegetables with remaining liquid on top of Chinese noodles. Makes 4 servings.

Finalist in 1979 Recipe Contest: BOB DIXON, Santa Cruz, CA

Another finalist from the Garlic Recipe Contest and Cook-off, this fireman who gets lots of practice cooking at the firehouse, claims this dish is a favorite. When you taste it you'll know why.

GILROY MEAT-AND-POTATOES QUICHE

Crust

1 lb. ground beef
¾ cup bread crumbs
1 egg
1 clove fresh garlic, minced
2 tablespoons Worcestershire sauce
2 tablespoons chopped fresh basil
½ teaspoon pepper

Combine all ingredients and press into a 9-inch pie pan. Bake in 350-degree oven for 15 minutes. Remove from oven and set aside.

Filling

3 cloves fresh garlic, minced
½ cup diced onion
2 tablespoons oil
3 medium potatoes, peeled, cooked and sliced
4 oz. Cheddar cheese, cubed
1 can (4 oz.) green chiles, chopped
1 teaspoon salt
½ teaspoon pepper

Saute garlic and onion in oil for 5 minutes. Combine potatoes (reserving enough to make ½ cup mashed for topping) and cheese with garlic and onion, chiles, salt and pepper. Mix well and spread over the beef crust.

Topping

½ cup potatoes, mashed with ½ cup milk
2 oz. Cheddar cheese
3 cloves fresh garlic, minced
1 egg
1 teaspoon dry mustard

Combine all the above ingredients and pour over the filling. Bake in 350-degree oven for 25 to 30 minutes.

Regional Winner 1983 Recipe Contest: DAVID LINDLEY, Union City, GA

Cooking for one? Pamper yourself with this delicious, garlic-laced veal chop with peppers.

VEAL GARLIC CHOP

1 veal chop (approx. 14 oz.)
1 tablespoon crushed black peppercorns
   Salt to taste
2 tablespoons butter
1 tablespoon olive oil
1 green bell pepper
1 red bell pepper
1 medium onion, peeled
6 cloves fresh garlic, minced
1 teaspoon finely chopped fresh parsley

Rub veal chop all over with crushed black peppercorns and salt to taste. In heavy skillet, combine butter and oil until hot, but not smoking; add veal and reduce heat to medium. Brown veal for about 7 minutes, then turn and brown other side. Meanwhile, remove seeds and membrane from peppers. Slice peppers and onion into julienne strips and add to skillet with veal. Add pinch of salt. Spread garlic evenly over chop; cover skillet and cook about 10 minutes, stirring vegetables occasionally, until tender. To serve, arrange bell peppers and onion on plate, top with veal chop and sprinkle with parsley. Serves 1 generously.

SCALOPPINE AL LIMONE

The term *scaloppine* describes the thin slices of veal that make this dish distinctive. Here lemon is used instead of wine and can be increased if a more *picante* flavor is desired.

1 lb. veal, cut for scaloppine
2 tablespoons flour
2 tablespoons salad oil
1 can (4 oz.) sliced mushrooms
¾ cup water
¼ cup onion, minced
2 tablespoons green pepper, chopped
1 tablespoon lemon juice
1½ teaspoons seasoned salt
1 teaspoon garlic powder
¼ teaspoon black pepper
¼ teaspoon nutmeg

Dredge veal with flour. Saute on both sides in hot oil until well browned. Add remaining ingredients, including liquid from mushrooms. Cover and simmer 10 minutes. Serve from platter attractively garnished with tomato wedges, potato cakes, parsley or paprika-rimmed slices of lemon. Makes 2 to 4 servings.

Finalist in 1979 Recipe Contest: ANN EPSTEIN, North Hollywood, CA

Ann Epstein, third place winner in the first Garlic Recipe Contest and Cook-off cooked with *four whole heads* of garlic in her recipe for veal shanks. Garlic and veal cook together in a wine sauce for about an hour or so and when ready, the garlic is gathered in a dish and offered to guests to spread, like butter, on toasty bread to eat with the meat. Be sure to select a robust red wine to go with it.

VEAL SHANKS WITH GARLIC

3   hind leg veal shanks, each cut into 3 or 4 1-inch pieces
½   cup oil (corn, peanut, soy, sesame, olive *or* a mixture)
3   large onions, thickly sliced
1   or 2 large carrots, thickly sliced
    Bouquet garni
1   cup dry white wine
2   to 3 cups brown veal stock *or* beef *or* chicken broth, enough to cover the meat
    Salt and pepper to taste
4   heads fresh garlic
    Fresh chopped parsley
    Bread, cut in thick slices and toasted

In a large braising pot, brown veal shanks in hot oil until golden on all sides. Remove meat. Into hot oil, add onions, carrots, bouquet garni and toss until soft and golden brown. Spoon off as much fat as possible. In the same pot, arrange cooked vegetables, then veal shanks, then wine. Reduce wine completely, taking care not to burn meat and vegetables. Add the veal stock or meat broth. Bring to a boil. Have ready all the cloves from the 4 heads of garlic—separated, peeled and mashed with a knife or mallet. Add these to simmering meat. Add salt and pepper. Cover with a layer of foil, the sides of which have been turned up so that the steam will not dilute the sauce. Cover with pot lid. Bake in 325-degree oven for 1 to 1½ hours. Meat will be done when it pulls easily away from the bones. There should be between 1½ to 2 cups of rich, thick sauce left. If more, reduce till required amount is reached. Onions and carrots can be left in the sauce as is; removed, pureed and added back; or removed entirely. Place meat on a pretty platter. Sprinkle with parsley. Gather all mashed garlic cloves and place in a dish. Serve meat and toasted slices of bread spread with mashed garlic. Because of the lengthy cooking, the garlic loses much of its pungency and becomes very rich and buttery in texture.

VEAL CUTLET PARMIGIANA

For the best flavor, be sure to use a good Italian Parmesan and grate it just before preparing the recipe.

Recipe contest entry: Carole A. Lake, Gilroy, CA

4 veal cutlets, pounded very thin
Flour
4 large eggs, beaten
Plain bread crumbs
¼ cup olive oil
½ cup butter
⅛ cup chopped chives
3 cloves fresh garlic, smashed and chopped fine
2½ cups marinara sauce (spicy tomato sauce)
4 slices prosciutto (thin sliced Italian ham)
4 slices Mozzarella cheese
Salt and pepper to taste
Grated Parmesan cheese

Dip cutlets into flour, then into egg and then bread crumbs. Repeat. Saute breaded cutlets for 6 minutes in oil and half of the butter. Melt remaining butter and add chives and garlic. Set aside and keep warm. Pour a layer of marinara sauce on the bottom of a baking dish. Place cutlets on top of sauce and pour a little sauce over. Cover each cutlet with a slice of prosciutto; then pour garlic, chives and butter over. Place a slice of cheese on top and lightly salt and pepper. Spoon remaining marinara sauce on top to cover meat. Sprinkle with grated cheese. Bake uncovered at 350 degrees for 20 minutes. Serve at once. Makes 4 servings.

VEAL PARMIGIANA

Parmigiana is the Italian word for Parmesan, the cheese that comes from Parma, Italy, and that has found such acceptance throughout the world because it grates and cooks better than almost any other cheese. Its flavor combines well with garlic and other seasonings in this well known and popular dish.

Sauce

1 can (6 oz.) tomato paste
1 can (6 oz.) water
1 tablespoon butter
1 tablespoon brown sugar
1 teaspoon Worcestershire sauce
1 teaspoon seasoned salt
½ teaspoon garlic powder
½ teaspoon Italian seasoning
¼ teaspoon oregano
⅛ teaspoon MSG (optional)

Mix all ingredients together. Cook until sauce has thickened, stirring constantly. Set aside.

2 lb. veal cutlets
2 teaspoons seasoned salt
¼ teaspoon black pepper
2 eggs
1 cup fine dry bread crumbs
½ cup olive oil
¼ cup grated Parmesan cheese
½ lb. Mozzarella cheese

Have cutlets sliced ½ inch thick; cut into serving-size pieces or leave whole. Add seasoned salt and pepper to eggs; beat lightly. Dip cutlets into egg mixture, then into bread crumbs. Brown on both sides in hot oil. Place cutlets in 8x13x1¾-inch baking dish. Pour sauce over meat and sprinkle with Parmesan cheese. Cover, using aluminum foil if necessary, and bake in 350-degree oven 30 minutes or until tender. Remove cover and top with slices of Mozzarella cheese. Continue baking until cheese melts. Makes 4 to 6 servings.

VEAL FRICASSEE WITH GARLIC

A buffet dish that is definitely company fare, but why not treat the family, too?

Recipe contest entry: Susan Grossman, Tucson, AZ

1 lb. veal stew meat cut in ½-inch cubes
6 tablespoons flour seasoned with salt and pepper
3 tablespoons butter
2 tablespoons cooking oil
1 cup coarsely minced onions
3 large cloves fresh garlic, minced *or* pressed
½ lb. fresh mushrooms, sliced thin
½ cup dry white wine
½ cup veal *or* chicken stock *or* water
½ cup heavy cream
1 tablespoon minced fresh parsley

Dredge veal in flour and shake off excess. Heat butter and oil in heavy skillet and brown veal in batches until golden. With slotted spoon, remove veal to platter and keep warm. Add onions, garlic and mushrooms to skillet, cover and cook until onions are soft. Remove all from skillet with slotted spoon and add to platter with veal. Pour off any remaining butter or oil from skillet and discard. Add wine and deglaze, scraping up all brown bits; cook for 2 minutes. Return veal and vegetables to skillet, add stock or water, cover and simmer for 30 minutes or until veal is tender and sauce is thickened. About 10 minutes before serving, add cream and simmer another 5 minutes until sauce is thick. Pour veal and sauce onto hot serving platter and sprinkle with minced parsley. Serve with broad egg noodles or rice. Makes 4 servings.

Finalist in 1985 Recipe Contest: DR. CARL JENSEN, Cotati, CA

According to Dr. Jensen, this hash was created for First Amendment garlic aficionados. It originated with his Danish father, and is called "uncensored" because "no sensitive or controversial ingredient should be left out of a true hash. . . . Everything in the kitchen is fair game."

DR. JENSEN'S UNCENSORED 7-CLOVE HASH

7 cloves fresh garlic, minced
½ cup diced red onion
⅓ cup diced celery
⅓ cup diced green pepper
⅓ cup diced mushrooms
⅓ cup chopped scallions
2 cups diced roast beef
1 cup diced cooked potatoes
Seasonings to taste: salt, pepper, basil, oregano, parsley, crushed red pepper, garlic powder, Worcestershire sauce, hot green chili salsa, Burgundy and Tabasco (sparingly)
4 extra-large eggs

In a large well-greased skillet, combine garlic, red onion, celery, green pepper, mushrooms and scallions and saute slowly and lovingly over medium heat. When golden brown, mix in meat and potatoes, raising heat to medium high. Cook until a crust starts to form on bottom, then stir constantly to let hash brown throughout while adding seasonings to taste. When nearly browned throughout, pat mixture down firmly to form a level cake. Carve out four evenly-spaced holes. Crack and slip an egg into each of the holes, being careful not to break the yolks. Turn heat back to medium and be patient. Serve on warmed plates when the egg whites are firm but the yolks still soft. Makes 4 terrific servings.

LENA'S MEATBALLS

The combination of pork and beef helps to keep these meatballs moist and juicy no matter how you choose to cook them.

Recipe contest entry: Lena Lico, Hollister, CA

1 lb. ground beef
½ lb. ground pork (lean)
⅓ cup grated Romano *or* Parmesan cheese
4 slices bread, soaked in water and squeezed tightly
2 eggs
5 cloves fresh garlic, minced
1 medium onion, finely chopped
1 tablespoon chopped parsley
2 teaspoons salt
1 teaspoon oregano
½ teaspoon black pepper

Combine all ingredients and mix well. Shape into balls. These can be fried, cooked in the oven or dropped into hot spaghetti sauce.

BUFFET MEAT LOAF

This recipe bakes in two loaf pans, making enough meat loaf for about six people. If there's any left over, it slices very well when chilled.

Recipe contest entry: Terry Santana, Saratoga, CA

3 lb. lean ground chuck
½ lb. fresh spinach, washed and coarsely chopped
8 cloves fresh garlic, minced
2 cups soft bread crumbs
1 large onion, chopped
1 tablespoon Madeira wine
2 teaspoons dried thyme
1 tablespoon salt
1½ teaspoons pepper
1 teaspoon ground cumin
½ teaspoon crumbled rosemary
3 raw eggs
8 hard-cooked eggs, whole

In large mixing bowl, combine ground chuck, spinach, garlic, bread crumbs, onion, wine and seasonings. Beat raw eggs lightly and add. Lightly toss all ingredients together. Using two 6-cup loaf pans, layer ¼ of meat mixture into each pan. Lay a row of 4 eggs down center of each loaf. Top eggs with remaining meat, smoothing top. Place on baking sheet in 350-degree oven and bake for 1½ hours. Allow loaves to cool 10 minutes, then invert on platter and serve. Makes 6 to 8 servings.

LIMAS AND SAUSAGE ITALIANO

Spicy sausage and herbs blend well with lima beans to make a low-cost and very appealing casserole.

1 lb. bulk Italian (*or* other spicy) sausage
¼ cup chopped onion
½ teaspoon garlic powder
¼ teaspoon rosemary leaves
¼ teaspoon thyme leaves
1 can (8 oz.) tomato sauce
2 cans (1 lb. *each*) lima beans
¼ cup butter
1 cup dry bread crumbs
1 tablespoon parsley flakes

Crumble sausage; add onion and garlic powder. Saute in a skillet until sausage is browned, stirring and breaking up with a fork while cooking. Crush rosemary leaves and add to sausage, along with thyme leaves and tomato sauce. Simmer 15 minutes. Drain limas; add to sausage mixture. Stir to mix well. Transfer to a 1½-quart casserole. Melt butter; stir into bread crumbs and parsley flakes, tossing lightly. Spoon over top of bean mixture. Bake in 350-degree oven 1 hour or until crumbs are golden. Makes 4 to 6 servings.

SPARERIBS A LA GILROY

Chinese Five Spice Powder, an essential ingredient in this easy-to-make recipe for spareribs, is available in Oriental markets or in the Oriental food section of most supermarkets.

Recipe contest entry: Lori Allen, Tacoma, WA

⅔ cup soy sauce
⅓ cup maple syrup
8 cloves fresh garlic, minced
3 tablespoons peach brandy
2 teaspoons *each* Five Spice Powder and ground ginger
2 lb. spareribs

In a bowl combine all ingredients except ribs and mix well. Place ribs in shallow dish, pour mixture over and turn ribs to coat. Marinate for 2 hours, covered, turning them about every 15 minutes. Place ribs in one layer on rack over shallow baking pan in 450-degree oven. Pour boiling water to 1 inch in bottom of pan. Brush ribs with marinade and bake for 30 minutes. Turn ribs, brush with more marinade. Reduce heat to 350 degrees and continue baking for 45 minutes, turning ribs once more. Transfer ribs to board and chop into 3-inch lengths. Makes 4 servings.

GARLIC SPARERIBS

Whether they are served as a main course or as an appetizer, these steamed ribs are outstanding. If you don't have a steamer, simply place ribs on a plate on a rack in large covered pot or wok.

Recipe contest entry: Erline Dair, South San Francisco, CA

3 lb. spareribs
8 cloves fresh garlic, finely chopped
6 tablespoons *each* soy sauce and oyster sauce
3 tablespoons dry sherry
Hot chili oil (optional)
Chopped green onions (optional)

Chop spareribs into bite-sized pieces. Cover with water and bring to a boil. Parboil spareribs for 10 minutes. Drain and rinse with cold water. Combine remaining ingredients except chili oil and green onion. Mix with spareribs and place on a heatproof dish on rack in steamer. Steam for 45 minutes. Garnish with green onions and serve with chili oil, if desired. Makes 4 servings.

TENTH ANNIVERSARY RIBS

This recipe was developed in honor of a tenth wedding anniversary. It combines the lightly sweet flavor Jill likes and the peppery spice Ron enjoys and "oh, that wonderful garlic!"

Recipe contest entry: Jill Goddard and Ron Kraus, Newhall, CA

8 cloves fresh garlic, minced
3 cans (8 oz. *each*) tomato sauce
3 small onions, minced
2 cups red wine
1 can (4 oz.) diced green chiles
5 tablespoons maple syrup
3 tablespoons *each* soy sauce and red wine vinegar
2 tablespoons prepared mustard
1 tablespoon Worcestershire sauce
1 teaspoon celery seed
½ teaspoon black pepper
¼ teaspoon *each* cayenne pepper and smoke salt
3 to 4 lb. beef or pork ribs

Combine all ingredients except ribs in a large enamel kettle. Bring to boil, reduce heat and allow to simmer uncovered for 1 hour, stirring occasionally. Meanwhile, place ribs in a deep pot; cover with water. Bring to boil, cover and simmer for 45 minutes to 1 hour to remove fat and tenderize ribs. Remove ribs to shallow baking pan, pour sauce over and bake for 30 minutes, at 350 degrees, turning and basting occasionally. Makes 2 to 3 servings.

SUMPTUOUS SPARERIBS

Cooking time in this recipe may vary depending on how meaty the ribs are. Check every half-hour and test for tenderness. When ribs are fork tender, they are ready to serve.

Recipe contest entry: Dorothy Jenkins, Livermore, CA

4 lb. pork spareribs, cut in serving-size pieces
10 cloves fresh garlic, peeled
1 onion, chopped fine
1 tablespoon margarine
1 cup *each* catsup and water
6 tablespoons brown sugar
¼ cup chopped celery *or* 1 tablespoon celery salt
4 tablespoons lemon juice
2 tablespoons *each* vinegar and Worcestershire sauce
1 tablespoon ground mustard
¼ teaspoon cayenne pepper

Place spareribs in baking pan with cover. Split 6 cloves garlic at the top to release flavor and sprinkle over ribs. Cover pan and bake at 350 degrees for 1 hour. Pour off the grease. Mince remaining 4 cloves garlic and fry with onions in margarine until onion is transparent, being careful not to burn garlic. Add all remaining ingredients and pour over ribs evenly. Cover and bake at 350 degrees, basting every 30 minutes and checking with fork for doneness. May take up to 2 hours. Bake uncovered for the last 30 minutes. Makes 4 servings.

ORANGE-GARLIC PORK CHOPS

The flavors of garlic, onion and ginger combined with the tang of fresh orange help to transform these pork chops into a truly exotic main course."

Recipe contest entry: Grace Maduell and Reid Brennen, San Rafael, CA

6 pork chops
1 medium orange
4 cloves fresh garlic
½ small onion
¼ teaspoon powdered ginger
Pepper to taste
1 to 2 tablespoons butter
Salt to taste

Remove fat from chops. Squeeze orange into small bowl, keeping as much pulp as possible. Press garlic into orange juice. Using garlic press, squeeze onion into orange-garlic mixture, being sure to remove onion skin. Add ginger and a pinch of pepper; stir well. Place chops in shallow baking dish, cover with marinade and let stand for at least 45 minutes. Melt butter in skillet with lid. Remove chops from marinade, reserving marinade, and brown chops on both sides in butter. Cover with remaining marinade and cook, covered, for 10 minutes. Remove cover and cook until fork tender. Add salt and more pepper to taste. Makes 6 servings.

Finalist in 1983 Recipe Contest: RAYMOND G. MARSHALL, Pasadena, CA

Some of the ingredients in this recipe may sound a bit exotic, but you'll like the results. The pork and chicken are marinated in advance to give the meat a rich flavor. Canned, peeled lichees are available in most supermarkets or you can substitute chunks of drained, canned pineapple, but it won't taste the same!

PORK AND CHICKEN LOS ARCOS

3 lb. pork shoulder
2 lb. chicken thighs
40 cloves fresh garlic, unpeeled
1 tablespoon salt
1 cup vinegar
2 tablespoons lemon juice
8 bay leaves
½ teaspoon *each* fresh ground pepper and caramel coloring
4 whole cloves
6 very thin slices fresh ginger (*or* prepared in light syrup)
2 tablespoons salad oil
2 tablespoons plain gelatin
2 cans (11 oz. *each*) peeled lichees
1 cup toasted pumpkin seeds

Cut pork into 1½-inch cubes. Bone chicken and cut each thigh into 3 or 4 pieces. Prepare marinade: Peel, chop and mash 4 cloves garlic in salt to make a paste. Add vinegar, lemon juice, bay leaves, pepper, caramel coloring, cloves and ginger; mix well. Pour over pork and chicken and marinate for 6 to 8 hours in the refrigerator, stirring frequently. Remove pork and chicken from marinade and reserve marinade. Saute pork in oil for 20 minutes. Add chicken and saute for another 20 minutes. Then add the remaining 36 cloves unpeeled garlic. Add gelatin to reserved marinade to soften, adding a little water if necessary. Stir marinade well, add to pork and chicken and cook about 30 minutes or until meat is done and tender. Add drained lichees and seeds to pot. Let cook about 5 minutes to heat through and serve, preferably with steamed rice. Makes 8 servings.

NOTE: The garlic cloves are eaten using the fingers to pinch the pump out of each skin.

SPICY CHOPS AND CABBAGE

Apples and cabbage are favorite ingredients in German cuisine. Combined here with garlic in a sauce for thick pork chops, they produce a deliciously different meal for the family.

Recipe contest entry: Margie Opresik, Phillips, WI

4 pork loin chops, ¾ inch thick
3 cloves fresh garlic, peeled
4 tablespoons water
1 teaspoon salt
½ small bay leaf
3 medium apples, peeled, cored and coarsely chopped
1 medium head cabbage, cored and coarsely chopped
½ small onion, chopped
¼ cup sugar
2 tablespoons *each* vinegar and water
1½ teaspoons flour

Trim fat from chops and cook fat in skillet to oil surface. Discard fat and brown chops in skillet. Add garlic, 2 tablespoons water, ½ teaspoon salt and bay leaf; cover and simmer for 30 minutes. Remove chops and discard garlic and bay leaf. To skillet add apples and cabbage. Blend onion, sugar, vinegar and water, flour and remaining ½ teaspoon salt. Pour over cabbage and stir to mix. Cover and simmer 5 minutes. Return chops to skillet; cover and cook 20 minutes, until chops are fork tender. Makes 4 servings.

PORK AND GREEN CHILES

Contrast the richness of pork with a snappy green chile sauce for a delicious, south-of-the-border flavor.

Recipe contest entry: Pat Haluza, Gilroy, CA

1 to 2 medium-sized onions, coarsely chopped
3 cloves fresh garlic, minced
Olive oil
1 lb. pork, diced
Flour, seasoned with salt and pepper
1 large or 2 small green chiles, chopped
1 can (10¾ oz.) chicken broth
1 jalapeno pepper (optional)
1 large or 2 small fresh tomatoes, chopped
1 teaspoon cornstarch mixed with 2 teaspoons water

Brown onions and garlic in olive oil. Set aside. Coat diced pork in seasoned flour and brown in the same oil, adding more if needed. After the pork is browned return the onion and garlic to the pan; add the chiles and the chicken broth. (One jalapeno pepper can be chopped up and added at this time if a sharper taste is desired.) Simmer mixture and add tomatoes 10 minutes or so before the pork is done. When pork is done, taste for seasoning; adding salt if needed. Stir in cornstarch mixture and heat until sauce has thickened.

ANNABELLE'S PORTUGUESE PORK IN ORANGE JUICE

We are pleased to present two time-honored Portuguese recipes from the wife of Ralph Santos, local garlic grower and shipper. You can give pork an exquisitely different flavor when you cook it Portuguese style.

Courtesy of: Annabelle Santos, Gilroy, CA

1   cup Burgundy
1   cup water
¼   cup orange juice
12   cloves fresh garlic, crushed
1   teaspoon ground cumin
½   teaspoon *each* cloves, all-spice, cinnamon (scant)
1   teaspoon salt
¼   teaspoon ground pepper
Pork loin roast *or* other cut of pork of your choice

Mix together all ingredients except meat. Pour mixture over pork and marinate for 48 hours, then drain off liquid and reserve. The pork may be roasted or barbecued. Brush meat with marinade while cooking.

ANNABELLE'S PORK IN VINEGAR

3   cups water
1   cup wine vinegar
1   tablespoon salt
½   teaspoon ground pepper
6   to 8 cloves fresh garlic, crushed
½   teaspoon ground cumin
½   teaspoon paprika

Combine all ingredients and follow the directions as above.

ADOBO

Filipino cooks have a way with garlic, as demonstrated in this classic pork adobo. It's easy to prepare and has a lovely, piquant sauce.

Recipe contest entry: Jean Baliton, Gilroy, CA

3   cloves fresh garlic, minced
3   lb. pork, cut in 2-inch cubes
15   whole black peppercorns
1   bay leaf
½   cup plus 1 tablespoon vinegar
6   tablespoons soy sauce
2   tablespoons sugar

Mix all ingredients together in large pot and simmer 1 hour. Serve with rice and green vegetables. Makes 4 servings.

Third Prize Winner 1982 Recipe Contest:

JOHN ROBINSON, Granada Hills, CA

This hearty award-winning entree which won a third prize for its originator requires 30 cloves of fresh garlic to achieve its robust flavor.
If you'd like even more garlic flavor, stud the lamb with slivers of fresh
garlic before cooking.

LAMB SHANKS WITH BARLEY AND GARLIC

Lamb
   4 lamb shanks
   ¼ cup *each* butter and olive
      oil
   ½ cup *each* red table wine
      and water
   ½ teaspoon rosemary (more
      if desired)
  30 cloves fresh garlic,
      peeled

In ovenproof pan with tight fitting
lid, brown lamb on all sides in butter and olive oil. Remove lamb, stir
wine and water into pan and heat,
scraping bottom and sides of pan.
Replace lamb and sprinkle with rosemary. Add at least 30 cloves garlic.
Put a sheet of foil over top, then the
tight fitting lid to seal thoroughly.
Bake at 350 degrees for 1½ hours.
Prepare barley.

Barley
   ½ to ¾ lb. fresh
      mushrooms, sliced
   ½ cup butter
  1½ cups pearl barley
  2½ to 3½ cups beef bouillon
   2 tablespoons mint jelly

Saute mushrooms in ¼ cup butter
and set aside. Brown barley in
remaining ¼ cup butter until golden
brown. Mix in mushrooms, turn into
casserole, and add 2½ cups beef
bouillon. Cover and bake 30 minutes
at 350 degrees. Add more bouillon
as needed, about 1 cup, and cook,
uncovered, until liquid is absorbed
and barley is done.

To serve, arrange lamb shanks
around edges of serving platter. Add
garlic cloves to barley, and heap
in center of platter. Stir mint jelly
into liquid remaining, cook 3 to 5
minutes, and spoon over lamb.
Makes 4 servings.

Finalist in 1985 Recipe Contest:

BARBARA WAYMIRE, assisted by Tim Lavalli, Manhattan Beach, CA

In this dish, the leg of lamb is stuffed with a puree made with eight heads of garlic, fresh rosemary and anchovy paste. For best results, use a good drinkable cabernet to marinate the meat, as the wine will later be reduced to sauce the meat.

GARLIC-STUFFED LEG OF LAMB WITH CABERNET SAUCE

1 leg of lamb, about 5 to 6 lb., boned
2 to 3 cups Cabernet Sauvignon
6 to 8 large heads fresh garlic, broken into cloves, unpeeled
1½ tablespoons finely minced fresh rosemary
1½ teaspoons anchovy paste
3 bunches fresh spinach (about 5 to 6 cups tightly packed)
1 to 2 teaspoons arrowroot
1 tablespoon whole fresh rosemary leaves, stripped from stem

Remove excess fat and skin from outside of lamb. Lay meat flat with boned-out side up. Make deep gashes in thick areas of the meat so that it is of consistent height and thickness. These gashes will also provide pockets for the stuffing, and meat will cook evenly. Place meat in a deep bowl and pour enough wine over to almost cover. Marinate for 1 to 2 hours. Place garlic in saucepan and cover with water. Simmer 10 minutes until cloves are soft. Do not overcook! Drain and rinse with cold water. Cut off stem end, pinch at bottom and pop cloves out. Mash garlic into a thick paste or process in blender. Add minced rosemary and anchovy paste and blend well. Remove meat from marinade, reserving marinade liquid. Lay meat flat with uncut side down and spread paste evenly over inside and down into pockets.

Wash spinach; remove stems and coarse ribs. Place in a nonstick pan and, using only the water left clinging to the leaves after washing, cook over high heat, covered, for 1 minute. Turn as necessary to evenly wilt spinach. Remove excess water by squeezing. Distribute spinach evenly over paste-covered meat surface. Roll lamb into roast form and truss with twine in 1-inch pattern.

Spread excess garlic mixture that may ooze out during trussing over exterior of finished rolled meat. Roast in preheated 500-degree oven for 10 minutes to sear outside of lamb. Reduce heat to 325 degrees for 10 minutes per pound. Allow lamb to "set up" for 15 minutes before carving.

Meanwhile, place marinade in saucepan and heat over medium heat until sauce is reduced by half. Skim if necessary. Thicken with arrowroot which has been dissolved in cold water. Add whole fresh rosemary leaves, reheat and serve with sliced lamb. Makes 10 to 12 servings.

LAMB SHANKS A LA BASQUE

This recipe was developed over 30 years ago and has been embellished and improved over the years to near perfection.

Recipe contest entry: M. Bernal, Morgan Hill, CA

4 lamb shanks
½ cup plus 2 tablespoons salad oil
10 cloves fresh garlic
½ lb. fresh mushrooms
½ to 1 cup chicken broth
½ cup dry red wine (Burgundy)
1 cup navy beans
Salt and pepper to taste
½ cup chopped fresh parsley
¼ cup wine vinegar

In heavy Dutch oven brown lamb shanks in 2 tablespoons salad oil. Remove lamb and reserve. Add 4 cloves garlic and mushrooms; brown well. Return lamb to Dutch oven and add wine and ½ cup broth. Cook, covered, in 350-degree oven for about 2 hours, adding more broth as needed, until meat falls from bones. Meanwhile cook beans with 4 cloves garlic in water to cover until soft. Drain and remove garlic. Remove bones from lamb. Add beans and salt and pepper to cooked meat and heat through. Serve with a sauce made by combining ½ cup salad oil, 2 minced cloves garlic, parsley and vinegar. Makes 4 servings.

Regional Winner 1982 Recipe Contest:

ROWENA BERGMAN, Toronto, Ontario, Canada

Plan ahead if you want to try this lamb dish. It is best if marinated for about four days in the refrigerator. For extra browning, run it under broiler for a few minutes just before serving.

RACK OF LAMB BREADBIN

1 rack of lamb, about 5 to 6 lb.
¾ cup fresh garlic cloves, peeled
½ cup olive oil
Juice of 4 lemons
3 heaping tablespoons dry mustard
2 heaping tablespoons bouquet garni
1 heaping tablespoon tarragon

Have the butcher cut through chine bone so meat can be carved into individual chops at the table and trim off fat around ends of ribs and around kidney area. Combine garlic and all remaining ingredients in food processor bowl (or in blender) and process until liquified. Place roast in large plastic bag, add marinade, spreading it all over roast and between cuts made by butchers. Seal bag and refrigerate at least 2 days. To roast, remove from bag, place in roasting pan and insert meat thermometer in thickest part of meat. Roast at 450 degrees until thermometer registers "medium" for beef. The lamb will be medium rare at this point. If you wish to have it done more, follow thermometer accordingly. Makes 4 servings.

T he main attraction was the cooking contest and it was a doozy. The winners were real winners.

Food and Wine Magazine

Regional Winner 1982 Recipe Contest:

CHAD REOTT, West Hollywood, CA

More than a seasoning, garlic is a major ingredient in this excellent dish. Chad recommends pouring a hefty glass of wine before starting to separate and peel the 30 heads of garlic. It will help to cheer you through the task.

CHAD'S GARLIC LAMB

1 6- to 7-lb. leg of lamb
30 heads fresh garlic, cloves separated and peeled
1 large onion, peeled
Garlic powder
Onion powder
Italian seasoning
½ gallon dry red wine such as Burgundy
3 tablespoons cornstarch

Coarsely chop 10 to 12 cloves garlic and onion; set aside. Spread remaining whole garlic cloves over bottom of roasting pan. With metal skewer poke holes in lamb (lengthwise). Stuff holes with chopped garlic and onion (a chopstick simplifies this step). Sprinkle lamb generously with garlic and onion powder and seasoning. Nestle lamb into bed of garlic cloves and pour enough wine over to reach a depth of ¾ inch. Roast lamb uncovered in 325-degree oven for about 30 minutes per pound. or until lamb is done to your liking. Remove lamb to warm platter. Pour contents of pan into blender and liquify. Transfer to saucepan. Mix 1 cup wine with cornstarch and add to liquid; heat until sauce is thickened. Carve lamb and pour some sauce over. Pass remaining sauce. Makes 6 servings.

Regional Winner 1981 Recipe Contest: HELEN MIZE, Lakeland, FL

Lamb and garlic go together in a "garlicious" dish of rolled, stuffed lamb cutlets, topped with Olive Sauce and served over broad noodles. "Mighty good eating," says Ms. Mize.

GARLICIOUS LAMB ROLL-UPS

1½ lb. lamb cutlets
1½ teaspoons garlic salt
¼ teaspoon black pepper
2 slices bacon
2 tablespoons chopped onion
1 cup soft bread crumbs
1 tablespoon chopped parsley
1½ teaspoons dried mint leaves, crumbled
1 teaspoon lemon juice
1 large clove fresh garlic
¼ teaspoon crushed rosemary
¼ cup flour
3 tablespoons butter
  Olive Sauce (Recipe below)
1 pkg. (8 or 9 oz.) pkg. broad noodles

Pound lamb cutlets to flatten (or have butcher do this for you). Trim off edges to make 8 rectangles, about 5x7 inches. Sprinkle with garlic salt and pepper. Finely dice lamb trimmings (½ to 1 cup) and bacon. Brown lightly in skillet. Add onion and cook until tender. Stir in bread crumbs, parsley, mint, lemon juice, fresh garlic and rosemary. Spread stuffing on cutlets. Roll up, fasten with toothpicks and dredge in flour. Slowly brown on all sides in 3 tablespoons butter over moderately-low heat. Continue cooking until meat is tender, about 30 to 40 minutes. Meanwhile, prepare Olive Sauce, and cook noodles in boiling salted water as package directs, then drain well. Serve lamb rolls over noodles with sauce and crusty chunks of garlic bread. Makes 4 servings.

Olive Sauce
2 beef bouillon cubes
1½ cups hot water
2 tablespoons butter
2 tablespoons flour
1 tablespoon tomato paste
1 bay leaf
⅓ cup sliced stuffed green olives
2 tablespoons dry sherry
  Garlic salt and pepper to taste

Dissolve 2 beef bouillon cubes in 1½ cups hot water. In a medium-sized saucepan melt 2 tablespoons butter and blend in 2 tablespoons flour. Slowly stir in broth. Cook, stirring, until thickened. Add remaining ingredients, stir and season to taste.

MARINATED GRILLED LEG OF LAMB

Menu suggestions from the chef to serve with the lamb: Baked Potatoes with Butter and Feta Cheese, Tomatoes and Sugar Snap Peas Vinaigrette, Homemade Sourdough Rolls and Fresh Raspberries and Cream.

Recipe contest entry: Linda Nee, Keller, WA

1 7- to 9-lb. leg of lamb
10 cloves fresh garlic, finely chopped
1 cup honey
1 cup soy sauce
⅓ cup dry sherry

Bone and butterfly lamb or have butcher do it. In a small bowl, combine garlic, honey, soy sauce and sherry. Place lamb in large roasting pan or large shallow baking dish. Pour marinade over, cover with plastic wrap and let stand at room temperature for at least 12 hours or overnight. If desired, lamb can be marinated for 3 or 4 days in refrigerator, but be sure to allow to come to room temperature before grilling. Grill lamb over hot coals to desired state of doneness. (For rare, allow approximately 15 to 20 minutes per side.) Let meat rest for 5 to 10 minutes before carving. If desired, heat remaining marinade and serve as sauce for the meat.

CRUSTY LAMB CON AJO

Tere Gonzales de Usabiaga from Celaya, Mexico, whose husband is a garlic grower, shares this exquisite method of preparing lamb that brings out a robust, garlicky flavor.

Courtesy of: Tere Gonzales de Usabiaga, Celaya, Mexico

3 extra-large heads fresh garlic (approx. 6 oz.)
¼ cup minced fresh parsley
¼ cup oil
  leg of lamb

Separate garlic into cloves and remove skins. Place garlic, parsley and oil in a blender or food processor and mix until a paste is formed. Remove excess fat from meat. Spread garlic mixture on all sides of meat. Bake uncovered in 350-degree oven 30 minutes per pound. This garlic mixture can also be used on other cuts of meat, such as rack of lamb, pork loin roasts, prime rib of beef, etc.

LAMB SHANKS DIVINE

Saucy lamb shanks are tender and tasty from long simmering in a spicy tomato sauce.

4 lamb shanks
2 tablespoons flour
1½ teaspoons seasoned salt
½ teaspoon black pepper
¼ teaspoon MSG (optional)
2 tablespoons shortening
1 can (8 oz.) tomato sauce
½ cup water
½ cup instant minced onion
2 tablespoons lemon juice
1 teaspoon garlic salt
1 teaspoon sage
½ teaspoon oregano
½ teaspoon celery salt

Roll lamb shanks in flour seasoned with seasoned salt, pepper and MSG; brown in hot shortening. Combine remaining ingredients; pour over meat. Cover and simmer gently 1½ hours or until tender. Makes 4 servings.

GOOD 'N GARLICKY KEBABS

Use this zesty marinade for your next barbecue. Grilled lamb and vegetables make a mouth-watering meal-in-one.

¾ cup dry red wine
¼ cup olive oil
¼ cup red wine vinegar
1 onion, chopped
5 cloves fresh garlic, pressed
1 teaspoon salt
1 teaspoon rosemary
1 teaspoon Worcestershire sauce
1 bay leaf
⅛ teaspoon pepper
2 lb. lamb, cut into 1½-inch cubes
16 mushrooms
16 cherry tomatoes
1 large green pepper, cut into 12 chunks
1 large onion, cut into 12 chunks

Combine wine, oil, vinegar, onion, garlic and seasonings. (To simplify preparation of marinade, combine all marinade ingredients in a food processor. The garlic can be left whole and the onion can be cut in large chunks. Process with quick on-and-off bursts until onion has been pureed.) Marinate lamb overnight in this mixture. Divide lamb into 4 portions and thread on 4 skewers. Divide vegetables into 4 portions and thread on 4 skewers. Grill lamb 4 inches from coals about 20 to 25 minutes, turning to cook all sides. Add vegetables the last 10 to 12 minutes. Baste meat and vegetables with marinade during the cooking process. Makes 4 servings.

DIANE'S BARBECUED MEXICAN LAMB CHOPS

Bathe loin lamb chops in a lemony marinade infused with aromatic herbs for a Mexican-style barbecue.

Recipe contest entry: Diane Truesdell, San Jose, CA

⅓ cup Chablis
½ cup oil
¼ cup fresh lemon juice
3 large cloves fresh garlic, minced
2 tablespoons brown sugar
2 teaspoons onions, minced
2 teaspoons cilantro leaves
½ teaspoon ground black pepper
½ teaspoon salt
¼ teaspoon basil
¼ teaspoon rosemary
⅛ teaspoon oregano
8 thickly cut lamb chops, center cut *or* shoulder

Combine all ingredients except lamb chops and mix thoroughly. Pour over lamb chops and marinate overnight. Barbecue over hot coals until chops are well browned and tender. Serve with green salad, hot steamed rice, zucchini cooked with basil and red Spanish onions, and crisp French bread.

MRS. JOSEPH GUBSER'S BARBECUED LAMB

You'll be surprised at the beautiful flavor you can impart to lamb by brushing with a simple combination of garlic and red wine, if you know the right technique.

Courtesy of: Mrs. Joseph Gubser, Gilroy, CA

12 to 16 cloves fresh garlic, minced
2 cups dry red wine
Choice young spring lamb, steaks *or* chops
Salt and freshly ground pepper (optional)
Melted butter *or* cream

Add garlic to wine. Let mixture stand overnight. Dip or brush (do not marinate) lamb with garlic-flavored wine and allow to stand 8 to 10 hours. Broil quickly over bed of hot coals. If desired, season with salt and freshly ground pepper. Baste with melted butter or cream. The flavor is far superior if cooked over a bed of oak or other hardwood coals.

RAGOUT OF LAMB

Simmer lamb with herbs and vegetable chunks for a classic stew.

2 lb. lean lamb, cubed
1 tablespoon oil
1 cup chopped onion
1 teaspoon seasoned salt
1 teaspoon celery salt
1 teaspoon beef flavor base
¾ teaspoon instant minced garlic
½ teaspoon mint flakes
½ teaspoon sugar
¼ teaspoon rosemary leaves
1 bay leaf
   Dash MSG (optional)
2 cups water
3 potatoes, peeled and cut in quarters
3 carrots, peeled and cut in 2-inch slices
2 tablespoons butter
2 tablespoons flour

Slowly brown lamb on all sides in oil. Add seasonings and water; gently simmer 1½ hours or until lamb is almost tender. Add potatoes and carrots. Simmer 40 minutes or until vegetables are tender. In a separate pan, melt butter; add flour and cook until flour is brown, stirring constantly. Stir into stew and cook a few minutes longer to thicken gravy slightly. Serve with noodles, dumplings or hot biscuits. Makes 4 to 6 servings.

CURRIED LAMB CHOPS

Lamb and curry have always made good partners. Here curry and garlic add a distinctive flavor touch to a basting sauce for grilled lamb chops.

½ cup salad oil
3 tablespoons lemon juice
2 tablespoons sugar
2 teaspoons curry powder
1 teaspoon salt
1 teaspoon instant minced onion
1 teaspoon seasoned salt
¾ teaspoon garlic salt
½ teaspoon black pepper
8 lamb chops, cut 1 inch thick

Combine all ingredients except lamb chops in saucepan. Bring to a boil, then simmer 10 minutes. Arrange chops on grill 5 to 6 inches from hot coals. Sear on both sides. Continue cooking, basting frequently with the curry sauce, 30 minutes or until chops are browned and done. Makes 4 servings.

MIGHTY GOOD MOUSSAKA

We all know the adage "You Are What You Eat," which happens also to be the title of a food column written by the third-generation winery owner who devised this recipe. If, indeed, we are what we eat, then we can count on being just that much better after a portion of this wonderful concoction of delectable ingredients.

Courtesy of: Louis Bonesio, Jr., Gilroy, CA

2 medium eggplants
½ cup polyunsaturated oil (approx.)
¼ cup olive oil
1 large onion, finely chopped
3 cloves fresh garlic, minced
1 lb. lean ground beef
1 can (8 oz.) tomato sauce
1 large ripe tomato, cut in pieces
1 bay leaf
¼ teaspoon Beau Monde seasoning
1 tablespoon honey
¼ teaspoon dried oregano
Freshly ground black pepper
10 fresh mushrooms, trimmed and sliced
½ teaspoon ground cinnamon
½ teaspoon ground allspice
1 cup partially creamed cottage cheese
½ cup dry red wine
¼ cup freshly grated Romano or Parmesan cheese
2 tablespoons parsley, chopped

Peel eggplant and cut into ½-inch slices. In skillet, heat enough polyunsaturated oil to brown eggplant quickly on both sides. Arrange half the slices in the bottom of an oiled 9x12x2 baking pan. Heat olive oil in skillet and cook onion and garlic until golden. Add meat and cook, stirring, for about 5 minutes, breaking up any lumps. In saucepan, heat tomato sauce, fresh tomato, bay leaf, Beau Monde, honey, oregano and pepper to taste. Cook for 10 minutes. In separate pan saute mushrooms in a little polyunsaturated oil until golden brown. Add to the meat mixture and mix. Put the chopped meat mixture over the eggplant slices. Sprinkle with cinnamon, allspice and cottage cheese, and cover with remaining eggplant slices. Pour tomato sauce mixture and wine over all and sprinkle with the grated cheese. Bake for 1 hour at 350 degrees until top is golden. Remove from oven and sprinkle with chopped parsley. Makes 6 servings.

GLORIA'S LAMB STEW

This is lamb stew with a difference—chile peppers, garlic and fresh cilantro are the seasonings.   *Recipe contest entry: Gloria Park, Los Gatos, CA*

1 cup fresh cilantro leaves
   (coriander)
1 whole head fresh garlic,
   peeled
2 or 3 fresh hot red *or*
   green peppers, seeded
½ cup olive oil
2 medium onions, finely
   chopped
4 lb. lean boneless lamb,
   cut into 1-inch cubes
   Salt and freshly ground
   pepper to taste
⅔ cup fresh orange juice
⅓ cup lime *or* lemon juice
   Water
2 lb. potatoes, peeled and
   sliced
1 lb. fresh green peas,
   shelled *or* 2 pkg. (10 oz.
   each) frozen

In blender or food processor puree cilantro, garlic and peppers; set aside. Heat oil in casserole or Dutch oven and saute onions until soft. Stir in cilantro mixture and cook for a minute or two longer. Add lamb pieces and cook for about 5 minutes, turning to coat with sauce. Season to taste with salt and a generous amount of pepper. Add orange and lime or lemon juice and enough water to cover, about 1½ cups. Cover and simmer until lamb is tender, about 1½ hours. If desired, this dish may be refrigerated at this point in order to solidify and remove any excess fat. Let stand to bring to room temperature before heating. Boil potatoes and peas separately in salted water until tender. Drain and add to casserole. Bring casserole to a simmer and cook just long enough to heat through. Makes 4 to 5 servings.

Finalist in 1983 Recipe Contest: JOHN ROBINSON, Granada Hills, CA

This two-time finalist specializes In hearty dishes made with grains and legumes. In this casserole, rabbit is paired with lentils and finished with the fruity sweetness of apple. An attractive and satisfying meal.

RABBIT WITH LENTILS

8 rabbit legs and thighs
   Flour, as needed
½ cup butter, unsalted
¼ cup olive oil
1 lb. dried lentils
   Salt and pepper to taste
   cayenne pepper
½ lb. thick-sliced bacon, cut into 2-inch pieces
20 to 25 cloves fresh garlic, peeled
1½ cups thickly sliced fresh mushrooms
½ cup gin (with strong juniper berry flavor)
½ cup crabapple jelly
½ cup finely chopped parsley
1 can (*or* jar) red spiced crabapples
1 bunch watercress

Dredge rabbit in flour and saute over moderately high heat in ¼ cup *each* butter and olive oil until brown on all sides. Remove rabbit and save pan with drippings. Cook lentils according to package instructions, except stop when *slightly* underdone. Drain lentils, stir in remaining ¼ cup butter, and season with salt, pepper and a generous dash cayenne pepper. Line bottom of heavy casserole (with tightly fitting lid) with bacon. Put layer of lentils on top of bacon, add rabbit pieces, heap garlic around rabbit and cover all with balance of lentils. Spread mushrooms on top and seal casserole with aluminum foil. Then carefully put on the lid and bake at 350 degrees for 1½ hours. Remove rabbit from casserole and place around edge of serving platter. Stir balance of casserole ingredients together and mount in center of platter. Heat pan with reserved drippings over moderately high heat, add gin and stir until thoroughly deglazed. Add crabapple jelly and stir until completely combined. Remove from heat, add parsley and stir. Pour over rabbit. Garnish with crabapples and watercress. Serves 4.

SHERRIED OXTAILS

On a cold, rainy night, these Sherried Oxtails will offer warming comfort. The meat is simmered with vegetables to tender perfection in a thick, bubbling broth.   *Courtesy of: Louis Bonesio, Jr., Gilroy, CA*

¼ cup flour
3 teaspoons paprika
1 teaspoon salt
4 lb. oxtails, cut into serving-size pieces
¼ cup butter *or* margarine
2 cups boiling water
½ lb. sliced mushrooms
1 red pepper, thinly sliced and seeded
2 large onions, thinly sliced
3 cloves fresh garlic, crushed
2 beef bouillon cubes
2 vegetable bouillon cubes
2 teaspoons curry powder
1 cup dry sherry *or* tomato juice

Blend flour, paprika and salt. Coat oxtails with this mixture and reserve remaining flour. In large frying pan with lid, melt butter. Brown floured oxtails in melted butter on all sides. Add boiling water; cover and simmer for about an hour. Stir in mushrooms, red pepper, onions, garlic, beef and vegetable bouillon cubes and curry powder. Cover again and continue cooking for about 2 hours longer, or until meat is very tender. Blend in sherry or tomato juice and simmer uncovered for about 15 minutes longer. In small bowl, gradually stir a little of the cooking liquid into reserved seasoned flour to form a smooth paste; blend flour paste into oxtails and cook, stirring constantly, until thickened and bubbling. Makes 4 to 6 servings.

CONEJO A LA CHILINDRON   *Sauteed Rabbit*

Tender rabbit, cooked the Spanish way, is an old country recipe submitted by a San Mateo family. You may want to include it in your family's cooking traditions after you taste its remarkably rich flavor.

Recipe contest entry: Fernandez-Carozzi family, San Mateo, CA

1   2-to 3-lb. rabbit, cut into 6 to 8 serving pieces
Salt to taste
Freshly ground black pepper
¼   cup olive oil
2   large onions, cut lengthwise in half and then into ¼-inch wide strips
1   teaspoon fresh garlic, finely chopped
3   sweet red *or* green peppers, seeded and cut lengthwise into ¼-inch wide strips
½   cup smoked ham, finely chopped
6   tomatoes, peeled, seeded and finely chopped
6   pitted black olives, halved
6   pitted green olives, halved

Rinse and pat rabbit pieces dry with paper towels; sprinkle liberally with salt and a little pepper. In heavy 10- to 12-inch skillet, heat oil over moderate heat until light haze forms; saute rabbit and as pieces become a rich brown transfer them to a plate. Add onions, garlic, pepper strips and ham to oil remaining in skillet. Stirring frequently, cook for 8 to 10 minutes over moderate heat until vegetables are soft, but not brown. Add tomatoes; raise heat and cook briskly until most of the liquid in the pan evaporates and mixture is thick enough to hold its shape lightly in a spoon. Return rabbit to skillet, turning pieces with a spoon to coat them evenly with sauce. Cover tightly and simmer over low heat for 25 to 30 minutes or until rabbit is tender. Stir in olives, and adjust seasonings to taste.

TRIPE A LA LOUIS

If you haven't tried tripe, here's a recipe to give you inspiration. Simmered with tomatoes, white wine, beef stock, vegetables, garlic and spices, this dish will make your kitchen smell heavenly as it cooks. A little chopped cilantro and oregano are pleasing garnishes.

Courtesy of: Louis Bonesio, Jr., Gilroy, CA

3 lb. honeycomb tripe
3 tablespoons olive oil
1 large onion, sliced
2 large carrots, sliced
1 large bell pepper, cut into ¾-inch pieces
½ cup tomato puree
1 cup chopped stewed tomatoes
2 cups dry white wine
1 cup beef stock *or* bouillon
1 bay leaf
4 cloves fresh garlic, crushed
4 to 6 dashes Tabasco sauce
½ teaspoon fine black pepper
¼ teaspoon thyme
1 can (1 lb.) hominy
Cilantro, chopped
Oregano

Cut tripe into 1x2-inch pieces and boil in lightly salted water for 15 minutes. Set aside to drain. Saute in a heavy Dutch oven with olive oil, onion, carrots and bell pepper for 5 to 15 minutes. Add tomato puree, stewed tomatoes, white wine, beef stock or bouillon, bay leaf, garlic, Tabasco, pepper, thyme and hominy. Add the tripe to the Dutch oven and simmer 2½ to 3 hours. Serve with chopped cilantro and a little oregano to garnish. Serves 6 hungry eaters!!

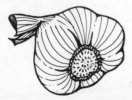

Poultry

Bob's Garlic Chicken   229
Joycie-A's Chicken Provincial   230
Spicy Garlic Chicken   231
California Chicken   232
Chicken Peperonata   233
Kiss Me Now-Chicken   234
Stuffed Chicken Breasts a L'ail   235
101 Garlic Chicken   236
Garlic-Chicken Phyllo Rolls   237
Mediterranean Chicken Breasts   238
Gin-Gar Chicken   240
Forty-Clove Chicken Filice   240
Thirty-Clove Chicken   241
Chicken in Garlic Mushroom Sauce   241
Vermouth Garlic Chicken   242
Burgundy Chicken Mozzone   243
Garlic Chicken with Artichokes
   and Mushrooms   243
Chicken Rosemary   244
Broiled Garlic and Lemon Chicken   244
Wild Rice and Chicken   245
Chicken Mama's Way   245
Garlic-Glazed Chicken for a Gang   246
Digger Dan's Chicken   246
Nofri's Garlic Chicken   247
Uncle Hugo's Chicken   247
Nehls' Saffron Chicken   248
Kelly's Asian Chicken   249
Shanghai Chicken on Shanghai Rice   250
Garlic Chicken with Plum Sauce   251
Woking Garlic Chicken   252
Chicken Maui   253
Hodge-Podge Chicken Bake   254
Chinesey Chicken Wings   254
Chicken a la Brazil   255
Pollo al Ajullo   255
Gypsy Garlic Chicken   256
Franco-Syrian Chicken   257

French Garlic Chicken a la Ingram   258
Chicken Pizzaiola   258
My Own Breathtaking Cacciatore   259
Chicken alla Toscano   259
Gilroy Chicken Paprika   260
Chicken Curry with Peaches   260
Chicken Karma   261
Crepes Poule a la Garlic   262
Herbed Cheese and Chicken in
    Puff Pastry   263
Chicken and Sausage Ragout
    alla Rosina   264
Phony Abalone   265
Squabs a la Santa Cruz   265
Helen's Baggy Henny   266
Oyster Sauce Turkey Breast with
    Peas and Mushrooms   267
Pheasant in a Bag   268
Oven-Fried Quail   268

Finalist in 1986 Recipe Contest: ROBERT FREEMAN, JR., Napa, CA

Once you've browned the chicken, this dish will take care of itself.

BOB'S GARLIC CHICKEN

14 chicken thighs
4 eggs
¾ oz. liquid garlic
1 lb. all-purpose flour
2 teaspoons salt
2 teaspoons pepper
¼ cup dehydrated garlic, or more if desired
Olive oil
6 to 10 cloves fresh garlic, crushed
Powdered garlic, as needed

Rinse and pat dry chicken thighs. Beat eggs and add liquid garlic. Combine flour, salt, pepper and dehydrated garlic. Dip chicken in egg mixture then dredge in flour mixture. In large frying pan brown thighs in $\frac{1}{16}$ inch olive oil to which 3 to 5 crushed garlic cloves have been added. Brown until just golden on both sides. Sprinkle browning chicken with powdered garlic. Remove browned chicken from pan and arrange in an ovenproof baking dish. Pour juices from frying pan over chicken in baking dish. Repeat procedure, being sure to add oil and crushed garlic to frying pan until all thighs have been browned and all juices added to baking dish. Bake chicken in 350-degree oven until the meat falls off the bones. Gravy may be made from leftover juices in baking dish. Makes 6 to 8 servings.

Finalist in 1985 Recipe Contest: JOYCE A. BROWER, San Diego, CA

The combined flavors of garlic and thyme permeate the chicken in this marvelous one-dish meal.

JOYCIE-A'S CHICKEN PROVINCIAL

1 whole head fresh garlic
1 chicken, cut into quarters
4 potatoes, peeled
3 carrots, sliced diagonally
2 onions, quartered
20 cherry tomatoes
20 mushrooms
1 cup pitted ripe olives, drained
1 cup olive oil
1 tablespoon dried thyme
Salt and pepper to taste

Break garlic into cloves, peel and cut into slivers. Place garlic under the skin of the chicken and in holes which have been poked into the chicken. Use entire head of garlic. Place chicken in roasting pan, add potatoes, carrots, onions, tomatoes, mushrooms and olives. Pour olive oil over all and sprinkle heavily with thyme, until chicken is nearly green in color. Bake, uncovered, 1½ hours at 350 degrees. Baste every 15 minutes. Serve with French bread to soak up the wonderful juices.

Finalist in 1984 Recipe Contest: CINDY NEVA, Acton, CA

Yum. Yum. This dish is good and spicy and at its best when the chicken is allowed to marinate overnight in the refrigerator.

SPICY GARLIC CHICKEN

1 bunch cilantro *with roots*
1 large whole head fresh garlic, peeled
2 tablespoons coarse black pepper
1 teaspoon ground curry powder
¼ teaspoon crushed red chile pepper
¼ cup peanut oil
⅓ cup soy sauce
1 whole chicken *or* 12 drumsticks, wings *or* thighs
Sweet Garlic Sauce for Dipping (recipe below)

Cut roots off cilantro and place with garlic, some cilantro leaves and a few stems in food processor and whirl until coarsely chopped, or chop by hand. Turn mixture into bowl, add remaining whole cilantro leaves, pepper, curry powder, chili pepper, peanut oil and soy sauce. Mix well. Pour mixture over chicken and marinate 4 hours or as long as overnight. Meanwhile prepare Sweet Garlic Sauce for Dipping. Barbecue chicken over low glowing coals about 1 hour, basting occasionally and turning chicken several times. Serve with Sweet Garlic Sauce for Dipping. Makes 4 servings.

Sweet Garlic Sauce for Dipping
3 cups sugar
1 cup vinegar
2 tablespoons coarse black pepper
1 teaspoon dry red chile pepper
½ teaspoon salt
1 drop red food coloring
1 whole head fresh garlic, peeled and chopped

In 2-quart saucepan bring sugar and vinegar to boil. Add pepper, chile pepper, salt and food coloring. Boil 5 minutes, stirring to prevent sticking. (Be careful not to permit mixture to boil over pan.) Remove from heat and stir in chopped garlic. Refrigerate.

Finalist in 1984 Recipe Contest: JAN E. SHELTON, Escondido, CA

In this recipe chicken breasts are browned in butter and then baked covered with a garlic cream sauce. When done they are beautifully presented garnished with colorful slices of California avocado and mandarin oranges.

CALIFORNIA CHICKEN

60 cloves fresh garlic (about 5 heads)
    Boiling water
 3 cups whipping cream
    Salt and white pepper to taste
¼ cup butter
 4 whole chicken breasts, split, skinned and boned
⅛ teaspoon *each* cinnamon and dried tarragon
 2 ripe avocados
    Juice of 1 lime
 1 small can (6 oz.) mandarin orange slices, drained
 1 tablespoon chopped fresh parsley
    Paprika

Place garlic cloves in a saucepan with boiling water to cover. Boil for 2 minutes. Drain, then peel cloves. Return garlic to pan and add whipping cream. Simmer, stirring occasionally, until garlic is very tender and cream is thickened and reduced by half. Rub garlic and cream through a wire sieve. Return to saucepan and season with salt and pepper. Set aside and place plastic wrap on cream surface. Heat butter in frying pan over medium-high heat. Add chicken and saute for 1 minute, turning chicken once. Do not brown. Place chicken on oven-proof platter. Bake in 325-degree oven 7 to 10 minutes. Meanwhile peel avocados, cut into ½-inch slices and toss with lime juice. Pour garlic mixture over chicken and return to oven for 2 or 3 minutes. Garnish with drained avocado and orange slices. Sprinkle with chopped fresh parsley and paprika to taste. Serve at once. Makes 4 to 6 servings.

Finalist in 1983 Recipe Contest: STACEY HAROLDSEN, Los Angeles, CA

Though not a winner, this tasty recipe was popular with the judges who thought the combination of garlic, peppers and balsamic vinegar made a wonderful sauce for the chicken. The fresh basil is an important ingredient also, but if not available dried basil can be substituted.

CHICKEN PEPERONATA

2 whole chickens, about 3 lb. *each*
2 tablespoons butter
2 whole heads fresh garlic
  Salt and pepper
2 large sprigs fresh rosemary
3 large green bell peppers
3 large red bell peppers
¼ cup pine nuts
¼ cup extra virgin olive oil
¼ cup Italian balsamic vinegar
1 tablespoon sugar
3 tablespoons chopped fresh basil
  Lettuce leaves and basil sprigs for garnish

Preheat oven to 375 degrees. Wash chickens and pat dry; rub with butter. Separate cloves of garlic but do not peel. Sprinkle cavities of chickens with salt and pepper; place a sprig of rosemary and half of the garlic cloves in each. Roast breast-side down for 1 hour, then turn breast-side up and continue roasting until tender, about 15 minutes. Remove from oven, when cool enough to handle, remove meat from bones, pulling the meat into strips. Reserve cooked garlic cloves. Broil peppers until skins are charred, then hold under running water while removing skins and seeds. Cut half the peppers into strips and reserve the rest. Remove skins from 6 of the cooked garlic cloves and mince finely. Toast pine nuts in a dry skillet over medium heat. Combine olive oil, vinegar and sugar in a bowl. Toss chicken, peppers, pine nuts, basil, minced garlic and dressing. Add salt and pepper to taste. Line serving platter with lettuce and mound chicken salad on top. Garnish with the reserved peppers, the cooked garlic cloves (skins and all) and basil sprigs. Serve at room temperature. Makes 6 to 8 servings.

Regional Winner in 1983 Recipe Contest:

EMMALEA KELLEY, Greenbelt, MD

One good way to be sure that the chicken you are preparing absorbs the flavors of the herbs and spices used in the recipe is to make a paste and rub it all over the bird between the skin and the flesh. This requires using your fingers to break the skin away from the chicken, leaving it in place, however, to hold the seasonings tightly.

KISS ME NOW—CHICKEN

2 heads fresh garlic
1 cup water
1 fryer-broiler chicken, about 3 to 4 lb.
¼ teaspoon *each* black pepper and dill weed
¼ teaspoon salad oil
¼ lb. fresh mushrooms, rinsed and trimmed
6 pieces of celery, 1 inch *each*
2 tablespoons flour
1 tablespoon cooking sherry
1 cup half-and-half

Separate garlic cloves and discard loose skin, but do not peel. Boil garlic in water in small saucepan for 30 minutes. Meanwhile, entering from both the neck section and rear of the chicken, break the membranes which attach the skin to the body of the chicken with the index finger. Remove all fat from chicken. Strain water from garlic into small bowl and reserve. Scatter garlic on plate to cool. Press each clove from the pointed end into a small bowl. Discard skins. Preheat oven to 350 degrees. Add pepper and dill to garlic paste in bowl and blend well. Spoon half the mixture under the skin of the chicken, patting gently to distribute evenly. Spread remainder of garlic mixture inside chicken. Place chicken in lightly oiled shallow baking dish and fill cavity with mushrooms. Arrange celery around chicken. Bake at 350 degrees for 1½ hours, basting every 15 minutes with reserved garlic liquid. Remove chicken to serving dish. Remove mushrooms and chop. Discard celery. Scrape drippings from baking dish into small pan. Stir flour in pan drippings. Add mushrooms, sherry and half-and-half. Bring to a boil, stirring constantly. Turn heat off and stir until well thickened. Quarter chicken and serve with sauce and hot cornbread or biscuits, rice, pasta, potatoes or grits. Makes 4 servings.

Regional Winner in 1983 Recipe Contest:

MRS. ROBERT SOELTER, Abilene, KS

Only three chicken breasts are used in this recipe, the skin from six is necessary to wrap the six stuffed half breasts. Reserve the remaining three whole skinned chicken breasts for use in another recipe or marinate and grill them when you prepare this recipe and freeze them to serve later.

STUFFED CHICKEN BREASTS A L'AIL

6 whole chicken breasts
3 cloves fresh garlic, minced
1½ cups Monterey Jack cheese, grated
Salt
Cracked black pepper
Nutmeg
1 jar marinated Brussels sprouts, drained
6 teaspoons capers
Basting Sauce (recipe below)

Carefully remove skin from 6 chicken breasts and set aside. Bone chicken breasts. (Use bones for stock and 3 breasts in another recipe.) Cut 3 chicken breasts in half. Cover chicken with piece of heavy plastic wrap and pound with wooden mallet until very thin. Combine garlic and cheese. Lightly sprinkle each chicken breast with salt and cracked black pepper. Place ¼ cup garlic/cheese mixture on each breast to within 1 inch of edge. Sprinkle with nutmeg. Cut Brussels sprouts in quarters and arrange evenly over chicken. Top with capers. Fold in sides of flattened chicken and roll to make neat packages, covering stuffing well. Wrap each breast in a chicken skin, securing with toothpicks. Grill over charcoal 30 to 40 minutes, basting with sauce. Makes 6 servings.

Basting Sauce
¾ cup dry white wine
⅜ cup olive oil
3 cloves fresh garlic, minced
½ teaspoon salt

Combine all ingredients and mix thoroughly.

Winner of Prize for Best Recipe Using Most Garlic, 1982:

HELEN McGLONE, Roseville, CA

When serving this recipe to guests, invite them into the kitchen to let them count as you place the garlic cloves around the chicken. They won't believe how sweet and delicious the cooked garlic will be until they eat it!

101 GARLIC CHICKEN

10 whole chicken breasts, split, boned and skinned
    Salt and pepper
 2 cups champagne
101 unpeeled cloves fresh garlic

Place chicken in ungreased baking pan, 12x16 or 18 inches. Sprinkle with salt and pepper and pour champagne over. Place garlic cloves around and between chicken pieces. Cover pan with foil. Bake at 350 degrees for 1½ hours. Remove chicken to large serving platter and place garlic around chicken. Tell guests to suck the garlic out of its skin, that it is deliciously sweet. Makes 20 servings.

There's no such thing as a little garlic.

San Diego *Union*

Finalist in 1981 Recipe Contest: MARY JANE HIMEL, Palo Alto, CA

This recipe turns out best when prosciutto is used. Look for it in an Italian grocery or deli if not available at your supermarket. It adds considerable flavor. Also, be sure to keep the phyllo dough moist as you work with it. Keep it covered with a dampened towel.

GARLIC-CHICKEN PHYLLO ROLLS

2 heads fresh garlic
½ cup dry white wine
½ cup water
    Juice of 1 lemon
¼ teaspoon salt
1 lb. boned, skinned chicken breasts
6 sheets phyllo
¼ cup butter, melted
2½ oz. thinly sliced prosciutto *or* 3 slices boiled ham, halved
2 cups grated Swiss cheese

Separate garlic into cloves and drop into boiling water. Simmer 1 minute, drain and peel. Bring wine, water, lemon juice and salt to simmer in large saucepan. Add chicken and garlic. Cook at a bare simmer, turning occasionally, just until chicken is cooked. Remove chicken and continue cooking garlic until tender, then drain. Cut chicken into large chunks and divide into 6 portions. Lay out 1 phyllo sheet, brush half with butter and fold in half crosswise. Brush with butter again. Top with a portion of chicken and garlic cloves lightly mashed with a fork along a short end. Top with ⅙ of the prosciutto, and ⅓ cup cheese. Fold in the sides and roll up. Repeat with remaining phyllo sheets. Work quickly so phyllo doesn't dry out. Place rolls on lightly greased baking sheet and brush them with butter. Bake at 400 degrees about 20 minutes, until golden. Makes 6 rolls.

Finalist in 1980 Recipe Contest: KAREN MAHSHI, Concord, CA

Still another mouth-watering Forty-Clove chicken. In this original version, succulent chicken breasts are marinated in seasoned lemon juice, lightly coated and combined with blanched fresh garlic cloves that are so sweet you can eat them by the handful.

MEDITERRANEAN CHICKEN BREASTS

2 lemons
4 large cloves garlic, minced
1½ teaspoons salt
1 teaspoon chopped fresh oregano
¼ teaspoon freshly ground pepper
¼ cup olive oil
¼ cup safflower oil
8 supremes (breasts from 4 frying chickens, boned and skinned)
1 cup freshly grated Parmesan cheese
1 cup fine, white, fresh bread crumbs
2 cups chicken stock (canned *or* homemade)
30 to 40 garlic cloves, peeled
Butter
1 cup dry white wine
⅓ cup minced fresh parsley leaves
Parsley sprigs

Remove lemon zest (yellow part of peel) with vegetable peeler and mince. With wide-bladed knife, make paste of minced garlic and salt. Combine lemon zest, 2 tablespoons lemon juice, garlic paste, oregano, pepper and oil. (Alternate method: Place unminced zest and garlic cloves in food processor and process a few seconds, using steel blade. Add salt, pepper, oregano leaves and lemon juice. With processor turned on, add oils in slow stream.) Coat chicken breasts with marinade; let stand several hours or overnight.

Remove supremes from marinade and scrape off excess. Roll chicken in mixture of Parmesan and bread crumbs. Lay coated supremes on waxed paper; allow to set 15 minutes to several hours. Heat chicken stock to boiling and blanch the 30 to 40 garlic cloves in it for 10 minutes. Remove and drain garlic. Reserve stock for sauce, reducing to 1½ cups while chicken is baking. Place supremes in shallow baking dish, coated with butter. Drizzle a little melted butter on each breast. Strew blanched garlic cloves over and around breasts. Cover with foil and bake in a preheated 375-degree oven 15 to 20 minutes, or until nearly done. Remove foil and place chicken under broiler until golden brown. Remove to heated platter and distribute the garlic around the breasts. Keep warm while preparing sauce.

Add dry white wine to juices remaining in the baking pan after chicken is removed. Deglaze pan over high heat, scraping up any brown bits clinging to bottom and sides. Pour mixture into saucepan and reduce over high heat to ¼ cup. Add reserved chicken stock and minced parsley and reduce mixture to about 1 cup. Remove pan from heat. Add lemon juice, salt and pepper to taste. Pour some sauce over chicken breasts and garnish platter with sprigs of parsley. Pass remaining sauce in a pitcher. Makes 8 servings.

Finalist in 1979 Recipe Contest: HELEN HEADLEE, South San Francisco, CA

Second place winner in the first Garlic Recipe Contest and Cook-off, this recipe combines the flavors of ginger and garlic with yogurt in an unusual marinade for barbecued chicken. Delicious hot or cold.

GIN-GAR CHICKEN

8   oz. plain yogurt
8   cloves fresh garlic
1   1-inch square piece ginger root
1½ teaspoons chili powder
1½ teaspoons salt
1   2½-lb. broiler-fryer chicken cut up (*or* equivalent chicken parts)

Put a small amount of yogurt in blender; add garlic and ginger and puree until smooth. Remove from blender and stir into remaining yogurt; add spices and blend well. Pour over chicken and marinate in covered container overnight, 12 to 24 hours, shaking occasionally. Cook over hot coals. Serve hot or cold with lemon slices.

FORTY-CLOVE CHICKEN FILICE

The head chef of Gourmet Alley, who is a garlic grower himself, has his own version of Forty-Clove Chicken which all who have tasted say is fantastic. Don't be timid. To enjoy this dish fully, pull out a hot, juicy garlic clove, hold one end and squeeze it into your mouth, discarding the skin. The garlic will be surprisingly mild, tender and buttery. Ahh . . .!   *Courtesy of: Val and Elsie Filice, Gilroy, CA*

1   frying chicken, cut in pieces
40 cloves fresh garlic
½   cup dry white wine
¼   cup dry vermouth
¼   cup olive oil
4   stalks celery, cut in 1-inch pieces
1   teaspoon oregano
2   teaspoons dry basil
6   sprigs minced parsley
    Pinch of crushed red pepper
1   lemon
    Salt and pepper to taste

Place chicken pieces into shallow baking pan, skin side up. Sprinkle all ingredients evenly over top of chicken. Squeeze juice from lemon and pour over top. Cut remaining lemon rind into pieces and arrange throughout chicken. Cover with foil and bake at 375 degrees for 40 minutes. Remove foil and bake an additional 15 minutes.

THIRTY-CLOVE CHICKEN

Not only will this dish banish evil spirits, but it will raise good ones, we're told, especially those of garlic lovers, for it contains thirty whole cloves! *Recipe contest entry: Leah Jackson, Marshfield, MA*

2 broiler-fryer chickens, cut in serving-size pieces
4 tablespoons olive oil
2 tablespoons butter
1 tablespoon flour
1 can (14½ oz.) chicken broth
30 cloves fresh garlic, peeled
1 cup rice
Fresh chives and parsley, minced

Brown chicken in 2 tablespoons oil and butter. Remove from pan and stir in flour, then broth and garlic. Bring to boil, return chicken to pan and simmer, covered, for 45 minutes. Saute rice in remaining 2 tablespoons oil until rice is opaque. Add to chicken, easing into liquid with fork. Cover and simmer another 25 minutes. Just before serving, stir in fresh herbs. Makes 8 servings.

CHICKEN IN GARLIC MUSHROOM SAUCE

A wonderful, rich creamy mushroom sauce turns this garlic chicken into a special event. *Recipe contest entry: Robin Lee Perkins, Covina, CA*

¼ cup butter
2 tablespoons vegetable oil
1 3-lb. broiler-fryer chicken, cut into serving pieces
30 cloves fresh garlic, minced
1 chopped onion
1 cup dry white wine
¼ cup water
¼ cup milk
1 teaspoon salt
Freshly ground pepper to taste
½ teaspoon cayenne pepper
1 lb. sliced mushrooms
3 egg yolks
1 cup heavy cream

In Dutch oven or kettle, melt butter with oil on medium heat. Add chicken, brown well, turning occasionally. When brown, remove pieces to bowl. Add garlic and onion to pan and saute until golden brown. Add wine, water, milk, salt, pepper, and cayenne pepper. Stir to loosen browned bits and bring to boil. Return chicken to pan and add mushrooms. Cover and cook at low heat until tender, about 45 minutes to 1 hour. Remove chicken to warm serving plate. Cover with foil and keep warm. Beat yolks into heavy cream until well mixed. Stir into pan drippings. Cook until thickened but do not boil. Spoon some of the sauce on the chicken; offer remainder separately. Serve with rice if desired. Makes 3 to 4 servings.

VERMOUTH GARLIC CHICKEN

"With the combination of vermouth and garlic, one needn't worry about garlic odor on the breath," says this chef whose recipe has been in the family for nearly 70 years. Actually when garlic is cooked whole for several hours, as it is here, it loses its pungency and becomes sweet and nutlike in flavor.   *Recipe contest entry: France D. Williams, Carlsbad, CA*

1   large onion, finely chopped
2   carrots, diced
2   celery stalks, diced
½   small rutabaga, diced
    Large sprig fresh parsley, minced
4   chicken thighs with bone
4   chicken breast halves, boned
½   cup safflower oil
30   cloves fresh garlic, peeled
    Dry vermouth

Combine onion, carrots, celery, rutabaga and parsley in large bowl and mix well. Remove skin from chicken pieces and wipe with a damp cloth. In large skillet, heat oil and brown chicken pieces on both sides. Start with thighs first as breasts take less time to brown. Drain chicken pieces on paper towels. Spread half the vegetables and half the garlic in a casserole. Arrange chicken on top and cover with the rest of the vegetables and the rest of the garlic. Over entire mixture pour vermouth and cover casserole. If lid does not fit tightly, cover with foil and then lid. Bake 2 hours in 325-degree oven, without removing lid. Serve with French bread on which the garlic cloves can be spread like butter. Delicious! A chilled Chablis is a good accompaniment.

BURGUNDY CHICKEN MOZZONE

The rich flavor of Burgundy seems to meld all the flavors into one in this recipe which combines green peppers and mushrooms with the chicken.

Courtesy of: Mary Mozzone, Gilroy, CA

2 medium-sized chickens,
   cut in pieces
   Flour
4 tablespoons oil
1 can (8 oz.) tomato sauce
½ cup Burgundy
   Salt and pepper to taste
   Dash of oregano
4 cloves fresh garlic,
   minced
3 large bell peppers, sliced,
   seeds removed
1 lb. sliced mushrooms
   Fresh parsley, chopped
   Parmesan cheese, grated

Dredge chicken with flour and brown in oil. While chicken is browning, mix tomato sauce, wine, salt, pepper and oregano in small bowl. After chicken is brown, put in ovenproof baking dish. Add garlic to pan drippings and saute 30 seconds. Add peppers and mushrooms, stir-fry 5 minutes, then add sauce. Simmer 3 to 4 minutes, and pour over chicken. Cover with foil and bake for 45 minutes at 350 degrees. Garnish with parsley and Parmesan cheese.

GARLIC CHICKEN WITH ARTICHOKES AND MUSHROOMS

A very elegant dish which draws its subtle, but delicious, flavor from the sweet and rich tasting Marsala wine which is added to complete the sauce.

Recipe contest entry: Carmela M. Meely, Walnut Creek, CA

8 cloves fresh garlic
¾ cup butter
6 chicken breasts, boned
   and pounded flat
   Salt and pepper
2 tablespoons olive oil
¼ lb. mushrooms, sliced
1 pkg. (9 oz.) frozen
   artichokes, cooked and
   drained
1 to 2 tablespoons Marsala,
   sherry *or* other white
   wine
   Parsley for garnish

Mince 5 cloves garlic and saute in ½ cup melted butter in skillet; add chicken breasts and sprinkle with salt and pepper. Brown, then remove chicken to a warm platter. Add remaining butter, olive oil and remaining 3 cloves garlic, minced. Brown garlic and toss in mushrooms; add artichokes. Heat. Stir in lemon juice and wine. Let thicken to desired consistency. Pour over chicken; garnish with parsley. Serve with rice.

CHICKEN ROSEMARY

The delicate taste of rosemary gives this dish its distinctive flavor but it's the garlic that adds zest.

1 3-lb. chicken
1 tablespoon flour
5 tablespoons oil
2 teaspoons garlic salt
1 tablespoon seasoned salt
1 tablespoon rosemary
¼ teaspoon black pepper
1 tablespoon vinegar

Cut chicken in pieces and dredge in flour. Heat 2 tablespoons oil in a skillet, and brown chicken on all sides. Remove chicken from skillet. Brush 1 tablespoon oil over bottom of a shallow baking dish and place pieces of browned chicken close together in dish, skin side down. Combine garlic salt, seasoned salt, rosemary, pepper and remaining oil; brush over chicken. Drizzle with vinegar; cover and marinate in refrigerator several hours before baking. Bake, covered, in 350-degree oven 45 minutes. Remove cover and turn chicken to skin side up; then continue baking 20 minutes or until tender. Makes 4 servings.

BROILED GARLIC AND LEMON CHICKEN

Just thinking about the tangy flavor of lemon, combined with fresh garlic, can get the juices flowing. Add a hint of oregano and you have a marinade for broiled chicken you'll want to use again and again.

Courtesy of: Karen Christopher, Gilroy, CA

6 oz. lemon juice (use 3 medium lemons)
¼ cup melted butter (or half butter, half corn oil)
3 large cloves fresh garlic, crushed or minced
½ teaspoon oregano
   Salt and pepper to taste
2 teaspoons corn oil
1 3-lb. broiler-fryer chicken, cut into quarters

Mix lemon juice, butter, garlic, oregano, salt and pepper. Preheat broiler and brush pan with 2 teaspoons of oil. Broil chicken, skin side down, for 25 minutes until golden brown, basting with garlic butter sauce. Keep chicken about 12 inches from the source of heat. Turn chicken pieces, skin side up; broil 20 minutes longer, basting frequently, until chicken is fork tender. Garnish with lemon slices and parsley if desired.

WILD RICE AND CHICKEN

Wild rice, which is not a rice at all but the grain of a tall, aquatic North American grass, is a true delicacy. It is prepared like ordinary rice, but takes a little longer to cook. It should maintain a bit of a chewy quality to be really good. *Recipe contest entry: M. Shipman, San Francisco, CA*

1 cup uncooked wild rice
2¼ cups chicken broth
8 to 10 cloves fresh garlic, minced *or* pressed
2 tablespoons soy sauce
2 teaspoons poultry seasoning
Coarsely ground black pepper
½ lb. mushrooms, sliced
1 green bell pepper, chopped
6 stalks of celery, chopped
6 chicken breast halves, boned and skinned
Chopped green onions for garnish

Rinse rice well at least 3 times. In casserole, place chicken broth, garlic, soy sauce, poultry seasoning and black pepper. Stir. Then add rice, mushrooms, bell pepper and celery. Mix well. "Bury" chicken in rice-vegetable mixture. Cover and bake at 350 degrees for 1 hour. Remove from heat and let stand for 30 minutes with cover still on. Garnish with sliced green onions and serve. Makes 6 servings.

CHICKEN MAMA'S WAY

Like the classic Spanish dish, paella, Mama's recipe combines chicken, sausage, seafood in a most complementary way.
Recipe contest entry: Ressie Crenshaw Watts, Porterville, CA

½ cup olive oil *or* cooking oil
4 medium-sized sweet red onions
2 2½-lb. broiler-fryer chickens, cut into pieces
2 cups rice
2 cups chicken broth
2 dozen clams
2 dozen shrimp
1 dozen slices Italian sausage
4 large cloves fresh garlic
1 teaspoon saffron
½ cup cooking sherry
Salt and coarsely ground pepper
Pimento strips
Grated Parmesan cheese

Heat oil in a large casserole. Add onions and chicken pieces. Saute until chicken is lightly browned on all sides; then add rice and 1 cup of the broth. Simmer until chicken and rice are almost tender; add clams and shrimp (if fresh, leave in shells), then sausage. Pound garlic, saffron and 1 cup of broth in a mortar. Strain into casserole and add sherry, salt and pepper to taste. Place strips of pimento and grated cheese on top. Broil 5 to 8 minutes.

GARLIC-GLAZED CHICKEN FOR A GANG

It isn't easy to find a party dish that will appeal to virtually everyone, but this one surely will. The chicken takes on a subtle garlic flavor that keeps everyone asking for seconds.

Salt and pepper
40 chicken quarters
2 tablespoons instant granulated garlic
3 teaspoons MSG (optional)
2 quarts chicken broth
4 cups apricot *or* peach preserves
2 cups white wine

Salt and pepper chicken and place in baking pan. Combine garlic, MSG and chicken broth. Pour over chicken and bake at 350 degrees for 1 hour or until tender. Combine wine and preserves, and spoon over chicken. Bake uncovered at 400 degrees for 15 minutes, spooning sauce over chicken every few minutes. Chicken should have a nice glaze when served. Makes approximately 20 portions.

DIGGER DAN'S CHICKEN

From the proprietors of a Gilroy restaurant who take pride in featuring garlicky dishes on the menu, especially at Festival time, comes this recipe for chicken in a garlic, tomato and wine sauce.

Courtesy of: Sam and Judy Bozzo, Gilroy, CA

1 3- to 3½-lb. broiler-fryer chicken
4 cloves fresh garlic, minced
4 tablespoons butter
4 tablespoons oil
Salt and pepper
2 cups white wine
1 lb. ripe tomatoes rubbed through a sieve (*or* use 1 lb. canned Italian peeled tomatoes)

Cut chicken into quarters. Saute garlic in butter and oil in a large pan, add the chicken legs first and brown them over high heat; then brown the breast pieces. Season with salt and pepper; lower heat and continue cooking until the chicken pieces are tender. Remove from the pan and keep hot. Scraping off bits adhering to the bottom and sides of the pan, stir in the wine and reduce over high heat. Add the pureed tomatoes, salt and pepper to taste; stir well and cook over moderate heat for almost 10 minutes. Return the chicken pieces to the pan, spoon over the sauce and cook for a few minutes longer. Serve the chicken in the sauce.

NOFRI'S GARLIC CHICKEN

This crispy-skinned chicken draws its great flavor from slivers of garlic and bits of sage which are inserted into slits in the flesh before cooking. It's easy to prepare.

Recipe contest entry: Jeanette Nofri Steinberg, Santa Monica, CA

1 frying *or* roasting chicken, whole or cut in pieces
Whole leaf sage
5 cloves fresh garlic, coarsely chopped
Corn oil
Salt and pepper

Rinse and dry chicken. Rub entire skin surface with a clove of garlic. With a sharp knife, make small random punctures in chicken about 2 inches apart and stuff each hole with a small piece of garlic and some sage. Salt and pepper entire chicken and place in a shallow baking pan. Brush chicken with corn oil and place in preheated 350-degree oven for 1½ hours, basting every 20 or 30 minutes.

UNCLE HUGO'S CHICKEN

Uncle Hugo likes his crunchy, garlicky chicken served with corn on the cob, tossed green salad and sourdough French bread with garlic butter. You will, too. *Recipe contest entry: "Hugo" David Hugunin, San Jose, CA*

⅔ cup dry French bread crumbs
⅔ cup grated Parmesan cheese
¼ cup minced parsley
½ teaspoon salt
¼ teaspoon pepper
3 cloves fresh garlic, minced
⅓ cup margarine *or* butter
1 3-lb. broiler-fryer chicken

Mix first 5 ingredients together in a 1-quart mixing bowl. Set aside. In 1-quart saucepan heat garlic and margarine over very low heat until margarine has melted. Remove from heat. Coat chicken pieces with margarine mixture, then thoroughly coat with crumb mixture. Place coated chicken on large, ungreased cookie sheet skin side up. Mix together any remaining crumb mixture and margarine and sprinkle over chicken. Bake for 1 hour in 350-degree oven. For crisper chicken, cook an additional 15 minutes.

NEHLS' SAFFRON CHICKEN

With saffron almost worth its weight in gold, it should be reserved for use on very special dishes. According to the woman who entered this recipe in the Garlic Recipe Contest, it never fails to receive raves whenever she serves it with French bread to soak up the sauce.

Recipe contest entry: Mrs. W. B. Nehls, San Clemente, CA

1 large broiler-fryer chicken
Salt
4 tablespoons oil *or* 2 tablespoons oil plus 2 tablespoons margarine
4 cloves fresh garlic, halved
2 bay leaves
½ teaspoon tarragon
¼ teaspoon saffron
¼ teaspoon thyme
Pinch of sage
Salt and freshly ground pepper to taste
4 to 5 ripe tomatoes, peeled and quartered
20 ripe olives *or* pimento-stuffed olives
1¼ cup Sauterne
1¼ cup chicken broth

Cut up chicken and rub pieces with salt. Saute on all sides in oil. When brown, blend in garlic, bay leaves, tarragon, saffron, thyme, sage and salt and pepper. Add tomatoes, olives, wine and chicken broth. Cook slowly for about 1 hour or until chicken is tender; sauce will be rather thin. Remove pieces of garlic before serving.

Finalist in 1979 Recipe Contest: KELLY GREENE, Mill Valley, CA

This absolutely mouth-watering chicken dish was unanimously selected as the First Place Winner in the Garlic Recipe Contest and Cook-off. It's a simple, inspired combination that takes only 20 minutes to put together. Serve with cooked Chinese noodles and then stand back and let the compliments fly!

KELLY'S ASIAN CHICKEN

1   3½-lb. frying chicken, cut into serving pieces *or* the equivalent in chicken parts of your choice
3   tablespoons peanut oil
1   head (not clove) fresh garlic, peeled and coarsely chopped
2   small dried hot red peppers (optional)
¾   cup distilled white vinegar
¼   cup soy sauce
3   tablespoons honey

Heat oil in large, *heavy* skillet and brown chicken well on all sides, adding garlic and peppers toward the end. Add remaining ingredients and cook over medium-high heat until chicken is done and sauce has been reduced somewhat. This will not take long, less than 10 minutes. If you are cooking both white and dark meat, remove white meat first, so it does not dry out. Watch very carefully so that the sauce does not burn or boil away. There should be a quantity of sauce left to serve with the chicken, and the chicken should appear slightly glazed. Serve with Chinese noodles, pasta or rice.

If you face toward Gilroy and take a deep breath, you can almost smell the good times being cooked up for the weekend.

San Jose Mercury News

SHANGHAI CHICKEN ON SHANGHAI RICE

For a potluck or to prepare this Oriental chicken dish in advance, bone chicken after it cools and combine chicken and sauce with rice in a casserole, then reheat before serving.

Recipe contest entry: John J. Moon, San Francisco, CA

Shanghai Chicken

  4 tablespoons oil *or* butter *or* combination
 12 medium onions, sliced
     Freshly ground pepper
  1 tablespoon soy sauce
  8 chicken thighs
 ¼ cup grated ginger root, or more if desired
 16 cloves fresh garlic, minced, or more if desired
 ½ cup oyster sauce
  2 tablespoons Worcestershire sauce

Heat oil or butter in large skillet over medium heat, add onions and pepper and saute until onions are golden. Stir in soy sauce. Add chicken, skin side down with skin touching skillet, and continue cooking. While skin browns, top chicken with equal amounts of grated ginger and minced garlic. Turn chicken over so that garlic and ginger are underneath and continue cooking, lowering heat if necessary to prevent burning. Cover chicken with onions and allow to cook for about 10 minutes more. Turn chicken again and top each thigh with oyster sauce. Cook for 5 minutes more and turn chicken again. Cook 5 minutes, turn chicken and add Worcestershire sauce, stirring into onions. Continue cooking until chicken is thoroughly browned and onions have reduced to form a sauce. Total cooking time is approximately 1 hour.

Shanghai Rice

  1 cup rice
 ½ lb. ham, cut into small chunks
  1 cup peas, fresh *or* frozen
     Small chunks of peeled ginger root (optional)

Prepare rice according to package directions. Cook the ham, peas and optional ginger in with the rice. Serve chicken over rice. Makes 4 to 6 servings.

GARLIC CHICKEN WITH PLUM SAUCE

Here are two recipes in one. The pickled garlic that is one of the main ingredients must be made at least 1 month before you prepare the chicken dish. Be sure to make several batches. Pickled garlic is an outstanding condiment.   *Recipe contest entry: Kathleen McElroy, Madison, WI*

Pickled Garlic
Put 2 or 3 heads of garlic, separated into cloves but unpeeled, into a small jar with tightly fitting lid. Add white vinegar and sugar to cover, adding ½ teaspoon sugar for each ½ cup vinegar. Refrigerate 1 month before using. Keeps indefinitely.

Garlic Chicken
  1 chicken breast, skinned, boned and partially frozen for easy slicing
  2 tablespoons Chinese plum sauce
  1 tablespoon Japanese soy sauce
  1 tablespoon cornstarch
  1½ teaspoons pickled garlic vinegar
  6 to 8 large dried Chinese mushrooms
  2 scallions
  4 large cloves pickled garlic
  2 thin slices fresh ginger
  3 tablespoons vegetable oil

Slice chicken breast thin and mix with 1 tablespoon plum sauce, soy sauce, cornstarch and pickled garlic vinegar. Let sit for 30 minutes. Meanwhile, soak mushrooms in lukewarm water for 30 minutes. Squeeze dry, cut out tough center stem and slice into thin strips. Split scallions lengthwise and shred into 1-inch lengths. Peel pickled garlic and mince. Chop ginger fine. Heat oil in wok or heavy skillet over high heat. Stir garlic and ginger in hot oil until they begin to brown. Add marinated chicken and stir until cooked through. Remove chicken and add remaining 1 tablespoon cooking oil. Quickly stir scallions, mushrooms and remaining 1 tablespoon plum sauce in oil until vegetables are wilted. Return chicken to mixture and stir until heated through. Serve with rice. Makes 2 servings.

WOKING GARLIC CHICKEN

The slightly Oriental touch in the recipe has great appeal, especially for kids. If you don't have a wok, use a large skillet or electric frying pan.   *Recipe contest entry: Marlene Sasaki Jose, Los Angeles, CA*

3 large dried shiitake mushrooms
1 lb. diced boned chicken breast
1 tablespoon dry white wine
¼ teaspoon *each* salt and pepper
1 can (14½ oz.) chicken broth
¼ cup tomato paste
2 tablespoons cornstarch
2 tablespoons brandy
   Salt and pepper to taste
2 tablespoons peanut oil
1 whole head fresh garlic, peeled and sliced
1 large green bell pepper, seeded and julienned
1 small onion, chopped
1 can (8 oz.) water chestnuts, drained and coarsely chopped
   Cilantro for garnish

Soak dried mushrooms in small bowl of hot water. Set aside for 20 minutes. Place chicken in bowl and cover with wine and salt and pepper. Set aside. Rinse soaking mushrooms, squeeze out excess water, cut stem off at base and discard. Slice mushrooms very thin. Combine broth, tomato paste, cornstarch, brandy and salt and pepper; set aside. Turn heat in wok on medium-high. Place 2 tablespoons oil in wok. When oil begins to smoke, lift and tilt wok slightly to coat cooking surface. Place chicken gently into oil and toss to stir-fry for 2 minutes or until chicken turns white with no pink showing. Remove from wok. Add 1 tablespoon oil and when it begins to smoke, add garlic, green pepper and onion. Stir-fry for 2 to 3 minutes. Add water chestnuts and mushrooms; stir-fry 1 minute. Return chicken to wok and pour sauce mixture over. Cook 5 minutes, stirring occasionally. Sauce will thicken. serve on rice, garnished with cilantro. Makes 4 servings.

CHICKEN MAUI

Pineapple slices, lichee nuts and kumquats add a touch of the Hawaiian islands to this recipe for stuffed chicken breasts.

Recipe contest entry: Barbara Cohen, Philadelphia, PA

1 lb. ground pork
1 small onion, minced
3 or more cloves fresh garlic, minced
2 green onions, chopped
2 tablespoons oil
½ cup bread crumbs
1 egg
¼ cup plus 1 tablespoon soy sauce
1 can (8 oz.) water chestnuts, drained and chopped
6 small whole chicken breasts, boned and skinned
½ cup chicken broth
1 tablespoon honey
Black pepper to taste
6 tablespoons sesame seeds
1 can (15¼ oz.) pineapple slices, drained
1 can (11 oz.) lichee nuts, drained
1 jar (8 oz.) kumquats, drained
Curly parsley

In large skillet, saute pork, onion, garlic and green onions in oil until pork loses pinkness. Remove from heat. Add bread crumbs, egg, ¼ cup soy sauce and water chestnuts. Stuff chicken breasts with this mixture, securing with toothpicks or wooden skewers if necessary. In large baking dish, mix broth, honey, 1 tablespoon soy sauce and pepper. Place chicken in pan and bake 35 minutes at 325 degrees, turning once and basting. Sprinkle with sesame seeds and top with pineapple. Broil for 3 minutes and remove to heated platter. Garnish with lichee nuts, kumquats and curly parsley. Makes 6 servings.

HODGE-PODGE CHICKEN BAKE

This delicious dish has a slightly Oriental flavor. True garlic lovers may wish to increase the garlic in this recipe to make its flavor more dominant.

Recipe contest entry: Cynthia Kannenberg, Brown Deer, WI

2   3½-lb. broiler-fryer chickens, each, each cut into 8 pieces
    Salt and pepper to taste
1   tablespoon paprika
1   can (1 lb. 4 oz.) pineapple chunks
1   can (8 oz.) tomato sauce
1   can (6 oz.) frozen orange juice concentrate
6   cloves fresh garlic, minced
¼   cup packed brown sugar
1   teaspoon cinnamon
½   teaspoon dry mustard
1   can (11 oz.) mandarin orange segments, drained

Sprinkle chicken on all sides with salt, pepper and paprika. Place in large 12x18-inch roasting pan. Drain pineapple, reserving juice. Mix 1 cup pineapple juice with tomato sauce, orange juice concentrate, garlic, sugar, cinnamon and mustard; pour over chicken. Bake at 350 degrees for about 1¼ hours, basting every 15 minutes. Add more pineapple juice if necessary. Add pineapple chunks the last 5 minutes of baking. Serve on bed of hot rice, garnished with orange segments. Makes 8 servings.

CHINESEY CHICKEN WINGS

This economical main dish can be baked a little quicker if you prefer. Try 375 degrees for 1 hour if you are in a hurry.

Recipe contest entry: Robyn Flipse, Ocean, NJ

3 to 4 lb. chicken wings
    Salt and pepper to taste
5   tablespoons honey
4   tablespoons soy sauce
3   tablespoons brown sugar
1   tablespoon minced fresh garlic
1   teaspoon lemon juice
6   peppercorns
1   cup hot water

Cut tips from chicken wings and reserve for another use. Cut remaining wing in half at joint. Rinse chicken and pat dry. Set in ungreased, shallow baking pan in single layer. Sprinkle with salt and pepper. Mix together in a small jar the remaining ingredients; cover and shake well. Pour over wings. Cover pan with foil and bake for 2 hours at 325 degrees. Remove foil, reduce heat to 300 degrees and continue baking another 30 minutes, basting wings with drippings every 10 minutes. When wings are brown, remove and drain on paper towels. Serve hot or cold. Makes 4 to 5 servings.

CHICKEN A LA BRAZIL

The use of garlic is a part of almost every cuisine. This recipe calls on Brazil for inspiration, but Brazil, in turn, draws on Africa. No matter the country, garlic and food are good companions.

Recipe contest entry: Lirian Connell, San Rafael, CA

5 cloves fresh garlic
Salt
2 medium-sized onions, minced
1 medium-sized chicken, cut into pieces
2 tablespoons vegetable oil
3 large peeled tomatoes, seeds removed
3 tablespoons chopped green pepper
⅛ teaspoon Tabasco sauce
Ground black pepper
2 tablespoons chopped parsley
2 cups whole kernel corn, fresh or frozen

Mash 2 cloves garlic with ½ teaspoon salt until salt is moist. Add half the minced onion and mix thoroughly. Brush chicken with this paste and let marinate overnight. In frying pan, brown chicken in oil. Remove and set aside. Mince remaining 3 cloves garlic; add to frying pan and brown with remaining onion. Add chicken, cover and cook for 10 to 15 minutes over low heat. Stir occasionally. Add tomatoes, green pepper, Tabasco, salt and pepper to taste, and let cook for about 20 minutes. Add parsley and corn and continue cooking for 10 minutes more. Serve with white rice.

POLLO AL AJULLO

No matter what language you say it in, garlic goes with chicken. In this Latin recipe the sauce is completed with a bit of sherry and thickened slightly before serving.

Recipe contest entry: the Fernandez-Carozzi family, San Mateo

2 medium-sized broiler-fryer chickens
1 cup olive oil
10 cloves fresh garlic, minced
1 large onion, chopped
1 teaspoon cornstarch
1 cup sherry
Salt and pepper to taste

Cut up chickens and fry in large pan with olive oil. When chicken is cooked, remove from pan and set aside. Add garlic and onion and saute in oil; when light brown add cornstarch and sherry. Return chicken to pan and let cook another 5 to 10 minutes. Season with salt and pepper.

GYPSY GARLIC CHICKEN

This is a true garlic lover's adaptation of a classic recipe that always begins: "First you steal the chicken . . . ."

Recipe contest entry: Jeanne D'Avray, Metairie, LA

21 or more cloves fresh garlic, peeled
 8 chicken breast halves and 4 legs
 2 tablespoons cooking oil
 2 medium onions, sliced
1½ cups water
 1 can (8 oz.) tomato sauce
 ½ cup dry sherry
 2 tablespoons sugar
 1 tablespoon vinegar
 1 teaspoon *each* salt and chervil
 2 large bay leaves
 1 heaping tablespoon whole peppercorns
 1 cheesecloth square, 4x4 inches
   Lemon slices and parsley for garnish

Cut 5 garlic cloves into thin slices. With sharp-pointed knife, pierce chicken skin at 1½-inch intervals and insert garlic slices between the skin and the flesh. Heat oil to medium-high and saute chicken, onions and remaining whole garlic cloves until chicken is slightly browned, being careful that onions and garlic do not burn. Stir often. Add water, tomato sauce, sherry, sugar, vinegar, salt and chervil; bring to a boil. Wrap bay leaves and peppercorns in cheesecloth and tie opposite ends to make a bag. Drop into boiling sauce; reduce heat, cover, and simmer for 25 to 30 minutes until chicken is tender. Remove spice bag. Secure a parsley sprig into center of 8 lemon slices with a toothpick. Place on top of larger pieces of meat, cover and simmer for 8 minutes. Arrange on platter, decorated with additional fresh parsley, if desired. Serve at once, accompanied by buttered noodles. Makes 8 servings.

FRANCO-SYRIAN CHICKEN

As the name implies this chicken recipe is a combination of French and Syrian cookery. If you prefer, the pine nuts can be ground and used to thicken the gravy. "Serve with French bread and cherry tomatoes" is the recommendation of the chef who created the dish. Definitely a "make-it-again" meal.

Recipe contest entry: Charles Perry, North Hollywood, CA

1 2- to 3-lb. broiler-fryer chicken
5 cloves fresh garlic
2 large lemons
2 tablespoons oil *or* clarified butter
1 cup dry white wine
¼ cup *pignoli* (Italian pine nuts)
1 teaspoon minced parsley
1 teaspoon salt
¼ teaspoon pepper

Cut chicken into frying pieces (wings, legs, thighs, deboned breast cut in quarters), discarding neck, back and giblets. Remove fat and skin. Press 3 large garlic cloves through garlic press onto chicken and rub all over with the garlic. Let stand 10 minutes. Squeeze juice of 1 lemon onto the chicken pieces and marinate chicken in garlic and lemon for 20 minutes, stirring once or twice. Wipe garlic off chicken and pat dry with paper towel. Reserve marinade. Fry chicken in oil over high heat, starting with drumsticks, until the meat stiffens and browns. Add wine and marinade and bring to a boil. Reduce and simmer, covered, over low heat for 25 minutes. Meanwhile brown pine nuts: Either put them in 350-degree oven for about 20 minutes until they are evenly beige, or fry in a little oil or butter over very low heat, stirring constantly until light brown. When chicken is done, remove and sprinkle with parsley. Keep warm. Add juice of second lemon and 1 or 2 more pressed garlic cloves and reduce pan juices over highest heat for 5 minutes. Season with salt and pepper and add pine nuts. Serve chicken with this gravy.

FRENCH GARLIC CHICKEN A LA INGRAM

This recipe was rated a "10" by our testers. What more can we say?

Recipe contest entry: Robert Ingram, Del Mar, CA

9 large cloves fresh garlic, peeled
4 tablespoons fresh lemon juice
4 chicken breasts, boned and skinned
3 tablespoons butter *or* margarine
1 tablespoon cooking oil
1 cup sliced mushrooms
¾ cup dry white wine
1 teaspoon salt
1 bay leaf
¾ cup chicken broth
1½ teaspoons Dijon-style mustard
1 tablespoon chopped parsley

Finely mince or press 4 cloves garlic in small dish with lemon juice. Rub mixture over chicken. Let stand 10 minutes. Meanwhile melt butter and oil over medium heat in large skillet and add chicken. Saute for 12 to 15 minutes, turning once. Add mushrooms, wine, salt and bay leaf and remaining garlic. Cover and cook for 10 to 12 minutes. Blend mustard and broth and add, cooking, covered, for 10 to 15 minutes more or until chicken is tender. Remove chicken and whole garlic cloves to platter and keep warm. Discard bay leaf. Bring pan liquids to boil and cook rapidly to reduce and thicken slightly. Pour liquids over chicken and sprinkle all lightly with parsley. Spread the garlic on bread accompanying the meal! Makes 4 servings.

CHICKEN PIZZAIOLA

So many wonderful Italian dishes are made with a tangy tomato sauce, and they're all good so long as they have plenty of garlic for satisfying flavor.

1 3-lb. broiler-fryer chicken
¼ cup butter *or* margarine
2 teaspoons seasoned salt
1 teaspoon Italian seasoning
½ teaspoon salt
½ teaspoon garlic powder
¼ teaspoon black pepper
1 cup milk
1 cup canned tomatoes
1 tablespoon flour
2 tablespoons water

Cut chicken in pieces. Brown on all sides in butter. Combine seasonings, milk and tomatoes; pour over chicken. Cover and simmer 45 minutes or until chicken is tender. Remove chicken to serving dish. Blend flour and water together; add to liquid in skillet. Simmer over low heat, stirring, until sauce thickens. Pour over chicken.

MY OWN BREATHTAKING CACCIATORE

The Italian word *cacciatore* literally means "hunter," but since this dish smells so good while it's cooking, you'll not likely have to hunt for an eager audience to sample it when it's ready.

Recipe contest entry: Mrs. Bern H. Gershick, Los Angeles, CA

1 3-lb. chicken, cut in pieces
3 tablespoons cooking oil
1 cup sliced onions
3 cloves fresh garlic, minced
1 can (1 lb.) tomatoes
1 can (8 oz.) tomato sauce
1 teaspoon salt
1 teaspoon oregano
1 teaspoon celery seed
¼ teaspoon pepper
½ lb. shredded Mozzarella cheese

In large skillet, brown chicken parts in hot oil. Remove chicken and drain on brown paper. Saute onions and garlic in remaining oil in skillet until soft, but not brown. Add tomatoes, tomato sauce, salt, oregano, celery seed and pepper. Bring to boil, then cover and simmer 30 minutes. Place chicken and sauce in 1½-quart casserole. Cover and bake at 350 degrees for 30 minutes, or until chicken is tender. Remove cover and sprinkle with cheese. Return to oven and bake until cheese melts. Serve with pride.

CHICKEN ALLA TOSCANO

This chicken entree can be made ahead in a large baking dish, covered with foil and refrigerated until ready to bake. May take slightly longer to cook if cold when placed in the oven.

Recipe contest entry: Carole A. Lake, Gilroy, CA

1 3- to 3½-lb. frying chicken, cut in serving pieces
Flour
Cooking oil
6 cloves fresh garlic, minced
3 medium leaves fresh basil, chopped fine
½ cup chopped fresh parsley
1 can (5 oz.) button mushrooms, drained
¼ cup butter
⅓ cup dry white wine
Salt and pepper to taste
Fresh parsley sprigs for garnish

Dredge chicken in flour and brown in oil over medium heat. Place browned chicken in large baking dish and set aside. Saute garlic, basil and parsley in butter. Drizzle evenly over chicken. Slowly pour wine and mushrooms over. Salt and pepper lightly; cover with foil and bake at 350 degrees for 40 minutes or until done. Garnish with parsley sprigs if desired. Makes 4 servings.

GILROY CHICKEN PAPRIKA

Hungarians also like garlic, especially when it's combined with sour cream and mushrooms with the spicy addition of paprika. Serve this dish with . . . what else? Buttered noodles!

1	3-lb. chicken
¼	cup flour
2	teaspoons seasoned salt
1½	teaspoons paprika
½	teaspoon garlic powder
¼	teaspoon black pepper
¼	teaspoon ginger
¼	teaspoon basil leaves
	Dash nutmeg
2	tablespoons butter *or* margarine
2	tablespoons shortening
¼	cup sherry *or* water
2	teaspoons Worcestershire sauce
1	teaspoon chicken-seasoned stock base
1	can (4 oz.) mushrooms
1	cup sour cream

Cut chicken in pieces; coat with mixture of flour, seasoned salt, paprika, garlic powder, pepper, ginger, basil leaves and nutmeg. Heat butter and shortening in heavy skillet. Brown chicken slowly. Combine sherry, Worcestershire sauce and seasoned stock base; pour over browned chicken. Add mushrooms, cover and simmer 45 minutes or until tender. Remove chicken to serving platter. Blend sour cream with drippings in skillet; stir 2 to 3 minutes until sour cream is heated but do not allow it to boil. Pour sauce over chicken; sprinkle with additional paprika. Makes 4 servings.

CHICKEN CURRY WITH PEACHES

Definitely a dish for company. It takes a little time to prepare, but is truly a delight.   *Recipe contest entry: Karen Harmatuik, San Francisco, CA*

½	cup butter
½	cup chopped onion
4	cloves fresh garlic, minced *or* pressed
2	teaspoons curry powder
3	teaspoons paprika
6	chicken breast halves thighs
1	bunch broccoli, cut into pieces
1	small head cauliflower, separated into florets
¾	cup dry white wine
12	canned *or* fresh peach halves, sliced
2	cups yogurt
½	cup mayonnaise
½	cup grated Monterey Jack cheese

Melt butter in small skillet. Add onion and garlic; saute until onion is soft. Stir in curry and paprika. Dip chicken in mixture until well coated; place in shallow baking dish. Steam broccoli and cauliflower briefly and arrange among chicken pieces. Carefully drizzle wine between chicken pieces. Cover loosely with foil and bake at 375 degrees for 30 minutes. Remove from oven and discard foil. Place peaches among chicken and vegetables. Mix yogurt and mayonnaise and spoon over chicken. Sprinkle with cheese. Place on lower rack of oven and broil for 8 to 10 minutes or until lightly browned. Makes 6 servings.

CHICKEN KARMA

This is a dish for lovers of Indian cuisine as well as garlic. Some may wish to cut back a bit on the ginger.

Recipe contest entry: Elizabeth Balderston, Ramona, CA

4 tablespoons butter
1 large onion, thinly sliced
6 cloves fresh garlic, diced
1 tablespoon fresh ginger, diced
¾ teaspoon whole cumin seed
½ teaspoon *each* coriander and mustard seed
½ teaspoon crushed red chiles
3 chicken breasts, skinned, boned and cubed
3 tablespoons raw almonds, ground in electric blender
1 teaspoon turmeric
½ teaspoon salt
¼ teaspoon *each* ground cloves and cinnamon
½ cup plain yogurt
¼ cup chopped fresh cilantro
1 tablespoon lemon juice

Melt butter in large, heavy skillet or Dutch oven over medium-high heat. Cook onion, garlic and ginger until onion is tender. Add cumin, coriander seed, mustard seed and chiles; cook 2 minutes. Add chicken; stir and cook until chicken begins to turn white. Stir in almonds, turmeric, salt, cloves and cinnamon; cook another minute. Add yogurt; stir until blended, then reduce heat, cover and simmer for 1 hour. Just before serving, stir in cilantro and lemon juice. Serve over rice. Makes 4 servings.

CREPES POULE A LA GARLIC

A little time consuming, but well worth the effort. For extra garlic flavor, be sure to have some garlic oil on hand to add to the crepe batter. Just add a few cloves of peeled fresh garlic to a bottle of vegetable oil a few days before you decide to prepare this recipe. You'll find it good for other uses, too.   *Recipe contest entry: Marty Tielemans, Gilroy, CA*

Veloute Sauce
⅓ cup butter
3½ tablespoons flour
1 cup chicken broth

Melt butter; stir in flour, cook over medium heat until golden in color. Gradually stir in broth. Cook, stirring, until thick. Set aside.

Filling
¼ lb. mushrooms, sliced
2 tablespoons butter
1 cup cooked chicken chunks
6 cloves fresh garlic, finely chopped
2 tablespoons chopped green onion
1 tablespoon sherry
½ teaspoon salt
3 dashes Tabasco
⅓ cup Veloute Sauce (above)

Brown mushrooms in butter. Add chicken, garlic, onion, sherry, salt and Tabasco. Mix well. Add Veloute Sauce to moisten.

Crepes
4 eggs
1½ cups milk
1 cup sifted flour
¼ cup sherry
2 teaspoons garlic-flavored oil
1 dash salt
1 dash nutmeg

Blend all ingredients and cook crepes in crepe pan or on hot buttered griddle. Use about 2 tablespoons batter for each crepe.

Topping for Crepes
1 cup Veloute Sauce
½ cup whipping cream
1 beaten egg yolk
¼ cup butter
1 cup grated Romano cheese
2 teaspoons paprika

Place remaining Veloute Sauce in pan; add cream and stir until smooth. Add egg and butter.

Assemble crepes by placing equal amounts of chicken filling across center of each crepe and roll up. Place rolled side down in shallow baking pan. Cover with topping; sprinkle with cheese and paprika. Broil until golden brown.

HERBED CHEESE AND CHICKEN IN PUFF PASTRY

A lovely main course for family and guests, this recipe is not at all difficult to prepare and makes a beautiful presentation.

Recipe contest entry: Mary Jane Himel, Palo Alto, CA

20 large cloves fresh garlic
6 chicken thighs
2½ cups chicken broth
9 slices bacon, fried
5 oz. cream cheese
1½ teaspoons tarragon
1 pkg. (10 oz.) frozen puff pastry patty shells, thawed
1 egg, slightly beaten

Blanch garlic in boiling water 1 minute. Peel. Place with chicken and broth in saucepan and simmer gently, covered, for 30 minutes. Remove chicken and garlic from broth. Skin chicken and remove bones. Place 1½ slices bacon where bones were. Puree garlic with 3 tablespoons broth, cream cheese and tarragon. On lightly floured board, roll out a pastry shell into an 8-inch circle. Put a stuffed chicken thigh on top, then 2 tablespoons garlic-cheese mixture. Moisten edges of pastry with a finger dipped in cold water. Gather edges at the top and crimp to seal. Repeat with remaining 5 shells. Place filled pastries on lightly buttered baking sheet. Brush tops with beaten egg and bake at 400 degrees for 25 minutes or until golden brown. Makes 6 servings.

The annual Gilroy Garlic Festival has grown from a small food editors' luncheon into one of America's largest urban fairs.

Family Weekly

CHICKEN AND SAUSAGE RAGOUT ALLA ROSINA

The definition of "ragout" is "a highly seasoned dish of stewed meat and vegetables." In this recipe the seasoning begins with 20 cloves of fresh garlic, the meat includes chicken and spicy Italian sausage and the vegetables, mushrooms and red peppers and the finished product is outstanding! And it's even better the next day!

Recipe contest entry: Rosina Wilson, Albany, CA

1 3-lb frying chicken, cut into pieces
1 1 lb. Italian-style fennel sausages, halved
¼ cup olive oil
1 large onion, minced
½ lb. button mushrooms
20 or more cloves fresh garlic, peeled
⅓ cup brandy
1 can (28 oz.) Italian-style plum tomatoes, chopped
2 cups red wine
3 bay leaves
½ teaspoon fennel seeds
1 roasted red pepper, cut in strips (canned may be used)
3 sprigs *each* fresh oregano and parsley
   Salt and pepper to taste
12 oz. fusilli (spiral noodles)
   Parmesan cheese, freshly grated

In large skillet, brown chicken and sausages in oil. Transfer to large heatproof casserole. Saute onion, mushrooms and garlic briefly in oil that remains; add brandy, then increase heat and ignite. Pour mixture, along with tomatoes, wine, bay leaves and fennel seeds into the casserole and simmer 1 hour, skimming fat frequently. Add roasted pepper, oregano and parsley; simmer 10 more minutes to blend flavors. Skim fat, add salt and pepper. Serve over fusilli which has been cooked *al dente* according to package directions. Sprinkle liberally with Parmesan cheese. Makes 4 to 6 servings.

PHONY ABALONE

The longer the chicken marinates, the more it tastes like abalone! Left-over clam juice can be used to make chowder by adding celery, potato, pepper, one can baby clams and milk for white chowder or a little water and cut-up fresh tomatoes for red chowder. And you can change the recipe to "Unreal Veal" by adding Parmesan cheese to the bread crumbs and omitting the tartar sauce.

Recipe contest entry: Sylvia Walker, Monterey, CA

4 chicken breast halves, boned, skinned and sliced into thin steaks
1 bottle (8 oz.) clam juice
6 cloves fresh garlic, peeled and halved
2 eggs, lightly beaten
1½ cups fine bread crumbs
4 to 6 tablespoons butter
Lemon wedges
Tartar sauce (optional)

Place chicken steaks between 2 sheets of waxed paper and pound thin. Place in flat airtight container. Pour clam juice over and add fresh garlic. Cover and refrigerate for 36 to 48 hours, turning chicken once or twice if clam juice does not cover completely. Drain chicken. Dip in beaten egg, then in bread crumbs. Saute lightly in butter. Serve with lemon wedges and tartar sauce if desired. Makes 4 servings.

SQUABS A LA SANTA CRUZ

Squab is a term used in the U.S. and Britain for a young pigeon, weighing usually no more than a pound. If not available, substitute Rock Cornish game hens which are available frozen at most supermarkets.

Recipe contest entry: Lisa Gorman, San Francisco, CA

2 squabs, 1 to 1¼ lb. *each*
6 tablespoons butter
8 cloves fresh garlic, peeled and finely chopped
1 medium tomato, peeled, seeded and finely chopped
2 tablespoons chopped parsley
Pinch of thyme
½ cup dry white wine
Garlic salt and pepper to taste
Lemon pepper and salt to taste (optional)
6 fresh mushrooms, sliced

Split squabs and remove breast-bones. In skillet, sear squabs on both sides in hot butter. Add garlic, tomato, parsley and thyme. Blend well, then add wine, salt and pepper. Cover and cook over low heat about 30 minutes. Add mushrooms and continue cooking for 10 to 15 minutes until squab is tender. Serve garnished with thin slices of orange with noodles or rice. Makes 2 to 3 servings.

Finalist in 1980 Recipe Contest:

HELEN HEADLEE, South San Francisco, CA

"So pretty with their golden brown glaze and even better to eat. Everyone will think that you spent all day slaving over a hot oven," says Helen Headlee, two-time finalist in the Great Garlic Cook-off.

HELEN'S BAGGY HENNY

1   pkg. (6 oz.) long grain and wild rice mixture (*or* use your favorite stuffing)
2   cups water
4 to 6 Cornish game hens (one per person)
½   cup soy sauce
½   cup honey
½   teaspoon paprika
1½   teaspoons salt
8   cloves fresh garlic, peeled and sliced
3   slices ginger root, peeled and cut coarsely
2   cups flour
4 to 6 small brown paper bags (lunch size)
      Salad oil

Cook rice using 2 cups water for 20 minutes. Allow to cool. Wash and dry hens. Cook soy sauce, honey, seasonings, garlic, and ginger together, stirring until it comes to a boil. Remove from heat.

Put flour into a large paper or plastic bag. Place hens in the bag and shake until hens are coated with flour. Roll the floured hen in the soy mixture or spoon this sauce on, coating the entire hen thoroughly.

Put small paper bags on a cookie sheet (do one at a time). Pour salad oil over the bag, saturating it well. (This is the messy part and you'll say "Ugh," but keep on.) When all the bags are soaked with oil set them aside. Wipe excess oil off cookie sheet. Spoon the cooked rice (or stuffing) into the hen. Slip the hen into the oiled paper bag. Staple the end shut. Place the bagged hens on cookie racks on the cookie sheet. Bake at 350 degrees for 1 hour. Split bag open. If not brown enough, return to oven for a few more minutes.

OYSTER SAUCE TURKEY BREAST WITH PEAS AND MUSHROOMS

Although this recipe could be made with soy sauce as a substitute for the oyster sauce, the dish has a much richer flavor made with the latter. Available in the Oriental section of most supermarkets, oyster sauce is a concentrated concoction of oysters cooked in soy sauce and brine.

Recipe contest entry: Cecilly Jacobsen, Fallon, NV

1½ lb. boned turkey breast
2 tablespoons vegetable oil
4 large cloves fresh garlic, peeled and minced
1 piece fresh ginger, 2 inches long, peeled and minced
½ cup chicken stock *or* bouillon
4 tablespoons oyster sauce
1 tablespoon *each* soy sauce and sherry
1 teaspoon sugar
1 pkg. (10 oz.) frozen green peas
1 can (4 oz.) button mushrooms, drained
2 teaspoons cornstarch mixed with 2 teaspoons water
1 green onion, chopped fine

Cut turkey into 1-inch cubes. Heat oil in wok or skillet; add garlic and ginger and stir-fry, being careful not to burn garlic. Add turkey and stir-fry to brown lightly. Mix chicken stock, oyster sauce, soy sauce, sherry and sugar and pour over turkey, stirring to coat turkey well. Cover and reduce heat; simmer for about 5 minutes. Stir in peas and mushrooms and stir until heated through, about 2 minutes. Stir cornstarch mixture and add to turkey. Cook, stirring, until mixture thickens slightly. Serve sprinkled with green onions. Makes 6 servings.

PHEASANT IN A BAG

1 pheasant
Salt and pepper
Butter
4 cloves fresh garlic, minced
1 chopped onion

Salt and pepper pheasant inside and out. Rub butter on outside of pheasant and add garlic, onion and a little butter to cavity of bird. Put bird in a brown bag and tie end. Set on cookie sheet and bake 1½ hours at 350 degrees.

OVEN-FRIED QUAIL

Here are two tempting recipes for preparing game birds from one of the area's best-known hunters—and chefs.

Courtesy of: Peter Moretti, Gilroy, CA

12 quail
1½ cups Sauterne
4 eggs
½ cup milk
1½ cups fine dry bread crumbs
2 teaspoons salt
1 teaspoon pepper
3 cloves fresh garlic, minced
⅔ cup butter *or* margarine

Tie legs of quail together; marinate in Sauterne overnight. Drain and dry thoroughly. Combine eggs and milk. Dip quail in this mixture and in bread crumbs that have been mixed with salt, pepper and garlic. Saute quail in butter until golden brown on all sides. Arrange quail in large shallow baking dish or roasting pan. Cover and bake in 400-degree oven 20 minutes until quail are fork tender.

Seafood

Grilled Fish with Garlic Salsa 271

Mouth-Watering Baked Fish 272

Bass and Swiss Chard 272

Baked Codfish Gilroy Style 273

Trout Saute alla Rosina 273

Baked Trout Montbarry 274

Trout Cantonese a la Gow 275

Herb-Broiled Salmon Steaks 276

Fillets Neapolitan 276

Alla Tamen Fillet of Sole Roll-Ups 277

Sharon's Garlic Monkfish 277

Garlic Shrimp 278

Roger's Scampi 278

Garlic Shrimp au Gratin 279

Tipsy Garlic Shrimp 279

Succulent Sauteed Shrimp 280

Rice a la Najar 280

Stuffed Calamari 281

Baked Squid Sicilian 282

Calamari del Mediterranean 282

Marinated Squid alla Rosina 283

Squid Gilroy for Two 283

Insalata di Calamari 284

Scallops Gilroix 285

Scallops and Mushrooms Brochette 285

Garlic Scallop Saute 286

Scallops in Garlic Mushroom Sauce 286

Garlic Clams 287

Clams Sailor Style 287

Cockles in Garlic Sauce 288

Dungeness Crab Dijonnaise 288

Renee's Seafood Fra Diavolo 289

Jambalaya a la Creole 290

Helen's Seafood Treat 291

Mixed Seafood Saute 291

Supersonic Fish Stew 292

Winner of 1984 Recipe Contest: BEVERLY STONE, Berkeley, CA

"To win first prize, improvise," said Beverly Stone, and improvise she did. Her recipe was developed out of necessity when she found herself with only a few ingredients in the house which, when combined, became an outstanding new garlic salsa to serve over fish. The judges agreed it was quite a catch.

GRILLED FISH WITH GARLIC SALSA

½ cup fruity olive oil
5 tablespoons lemon juice
4 cloves fresh garlic, peeled and slivered
1 bunch fresh cilantro, chopped to make ½ cup, reserving some whole leaves for garnish
Salt and freshly ground pepper to taste
6 firm-fleshed fish fillets, about 6 oz. each and ¾ inch thick*
¼ lb. sweet butter
¼ cup chopped sweet red onion
2 small hot green chiles, finely minced
1 tablespoon finely minced fresh garlic
1 lb. ripe tomatoes, peeled and chopped
Lemon wedges

Mix together olive oil, 4 tablespoons lemon juice, slivered garlic, ¼ cup chopped cilantro and salt and pepper to taste. Add fish fillets and marinate for 1 hour or as long as overnight. Meanwhile prepare Garlic Salsa. In a frying pan over medium heat, melt 2 tablespoons butter. Saute onion, chiles and minced garlic until soft, stirring. Add tomatoes and the remaining 1 tablespoon lemon juice. Cook, stirring, for 10 minutes. Remove from heat and add salt and pepper to taste. Stir in remaining ⅓ cup chopped cilantro. Slowly stir in remaining butter until melted. Barbecue fish over low glowing coals about 7 minutes or until done to your liking, turning fish once. Remove to warm serving platter. Top with Garlic Salsa. Garnish with lemon wedges and reserved cilantro leaves. Makes 6 servings.

* Angler (sometimes called monkfish) is particularly good in this recipe.

Finalist in 1979 Recipe Contest: JEANNE MARKS, Aptos, CA

Jeanne Marks says of her truly mouth-watering baked fish, "The aroma knocks you out." Whole fish are not easy to come by and it's the fortunate chef whose good luck brings him a freshly caught salmon, bass or snapper so he can enjoy this nearly effortless method for cooking it. It is good enough to qualify the author as one of the ten finalists who competed in the Garlic Recipe Contest and Cook-off.

MOUTH-WATERING BAKED FISH

8 to 10 lb. whole fish (salmon, sea bass, red snapper, etc.)
Non-stick vegetable spray coating
¼ cup brandy *or* apple juice
½ cup onion flakes
¼ cup oil *or* melted butter
¼ cup lemon juice
¼ cup soy sauce
4 cloves fresh garlic, minced *or* pressed
2 tablespoons Worcestershire sauce
Salt and pepper to taste
Lemon slices
Paprika

Rinse and dry fish and put into baking dish that has been sprayed with a non-stick spray. Combine all ingredients and pour over fish. Let stand at least 1 hour. Bake in 400-degree oven for about 30 minutes or until fish flakes and has lost its transparency. Baste at least once during baking process. Decorate top with lemon slices and paprika.

BASS AND SWISS CHARD

Long a favorite with Europeans, chard is becoming more popular in this country as people begin to appreciate the need to include more dark, leafy greens in the diet. The chard in this recipe helps to keep the fish moist and benefits from the taste imparted by the other ingredients.   *Courtesy of: Emma Morretti, Gilroy, CA*

2 tablespoons olive oil
1 whole bass, about 4 lb.
Salt and pepper to taste
2 large bunches Swiss chard
4 cloves fresh garlic, minced
2 medium onions, chopped
2 cans (1 lb. *each*) solid pack tomatoes

In large covered roasting pan or casserole, place oil and then bass; sprinkle with salt and pepper. Cut chard in 3-inch pieces and lay on top of bass with garlic and onion. Pour tomatoes on top. Bake at 350 degrees for 1½ hours with cover on. Remove cover and bake another 30 minutes. Serve immediately from the baking dish.

BAKED CODFISH GILROY STYLE

There are many different kinds of fish, including codfish, available from nearby Monterey Bay and the Pacific Ocean. This recipe, which includes both potatoes and tomatoes, becomes a meal-in-one. Just serve it with a green salad and your favorite wine.

Recipe contest entry: Aurelia Verissimo, Gilroy, CA

⅔ cup salad oil
4 cloves fresh garlic, crushed
8 sprigs fresh parsley, chopped
6 large new potatoes
2 green onions, chopped
Salt
2 lb. fresh codfish
1 large tomato
1 lemon
Fresh parsley sprigs

Mix salad oil, garlic and parsley in a measuring cup. Peel and slice potatoes ¼ inch thick. Mix well with ½ garlic mixture and green onions. Spread in a 9x13 baking dish. Salt generously. Bake 20 minutes at 450 degrees. Remove from oven and place fish fillets on potatoes. Pour remaining garlic mixture evenly over fish. Salt again. Return pan to oven and bake 15 minutes. Garnish with thinly sliced tomatoes, lemon wedges and parsley. Makes 6 servings.

TROUT SAUTE ALLA ROSINA

Contest winner Rosina Wilson definitely has a way with garlic, and her recipes are always relatively easy to prepare, something other busy people will appreciate.

Recipe contest entry: Rosina Wilson, Albany, CA

4 trout, 12 oz. *each*
¼ cup olive oil
½ cup *each* fine cornmeal and freshly grated Parmesan cheese
¼ teaspoon salt
¼ cup butter
20 cloves fresh garlic, minced
¾ cup dry white wine
¼ cup minced parsley
4 tablespoons capers, including juice
Juice of 2 lemons
4 lemon wedges

Remove heads, tails and scales from trout. Rinse well; pat dry, then rub skin with a little of the oil. Combine cornmeal, cheese and salt in a long bowl or dish and coat trout generously with the mixture. In a large skillet, saute trout in butter and oil over medium heat for 5 minutes on each side. Add garlic to fish and stir in oil for 2 to 3 minutes. Add wine, parsley, capers and lemon juice and cook for 5 to 10 minutes more, turning once, until trout flakes when tested with fork. Spoon reduced wine sauce over the trout and serve with lemon wedges. Makes 4 servings.

BAKED TROUT MONTBARRY

Mrs. Morretti, whose recipe this is (and whose husband, by the way, is with the Fish and Game Department), did not share with us the secret of the name "Montbarry." However, we are grateful she has shared her most unusual treatment for trout and that we, in turn, can pass it along to you.   *Courtesy of: Emma Morretti, Gilroy, CA*

4   tablespoons butter
1   teaspoon parsley, finely chopped
1   teaspoon onion, finely chopped
4   cloves fresh garlic, minced
3   heaping tablespoons finely chopped raw mushrooms
6   trout
      Salt and pepper to taste
4   egg yolks
3   tablespoons brandy
5   tablespoons soft bread crumbs
5   tablespoons grated cheese (Parmesan *or* Romano)
      Dash of paprika

Using about 1 tablespoon, butter a baking dish thoroughly. Line with mixture of parsley, onion and garlic. Sprinkle mushrooms over and place trout which have been seasoned with salt and pepper on top. Pour over 2 tablespoons melted butter and cover the dish with parchment paper (or brown or waxed paper), heavily buttered with the remaining 1 tablespoon butter. Bake in hot (400- degree) oven for 10 minutes. Meanwhile beat egg yolks well; add brandy. Remove paper from trout and pour egg-brandy mixture over. Sprinkle with bread crumbs and cheese, then paprika. Serve in its own baking dish.

TROUT CANTONESE A LA GOW

One advantage of Chinese cooking is that it preserves the firm texture of fish, and the spices selected tend to highlight the flavor of the fish, bringing all into harmony. Though not traditional by any means, this recipe does call on classic methods and seasonings and produces a dish well worthy of the trout.

Recipe contest entry: Lorraine Soo Storck, Fullerton, CA

2 large trout
1 large bunch scallions
4 cloves fresh garlic, finely chopped
Fresh ginger root
2 tablespoons soy sauce
4 thinly sliced onion rings
¼ cup bacon drippings
4 large tomatoes
Salt, pepper and garlic powder to taste
1 cup water

Clean and slit trout; place in shallow baking dish. Chop scallions and cover fish. Insert some garlic in slits of fish and sprinkle remainder on top of fish with scallions. Slice thin ginger strips and lay on fish lengthwise. Sprinkle soy sauce on fish. Arrange onion rings in circle around fish. Pour bacon drippings over. Quarter tomatoes and circle fish; season with salt, pepper and garlic powder. Sprinkle water over all; cover with aluminum foil and bake in oven slowly for 1 hour at 350 degrees. Reduce heat to 275 degrees and bake for another hour. Baste frequently. Serve with steamed rice. Makes 4 servings.

It can be gentle, alluring and enticing, giving a marvelous subtle flavor to various dishes—a superb herb.

Marie Ryckman
Cincinnati Enquirer

HERB-BROILED SALMON STEAKS

Custom dictates that the cook be gentle when choosing the spices to use in cooking salmon, lest the fish lose its own distinguishing flavor in the process. The seasonings used in this recipe have been carefully selected to blend with and enhance the flavor of the salmon steaks as they broil. However, prejudiced though we may be, the recipe could use just a bit more garlic.

½ cup melted butter
2 teaspoons lemon juice
2 teaspoons seasoned salt
1 teaspoon tarragon
½ teaspoon garlic powder
½ teaspoon ground marjoram
½ teaspoon lemon peel
Dash cayenne or red pepper
2 lb. salmon steaks

Combine melted butter and lemon juice with seasonings. Arrange salmon steaks on greased broiler rack and brush with one half of seasoned butter. Broil 2 inches from heat 5 to 10 minutes. Carefully turn and brush with remaining butter mixture. Broil steaks 7 minutes longer or until they can be flaked easily with a fork. Serve hot, garnished with lemon wedges and sprigs of parsley.

FILLETS NEAPOLITAN

Probably the most famous example of the cooking of Naples is pizza and, although this fish recipe does not contain the cheese usually associated with pizza, it does call for many of the seasonings and familiar tomato sauce, hence the description, Neapolitan.

¼ cup flour
1 teaspoon MSG (optional)
½ teaspoon salt
¼ teaspoon black pepper
2 lb. fish fillets (sole, flounder, perch, etc.)
¼ cup olive oil
1 cup chopped onion
1 can (8 oz.) tomato sauce
1 can (6 oz.) tomato paste
¼ cup water
2 teaspoons parsley flakes
½ teaspoon sugar
½ teaspoon garlic powder
½ teaspoon Italian seasoning

Combine flour, MSG, salt and pepper. Dip fish fillets in seasoned flour, then saute in hot oil until lightly browned on both sides. Remove. Brown onion, then add remaining ingredients. Mix well and simmer 10 minutes. Place fish in sauce and simmer 5 minutes longer or until heated through. Serve with lemon wedges. Makes 4 to 6 servings.

ALLA TAMEN FILLET OF SOLE ROLL-UPS

The influence of the Orient can be found in this recipe—an exotic treatment for a familiar fish. *Recipe contest entry: Stella Wolf, Culver City, CA*

1 lb. fillet of sole
¼ cup peanuts
6 cloves fresh garlic, peeled
4 slices fresh ginger root, about ¼ inch thick, peeled
1 tablespoon salad oil
1 tablespoon lemon
4 teaspoons sesame oil
1 pkg. (10 oz.) frozen peas
1 cup sliced fresh mushrooms (optional)
1 tablespoon *each* soy sauce and lemon juice
1 teaspoon dry mustard powder
2 tablespoons sesame seeds

Rinse sole with cold water and set aside. In blender or food processor, combine peanuts, garlic, ginger, salad oil, lemon juice and 1 teaspoon sesame oil. Spread ¼ of paste on each fillet and roll up. Arrange fish rolls in 7x12x2-inch glass baking dish, surrounded by peas and mushrooms. Blend together remaining sesame oil, soy sauce, lemon juice and mustard. Pour over fish, allowing excess to dribble down to bottom of dish. Sprinkle sesame seeds over. Cover with aluminum foil. Bake at 350 degrees for 15 to 20 minutes or until fish tests done. Serve at once. Makes 4 servings.

SHARON'S GARLIC MONKFISH

Monkfish is also called angler or lotte. It is a firm-fleshed fish that has a flavor and texture resembling lobster.

Recipe contest entry: Sharon Cordonier, San Jose, CA

2 lb. monkfish
20 large mushrooms, sliced
8 large cloves fresh garlic, chopped
3 green onions, with tops, chopped
Salt and pepper to taste
½ lb. butter
1 cup dry white wine
3 tablespoons Worcestershire sauce

Clean monkfish and cut into chunks. In skillet, saute mushrooms, garlic, onions, salt and pepper in ¼ pound butter for 1 minute. Add ½ cup wine and saute until vegetables are tender. Set aside. In another large skillet, melt remaining ¼ pound butter. Add fish and fry until fish turns white. Add Worcestershire sauce and continue cooking, covered, until liquid is reduced to half. Add mushroom-garlic mixture and remaining ½ cup wine. Cook, covered, until liquid is reduced to ¼. Serve over rice, if desired. Makes 4 servings.

GARLIC SHRIMP

A very low-calorie dish which is easy to prepare and would be enjoyed by the whole family, not just the dieters.

Recipe contest entry: Gloria Park, Los Gatos, CA

2 lb. raw shrimp (about 24)
6 cloves fresh garlic, chopped
6 scallions *or* green onions, with tops, minced
⅓ cup chopped fresh parsley
2 teaspoons dry vermouth
½ teaspoon soy sauce
¼ teaspoon Tabasco
8 fresh mushrooms, sliced

Rinse shrimp; remove legs, leaving tails and shells intact. With sharp knife, cut through shells down the back, leaving shells on. Devein shrimp. Mix garlic, onion, parsley, vermouth, soy sauce and Tabasco and toss with shrimp. Marinate in refrigerator for about 1 hour. Add mushrooms and toss again. Cut 2 sheets of heavy-duty foil 18x36 inches. Double each by folding to 18x18 inches. Divide shrimp mixture evenly between the 2 foil sheets, making single layers. Enclose shrimp with double folds on the tops and both sides of the packages so that none of the juices can escape. Place each package on a cookie sheet and bake at 400 degrees for 15 to 20 minutes, until shrimp have turned pink. Serve immediately. Makes 6 servings.

ROGER'S SCAMPI

This seafood dish is equally good served over pasta or rice. It can easily be increased to serve six.   *Recipe contest entry: Roger Kirsch, San Jose, CA*

1 lb. large prawns (12 to 16 per lb.)
4 tablespoons sweet butter *or* margarine
¼ cup olive oil
5 cloves fresh garlic, minced
⅛ teaspoon *each* sweet basil and oregano
   Juice from 1 lemon
   Salt and pepper to taste
¼ cup Triple Sec *or* Cointreau

Shell and devein prawns; rinse and drain. Melt butter in medium skillet; add olive oil, garlic, basil and oregano and lemon juice. Saute for 1 minute. Add prawns and cook until pink. Add salt and pepper and Triple Sec and cook on high until liquid is reduced by ¾. Serve over pasta or rice. Makes 2 to 3 servings.

GARLIC SHRIMP AU GRATIN

This dish is simplicity itself, requiring only a few ingredients and a few minutes of preparation time.

Courtesy of: Fresh Garlic Association

2 lb. raw shrimp
1½ sticks butter (¾ cup)
2 cups fine dry bread crumbs
½ cup finely chopped parsley
4 cloves fresh garlic, minced *or* pressed
Salt and pepper to taste
1 cup dry sherry

Shell and devein shrimp. Toss into boiling water, return to boil and cook for about 2 minutes until shrimp turn all pink. Drain. In large skillet melt 1 stick butter (½ cup) over low heat. Add bread crumbs, parsley, garlic and salt and pepper. Stir a few minutes over low heat; pour in sherry and cook 1 minute more. Place alternate layers of shrimp and bread crumbs in well-buttered gratin dish, ending with bread crumbs. Dot with remaining butter. Bake at 350 degrees for 10 to 15 minutes. Makes 4 servings.

TIPSY GARLIC SHRIMP

This sauteed shrimp recipe calls on white wine to make the sauce, and the report is it makes a delightful contribution to the flavor of the dish.

Recipe contest entry: S. Louise Gershick, Los Angeles, CA

¼ cup butter
3 cloves fresh garlic, crushed
½ lb. whole mushrooms, stems removed
1 tablespoon lemon juice
12 oz. fresh shrimp, shelled and deveined
1 cup white wine
2 tablespoons cornstarch mixed with just enough water to dissolve

Melt butter in large skillet. Add crushed garlic and whole mushrooms. Gently mix in lemon juice and shrimp. (Add more butter, if needed, at this time.) Saute 1 minute on each side, or until pink. Add wine; increase heat and bring to a boil. Remove from heat and add cornstarch mixture. Return to flame until sauce is thickened. Serve over rice.

SUCCULENT SAUTEED SHRIMP

Shrimp vary in flavor, depending on the area and how fresh they are when served. Garlic is a very good seasoning to use with shrimp whether they are highly flavorful or bland.

1 lb. raw shrimp
¼ cup butter
2 tablespoons lemon juice
1 teaspoon parsley flakes
1 teaspoon chives
¾ teaspoon seasoned salt
½ teaspoon garlic powder
½ teaspoon dry mustard
½ teaspoon tarragon leaves
⅛ teaspoon cayenne *or* red pepper

Shell and devein shrimp. Melt butter in chafing dish or skillet; add lemon juice and seasonings. Saute shrimp in hot herb butter over medium heat 8 minutes or until pink, turning once. Serve hot, preferably on a bed of rice. Makes 2 or 3 servings.

RICE A LA NAJAR

Rice can be the star of the meal when cooked to fluffy perfection with chicken stock, tomato juice, garlic and other seasonings. Bright green peas and plump pink shrimp add color and eye appeal.

Recipe contest entry: Marina V. Najar, Gardena, CA

2 tablespoons corn oil
2 cups long grain rice
3 cloves fresh garlic, minced
3 medium-size green onions, chopped
1 teaspoon vinegar
4 cups chicken stock
1 cup sweet peas
½ cup tomato juice
1 teaspoon mustard
Salt and pepper to taste
1 teaspoon thyme
¼ cup margarine
2 cups cooked shrimp, cleaned and deveined
Minced parsley for garnish
Paprika for garnish
Pimento for garnish (optional)

Heat oil in non-stick skillet or pan. Saute rice (do not brown); add garlic, onions and vinegar. Stir gently. Add stock, peas, tomato juice, mustard, salt, pepper and thyme. Stir 2 or 3 times gently. Turn heat to medium-high and boil until water comes to about ½ inch above rice. Reduce heat and simmer for about 25 to 30 minutes, or until rice is done. Grains should look whole and be easy to separate with a fork. Dot generously with margarine. Top with shrimp and cover for about 10 minutes. Sprinkle with minced parsley and a little paprika and serve piping hot. Tiny pieces of pimento can also be used if desired. Makes 6 to 8 servings.

Finalist in 1986 Recipe Contest: TIM E. JONES, San Jose, CA

Squid tubes are filled with a stuffing made with shrimp and crab, then baked in a highly seasoned tomato sauce. It won't matter if some of the filling escapes. It will all go into the sauce.

STUFFED CALAMARI

12 squid tubes, approx.
     1½-inch diameter*
1   bell pepper, finely
     chopped
3   stalks celery, finely
     chopped
5   green onions, finely
     chopped
10 cloves fresh garlic,
     minced
½   lb. shrimp meat, chopped
½   lb. crabmeat, chopped**
     Juice of ½ lemon
2   tablespoons olive oil
2   cans (16 oz. *each*) tomato
     sauce
⅓   cup cooking sherry
2   teaspoons thyme
1   teaspoon *each* oregano,
     basil, garlic salt, crushed
     bay leaves and black
     pepper
1   lb. linguine, cooked and
     drained

Preheat oven to 350 degrees. Rinse squid and pat dry. Mix together bell pepper, celery, onions and garlic. Add ⅓ of mixture to shrimp and crabmeat with lemon juice. Stuff this mixture into the squid tubes and place them in a 9x15-inch baking dish. Heat oil in large skillet and saute remaining pepper, celery, onion and garlic mixture. Add remaining ingredients and simmer 10 to 15 minutes. Pour this sauce over the stuffed squid tubes and bake for 30 minutes. Serve over bed of linguine. (Be sure to have some garlic bread to soak up the sauce.) Makes 6 servings.

* Pre-cleaned squid tubes should be available at fish markets; if you can't find any just cut the tentacles off of fresh squid and clean the tubes.

** Mock crabmeat (again, available at fish markets) is just as good and considerably cheaper than the real stuff.

BAKED SQUID SICILIAN

This recipe can be prepared ahead of time, refrigerated and baked just before serving.

Recipe contest entry: Kay Lucido, Hollister, CA

2 lb. squid, cleaned and drained
1/4 cup vegetable oil
1 bunch parsley, chopped
1 cup toasted bread crumbs
1/2 cup *each* grated Parmesan and Romano cheese
3 cloves fresh garlic, minced
1 teaspoon oregano
Salt and pepper to taste

Dip squid in oil. Combine remaining ingredients. Roll oiled squid in bread crumb mixture; roll up and place on oiled jelly roll pan, cut side down. Bake in preheated 425-degree oven for 20 minutes. Makes 4 servings.

CALAMARI DEL MEDITERRANEAN

An outstanding dish, best served over fresh fettuccine or linguine with freshly grated Romano cheese.

Recipe contest entry: Karen Occhipinti, Los Gatos, CA

4 lb. calamari (squid), cleaned
1 cup plus 3 tablespoons butter
1/2 cup olive oil
10 cloves fresh garlic, minced
Salt and pepper to taste
1/3 cup dry white wine
1 lb. small to medium fresh mushrooms, cut in quarters
3 medium ripe tomatoes, peeled and chopped
1/2 cup chopped fresh parsley
4 to 5 tablespoons fresh chopped basil *or* 1 teaspoon dried basil

Cut calamari into wide strips and rings. Melt 3 tablespoons butter in large skillet; add 3 tablespoons oil, half the garlic, calamari, salt and pepper and saute for 2 minutes. Do not overcook. Drain and reserve liquid. Set calamari aside. In same skillet, melt 1 cup butter, then add remaining oil, all but 1 tablespoon garlic and wine and simmer for 1 to 2 minutes. Add mushrooms, tomatoes and 1/4 cup parsley. Simmer over low heat for 8 to 10 minutes. Add basil and remaining garlic. For thinner consistency, if desired, add reserved liquid. Simmer 2 minutes longer. Serve sprinkled with remaining parsley. Makes 8 servings.

MARINATED SQUID ALLA ROSINA

An outstanding recipe from the winner of the 1982 Recipe Contest. For best flavor, be sure to prepare this several hours before serving time.

Recipe contest entry: Rosina Wilson, Albany, CA

3 lb. squid
¼ cup olive oil
⅛ cup *each* lemon juice and red wine vinegar
1 tablespoon Dijon-style mustard
Salt and pepper to taste
1 medium purple onion, coarsely chopped
1 roasted red bell pepper, cut in strips
½ cup diagonally sliced baby carrots, lightly poached
½ cup Nicoise olives
¼ cup chopped parsley
6 cloves fresh garlic, sliced
3 tablespoons capers
1 tablespoon slivered lemon peel
Lettuce, if desired

Clean squid and cut in rings. Poach in boiling water in small batches for 30 seconds. Drain well. Prepare marinade by mixing olive oil, lemon juice, vinegar, mustard and salt and pepper. Set aside. Combine squid and remaining ingredients in large bowl and pour marinade over. Refrigerate several hours. Serve over lettuce or as an appetizer salad. Makes 8 servings.

SQUID GILROY FOR TWO

Serve this squid dish alone or over spaghetti with a light, fruity Zinfandel and fresh vegetables.

Recipe contest entry: Dr. E. Stoddard, Monterey, CA

2 lb. squid, cleaned and drained
3 or 4 green onions, sliced
3 large cloves fresh garlic, sliced
4 teaspoons olive oil
1 can (8 oz.) tomato sauce
½ cup red wine
½ cup chopped parsley
3 teaspoons Italian seasoning
½ cup grated Parmesan cheese

Cut squid in rings. In large skillet cook onions and garlic in oil until lightly brown, about 2 minutes. Add squid when pan is quite hot and cook approximately 10 minutes, stirring occasionally. Add tomato sauce, wine, parsley and seasoning. Simmer for 10 minutes. Sprinkle with Parmesan, stir well and leave for 1 minute to blend flavors before serving. Makes 2 servings.

INSALATA DI CALAMARI

The Italians like their calamari deep fried, in seafood stews, in sauces for pasta and in many other popular dishes. It is also absolutely delicious served cold as a tangy fresh salad. This recipe could be served in small portions as an appetizer. *Courtesy of: John Filice, Aptos, CA*

5 lb. calamari (squid), cleaned (bodies cut into rings and tentacles separated)
¼ cup olive oil
1 medium-sized bunch parsley, chopped
5 jars (4 oz. *each*) whole pimentos
½ cup olive oil
5 to 10 cloves fresh garlic
1 to 2 cans (2 oz. *each*) anchovy fillets
Worcestershire sauce
1 teaspoon French-style mustard
Red wine vinegar
4 lemons
1 can medium-sized ripe olives

Place cleaned squid in large skillet with natural juices and ¼ cup olive oil. Saute over medium heat until squid is barely cooked, turning frequently. Remove, drain well, and let stand. Chop parsley and pimentos. Pour olive oil into large salad bowl and press half the garlic into the oil. Slice remaining garlic and add to oil. Add anchovy fillets and mash well. Add 2 shakes Worcestershire sauce and mustard. Add red wine vinegar to taste (approximately ¼ cup) and squeeze juice of 2 lemons into mixture. Mix well. Add squid, chopped parsley, pimentos and olives. Toss and refrigerate for at least 5 hours. Mix occasionally. Serve in decorative shallow salad bowl. Garnish with parsley and slices of lemon. Just before serving squeeze 1 or 2 additional lemons on salad.

Finalist in 1980 Recipe Contest: JAMES JEFFERSON, Los Gatos, CA

An aromatic sauce, thick and bubbling, enfolds tender scallops in this luscious appetizer that's served in individual bowls.

SCALLOPS GILROIX

6   tablespoons butter
3   large cloves fresh garlic, finely chopped
½   teaspoon garlic salt
½   teaspoon tarragon, crushed
½   teaspoon pepper medley
¼   cup white wine
½   lb. fresh scallops, rinsed and drained
1   teaspoon cornstarch
½   cup sour cream

Melt butter in a small saucepan. Add garlic, garlic salt, tarragon, pepper medley, and wine. Stir well and bring to a boil. Add scallops and saute 3 minutes. Thicken the sauce with cornstarch. Reduce heat. When mixture stops boiling, stir in the sour cream. Serve in small bowls. Serves 4. The recipe is best used as an appetizer. If used as an entree, double the recipe.

SCALLOPS AND MUSHROOMS BROCHETTE

In some areas fresh scallops are becoming difficult to find and small pieces of shark or other fish are being substituted in the marketplace. Our first choice would be scallops, of course, but this recipe could be used with any similar fish. Be sure not to overcook, particularly if using scallops. They should be slightly *under*done to be at their best flavor.

2   lb. fresh scallops
½   cup olive oil
2   tablespoons lemon juice
2   teaspoons seasoned salt
½   teaspoon garlic salt
¼   teaspoon black pepper
1   bay leaf
8   coriander seeds
    Dash of MSG (optional)
1   can (8 oz.) mushroom caps, drained

Wash and drain scallops and put in flat baking dish. Combine remaining ingredients, except mushrooms, and pour over scallops, turning to coat all sides. Marinate in refrigerator several hours. Thread scallops onto skewers alternately with mushroom caps. Place on rack and broil 3 to 4 inches from heat 8 to 10 minutes. Turn and broil 8 to 10 minutes longer. Brush several times with marinade during broiling. Serve with tartar sauce. Makes 6 to 8 servings.

GARLIC SCALLOP SAUTE

A very simple dish with elegance and good flavor.

Recipe contest entry: Anne McDonald, Morgan Hill, CA

1 lb. scallops
¾ cup milk or enough to cover
⅓ cup flour
4 tablespoons *each* butter and cooking oil
4 cloves fresh garlic, minced
10 fresh mushrooms, thinly sliced
2 shallots, chopped (about 3 tablespoons)
1 teaspoon lemon juice
Sherry

Wash scallops well to remove sand. Place in small bowl and cover with milk. Let stand for 10 minutes. Drain well and coat with flour. Shake off excess flour and set aside. Melt butter in large skillet, add oil and half the garlic and cook a few seconds. Add mushrooms, shallots and remaining garlic. Stir constantly until done. Add scallops and lemon juice; cook for 2 to 3 minutes, stirring occasionally, until scallops are just done. Remove scallops to serving platter and keep warm. Add a dash of sherry and deglaze the pan. Pour over scallops and serve. Makes 4 servings.

SCALLOPS IN GARLIC MUSHROOM SAUCE

When preparing scallops it is extremely important not to overcook them as they can become quite tough and chewy. They are best when cooked until just barely done or even slightly undercooked.

Courtesy of: Fresh Garlic Association

1 lb. scallops
1 tablespoon vegetable oil
4 cloves fresh garlic, minced
1 can (5 oz.) water chestnuts, drained and sliced
2 to 3 tablespoons soy sauce
2 tablespoons cornstarch mixed with 2 tablespoons water
1 teaspoon salt
⅛ teaspoon white pepper
1 cup sliced fresh mushrooms
⅓ cup sliced green onions, including stems

Place scallops in 2 quarts lightly salted water. Bring to a boil. Drain immediately. Heat vegetable oil in wok. Add garlic and stir-fry until golden. Add water chestnuts, soy, cornstarch mixture, salt and pepper and mix. Add scallops and mushrooms and cook, stirring gently, until suace thickens and coats scallops. Remove to platter. Sprinkle with sliced green onion. Makes 2 to 3 servings.

GARLIC CLAMS

Lots of hot sourdough French bread is a must to sop up the delicious juices!

Recipe contest entry: Roberta Robinson, Campbell, CA

12 cloves fresh garlic, minced
 1 bunch green onions, minced
½ cup butter
¼ cup vegetable oil
½ cup chopped parsley
 1 teaspoon Italian seasoning
 1 cup *each* dry white wine, clam juice and water
24 cherrystone clams, brushed and cleaned

In large skillet, saute garlic and onion in butter and oil for 1 minute. Add parsley and seasoning. Add wine, clam juice and water and cook 2 minutes. Now add clams and cook, covered, until clams open, about 10 to 12 minutes. Serve in bowls. Makes 2 servings.

CLAMS SAILOR STYLE

Although the author of this recipe says the chopped chile is optional, we recommend you include it, for it gives the dish a most distinctive flavor.

Recipe contest entry: Fernandez-Carozzi family, San Mateo, CA

20 medium-size clams
 8 cloves fresh garlic, minced
 6 tablespoons olive oil
 3 tablespoons chopped parsley
 2 tablespoons fine dry bread crumbs
    Salt to taste
 1 cup white wine *or* sherry
 1 chile, chopped (optional)

Soak clams in salty water for 5 hours before preparing dish, and rinse. In a large pan, saute garlic in oil. Add parsley and clams; cover 5 to 10 minutes to open the clams. Once clams are open, add bread crumbs, salt, white wine and chile. Move pan back and forth for about 5 minutes over medium heat until sauce thickens. Makes 4 servings.

COCKLES IN GARLIC SAUCE

In England and Ireland, cockles are eaten cold with a little vinegar, but Californians like their cockles prepared with. . .you guessed it! Garlic! We think you will enjoy this simple dish.

Recipe contest entry: Donald A. Hunter, Novato, CA

35 cockles (hard-shell clams) ½ yellow onion, sliced in rings 1 cup water ½ cup white wine 4 tablespoons butter 3 cloves fresh garlic, minced ¼ teaspoon thyme ½ teaspoon minced parsley 1 tablespoon flour, heaping	Steam clams with onion rings, water and white wine until shells open. Remove clam meat and chop well. Reserve 1¼ cups of clam broth. Melt butter and saute garlic. Add thyme, parsley and flour. Stir well. Slowly add reserved clam broth and then chopped clams. Simmer for 10 minutes. Serve over noodles or fresh pasta.

DUNGENESS CRAB DIJONNAISE

Dungeness crab, usually weighing about 3 pounds, are native to the Pacific Northwest and have a distinctively sweet taste. Any crabmeat can be substituted in this recipe if Dungeness is not available. Best served over a pasta such as fettuccine.

Recipe contest entry: Norman Noakes, Corvallis, OR

1 lb. Dungeness crabmeat 4 tablespoons butter 3 cloves fresh garlic, minced ½ lb. fresh mushrooms, thinly sliced 2 tablespoons finely chopped shallots, scallions *or* green onions ½ cup dry white wine ½ cup whipping cream 1 tablespoon Dijon-style mustard Salt and pepper to taste Lemon juice to taste Minced fresh parsley	In skillet, saute crab in butter for 3 to 4 minutes. Remove crab and keep warm. Add garlic, shallots and mushrooms. Cook for 1 minute. Deglaze pan with wine. Reduce to 2 tablespoons. Add cream and reduce until thick. Whisk in mustard. Do *not* boil. Add salt, pepper and lemon juice. Return crab to pan and toss quickly in sauce. Serve over fettuccine. Sprinkle with parsley. Makes 4 servings.

Winner of 1985 Recipe Contest: RENEE N. TELESE, Saugus, CA

The base for the sauce in this dish is a puree of mushrooms, onions, red peppers, mint, basil, oregano and, of course, garlic—½ cup of it. Try this seafood pasta casserole and you'll know why it took first prize in the '85 Cook-off.

RENEE'S SEAFOOD FRA DIAVOLO

½ cup chopped fresh garlic
¼ cup olive oil
1 small lobster in the shell (about 1 lb.), cleaned, small claws and antennae removed
6 large shrimp, cleaned and deveined
¼ lb. fresh mushrooms, sliced
1 small onion, chopped
5 leaves *each* fresh mint, fresh basil and fresh oregano, chopped
¼ to ½ teaspoon crushed dried red pepper
1 teaspoon clam *or* chicken soup base (paste *or* granulated)
1 cup dry white *or* red wine
1 can (28 oz.) whole Italian tomatoes with basil, including juice
8 large mussels, scrubbed
6 large clams, scrubbed
¼ cup chopped fresh parsley
1 lb. thin spaghetti *or* vermicelli, cooked and drained

In 14-inch skillet, cook ¼ cup garlic in hot oil over high heat for 2 to 3 minutes, being careful not to burn. Add lobster and shrimp to skillet and cook on high heat for 3 to 4 minutes, until lobster turns pink. Remove lobster and shrimp and set aside. Add remaining ¼ cup garlic, mushrooms, onion, mint, basil, oregano and red pepper. Cook over medium heat 7 to 9 minutes, stirring frequently. Pour mixture from skillet into blender or food processor. Add clam or chicken soup base, wine and tomatoes and puree. Pour puree into 2- to 3-quart saucepan and cook over medium-high heat, adding mussels and clams when mixture begins to boil. Stir often until mussels and clams open, then add parsley. Remove clams and mussels to dish with lobster and shrimp. Toss pasta with 2 cups of sauce and line bottom of large ovenproof serving platter with coated pasta. Place lobster in center on top of pasta and place shrimp, mussels and clams decoratively on both sides. Pour remaining sauce over the top, being careful not to hide the shellfish. Cover with foil and place in preheated 375-degree oven for 7 to 10 minutes. Serve when piping hot. Makes 4 to 6 servings.

JAMBALAYA A LA CREOLE

To make Jambalaya "Santa Cruz-style" just substitute calamari for the shrimp in this recipe. Great dish for a crowd. Serve with hot cornbread or sweet French bread.

Recipe contest entry: Bruce Engelhardt, Santa Cruz, CA

1½ lb. cooked shrimp (*or* cooked calamari)
1 lb. smoked rope-style sausage, cut in ¼-inch slices
1 lb. ham, diced
½ cup cooking oil
½ cup flour
1 red onion, finely chopped
1 cup chopped green bell pepper
2 stalks celery, finely chopped
2 shallots, chopped
4 or more cloves fresh garlic, chopped
2 tomatoes, chopped
1 can (16 oz.) tomato sauce
1 tablespoon crushed oregano
1 teaspoon salt
½ teaspoon chopped fresh cilantro
¼ teaspoon *each* red pepper, black pepper, ground cloves, allspice and cumin
1 cup red wine
2 bay leaves
½ cup chopped parsley
1 cup hot water
2 cups long grain white rice
¼ cup chopped green onion tops for garnish
Louisiana-style hot sauce, if desired

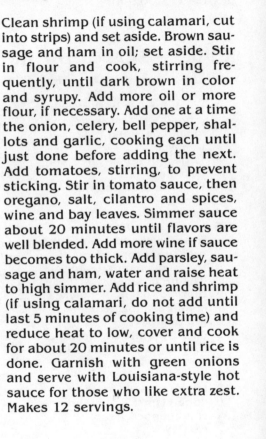

Clean shrimp (if using calamari, cut into strips) and set aside. Brown sausage and ham in oil; set aside. Stir in flour and cook, stirring frequently, until dark brown in color and syrupy. Add more oil or more flour, if necessary. Add one at a time the onion, celery, bell pepper, shallots and garlic, cooking each until just done before adding the next. Add tomatoes, stirring, to prevent sticking. Stir in tomato sauce, then oregano, salt, cilantro and spices, wine and bay leaves. Simmer sauce about 20 minutes until flavors are well blended. Add more wine if sauce becomes too thick. Add parsley, sausage and ham, water and raise heat to high simmer. Add rice and shrimp (if using calamari, do not add until last 5 minutes of cooking time) and reduce heat to low, cover and cook for about 20 minutes or until rice is done. Garnish with green onions and serve with Louisiana-style hot sauce for those who like extra zest. Makes 12 servings.

HELEN'S SEAFOOD TREAT

Fresh shrimp and crabmeat baked in individual casseroles with a rich and buttery garlic sauce.

Recipe contest entry: Helen Cairns, Marblehead, MA

1½ lb. fresh shrimp
8 cups water
3 cloves fresh garlic, chopped
1 onion, quartered
1 bay leaf
8 tablespoons butter
1 teaspoon lemon juice
¾ cup cracker crumbs
½ lb. fresh crabmeat, lobster, scallops *or* other seafood
Lemon wedges and fresh parsley for garnish

Clean shrimp. Boil in water with 1 clove garlic, onion and bay leaf for 5 minutes. Drain. Melt butter in skillet; add remaining garlic and lemon juice. Add half the garlic butter to cracker crumbs. Mix well and set aside. Place shrimp and crabmeat in 4 individual casseroles. Pour remaining garlic butter evenly over seafood. Sprinkle with cracker crumbs and bake at 400 degrees for 5 minutes. Serve piping hot garnished with lemon wedges and parsley. Makes 4 servings.

MIXED SEAFOOD SAUTE

Seafood lovers will recognize quickly how good they can expect this combination to be, and indeed it is. Although not a winner in the 1979 Garlic Recipe Contest, it merited an Honorable Mention. All who tested it rated it excellent.

Recipe contest entry: Carmela Meely, Walnut Creek, CA

½ cup butter
2 tablespoons olive oil
½ lb. raw prawns, shells on
½ lb. scallops
½ lb. crab legs, shells on
⅓ cup chopped parsley
6 cloves fresh garlic, minced
3 chopped shallots
2 tablespoons white wine
2 teaspoons lemon juice
Salt and pepper to taste
1 tablespoon sherry *or* Marsala

Melt butter in pan, and add olive oil. Toss in seafood. When prawns turn pink, add parsley, garlic, shallots, white wine, lemon juice, salt and pepper. Heat through. Stir in sherry. Garnish with lemon slices and serve over rice. Makes 4 servings.

Now garlic is to Gilroy what Mardi Gras is to New Orleans . . .

Los Angeles Herald-Examiner

SUPERSONIC FISH STEW

Whether you call it stew or chowder, this dish has plenty of flavor and is very easy to prepare.

Recipe contest entry: Jacqueline McComas, Frazer, PA

2   tablespoons cooking oil
1   cup chopped onions
3   cloves fresh garlic, minced
¼   cup *each* chopped green bell pepper and celery
2   lb. seafood, cut up (scallops, shrimp, flounder, etc. *or* mix)
1   can (10¾ oz.) condensed tomato soup, undiluted
1   can (10¾ oz.) condensed clam chowder, undiluted
1   soup can water
¼   cup dry white wine
4   tablespoons minced parsley
     Salt and pepper to taste
2   tablespoons minced chives for garnish

In large saucepan, heat oil; add onions, garlic, bell pepper and celery. Saute until vegetables are lightly cooked. Add fish, soups, water, wine, 2 tablespoons parsley and salt and pepper. Bring to boil and simmer for 20 minutes, or until fish is done. Sprinkle with remaining parsley and/or chives and serve with plenty of crusty bread. Makes 6 to 8 servings.

Breads

Mahony's Bruschetta	296
California Gourmet Garlic Loaf	297
Classic Garlic Bread	298
Grilled Garlic Bread	298
Speedy Garlic Cheese Bread	298
Mary's Garlic Bread	299
Leo's Special Garlic Bread	299
Dilly Garlic Rolls	299
Southern California's Best Bread in the West	300
Busy Day Garlic Casserole Bread	301
Bacon-Greens-and-Garlic Bread	302
Krusty Garlic Kuchen	303
Calzone	304
Croissants d'Ail	306
Mamma's Sfeenjunee	308
Garlic Clove Bread	309
Hobo Bread	309
Country Picnic Loaf	310
Garlic Focaccia	311
Golden Garlic Clouds	312

QUICK TIPS FOR MAKING GARLIC BREADS

Take a tip from the French, who love their garlic. Rub toasted bread with a cut clove of garlic before buttering. The toast acts as a grater and leaves a layer of fresh garlic flavor on the bread.

Garlic toast can also be made by toasting bread and spreading with garlic puree or granulated garlic, then adding a sprinkle of grated bread crumbs and olive oil before browning in the oven.

Toasted English muffins or bagels can be good substitutes for French bread. They taste great with garlic butter.

For impromptu parties, keep garlic bread in the freezer. It will last for months if well wrapped. When needed, just pop into the oven still frozen.

Use baked garlic cloves to spread on hot French bread. Bake whole heads with the skin left on in a little oil, either in a casserole or wrapped in foil in a moderate oven until soft. The cloves will pop right out of their skins and spread like butter.

Winner of 1983 Recipe Contest: NEIL MAHONY, Ventura, CA

This recipe is one of the all-time favorite prize-winners. An unusual and outstanding dish. The Mahonys recommend keeping a bottle of olive oil in the refrigerator to which have been added four to five heads of peeled garlic. That way you'll have it ready when you want to make Bruschetta or you can add lemon juice for a salad dressing, to prepare oysters and linguine or to add to pasta water for flavor and to prevent boilover.

MAHONY'S BRUSCHETTA

1 loaf French *or* Italian
   bread without seeds
   (day-old bread works fine)
10 large cloves fresh garlic,
   peeled
¾ cup olive oil, preferably
   extra virgin
1½ cups whipping cream
½ cup grated Locatelli
   cheese (hard Romano
   cheese)
½ cup grated Parmesan
   cheese, preferably
   imported Italian
3 tablespoons butter
1 tablespoon chopped
   parsley
   Paprika

Cut bread diagonally in 1-inch slices, without cutting through bottom crust. In food processor or blender, chop garlic fine with steel blade and add olive oil with processor running to make a thin paste. Slather garlic paste on cut surfaces and on top and side crusts of bread. Place in 350-degree oven, directly on rack (with pan on shelf below to catch drippings), and bake for 10 to 12 minutes, until top is crispy looking. While bread is in oven, heat whipping cream in heavy saucepan. Do not boil. Stir in cheeses slowly so that sauce is absolutely smooth (a wire whip works well for this). Stir in butter and keep sauce warm until bread is ready. Wait until everyone is seated at the table. Then place crispy bread in a warmed, shallow serving dish with sides. Finish cutting through bottom crust and pour sauce over. Sprinkle with parsley and paprika and serve IMMEDIATELY. This dish cools very quickly. Makes 6 servings.

NOTE: Each guest should be provided with a small saucer for the Bruschetta, as it is best eaten with a knife and fork.

Finalist in 1982 Recipe Contest: LEONA PEARCE, Carmichael, CA

This recipe for a split loaf of French bread, stuffed with artichoke hearts, cheese, sour cream, olives and garlic makes eight generous servings of crusty, cheesy, garlicky goodness.

CALIFORNIA GOURMET GARLIC LOAF

1 (1 lb.) long loaf sweet French bread
½ cup butter
6 cloves fresh garlic, crushed
1½ cups sour cream
2 cups cubed Monterey Jack cheese
¼ cup grated Parmesan cheese
2 tablespoons dried parsley flakes
2 teaspoons lemon pepper seasoning
1 can (14 oz.) artichoke hearts, drained
1 cup shredded Cheddar cheese
1 can (6 oz.) pitted ripe olives
Tomato slices and parsley sprigs for garnish

Cut French bread in halves lengthwise. Place halves on aluminum foil-covered baking sheet. Tear out soft inner portion of bread in large chunks, leaving crusts intact. Melt butter in large skillet and stir in garlic and sesame seeds. Add bread chunks and fry until bread is golden and butter is absorbed. Remove from heat. Combine sour cream, Jack cheese, Parmesan cheese, parsley flakes and lemon pepper seasoning. Stir in drained artichoke hearts and toasted bread mixture; mix well. Spoon into bread crust shells and sprinkle with Cheddar cheese. Bake at 350 degrees for 30 minutes. Meanwhile, drain olives well. Remove bread from oven and arrange olives around edges of bread and tomato slices and parsley sprigs down center. Makes 8 servings.

CLASSIC GARLIC BREAD

Here's a classic bread treatment that makes perfect garlic bread every time. Just watch carefully to prevent burning!

Courtesy of: Karen Christopher, Gilroy, CA

¾ cup melted butter
3 large cloves fresh garlic, minced *or* pressed
1 loaf fresh French bread (sweet)

Combine butter and garlic in pan over low heat until butter melts. Do not brown! Cut bread in half lengthwise. Cut diagonal slices 2 inches wide, but not all the way through the crust. Spoon garlic butter evenly on bread. Place bread halves on cookie sheet in preheated broiler about 9 inches from the source of heat. Broil until lightly browned. Watch carefully!

GRILLED GARLIC BREAD

When it's barbecue time, be sure to toss some garlic bread on the grill. Served piping hot, its zesty flavor adds a special touch to any outdoor meal.

1 loaf French bread
¾ teaspoon garlic powder
½ cup softened butter *or* margarine

Slice bread but not through the bottom crust. Add garlic powder to butter and blend thoroughly. Spread between slices and over top of bread. Wrap in aluminum foil; seal edges. Heat on back of grill 45 minutes to 1 hour, depending on heat of coals. Serve hot. Makes 6 to 8 servings.

SPEEDY GARLIC CHEESE BREAD

No time to cook? Here's a garlic bread recipe that's a snap to prepare, relying on garlic powder for its mouth-watering appeal.

1 loaf French bread
¾ teaspoon garlic powder
½ cup butter *or* margarine
1 cup Parmesan *or* sharp cheese, grated

Cut bread into 1-inch slices. Heat garlic powder and butter slowly until butter is melted. Brush each slice of bread on both sides with garlic butter and place on baking sheet. Sprinkle with cheese and bake in 425-degree oven 10 minutes or until cheese melts. Serve hot. Makes 6 servings.

MARY'S GARLIC BREAD

The Gilroy merchant who developed this recipe adds mayonnaise, cheese and herbs to her garlic butter mixture to achieve a fabulous flavor.

Recipe contest entry: Mary Mozzone, Gilroy, CA

1 cup butter, softened
1 cup grated Parmesan cheese
½ cup mayonnaise
5 cloves fresh garlic, minced *or* pressed
3 tablespoons chopped fresh parsley
½ teaspoon oregano
1 large loaf French bread, cut lengthwise

Mix all ingredients in bowl and spread on bread. Wrap in foil and bake at 375 degrees for 20 minutes. Unwrap and brown slightly under the broiler.

LEO'S SPECIAL GARLIC BREAD

Gourmet Alley chef Leo Goforth shares his version of garlic bread. You don't even have to mince or press fresh garlic to make Leo's specialty. Just cut cloves in half and rub over toasted French bread. It's fabulous!

Courtesy of: Leo Goforth, Gilroy, CA

1 large loaf French bread, sweet *or* sourdough
4 large cloves fresh garlic, peeled and cut in half
½ cup melted butter *or* margarine
2 tablespoons parsley, minced

Cut bread lengthwise and place on cookie sheet under broiler. Toast very lightly. Immediately rub cut end of garlic cloves over surface of bread. Brush on melted butter, sprinkle with minced parsley and return to oven to keep warm. Slice and arrange in serving basket.

DILLY GARLIC ROLLS

Buttery, herbed rolls, piping hot from the grill are easy to make when you start with the ready-to-serve variety and add your own creative touches.

¼ cup softened butter
½ teaspoon dill weed
¼ teaspoon garlic powder
6 ready-to-serve pull-apart rolls

Cream together butter, dill weed and garlic powder. Break rolls apart from the top and spread butter mixture between sections. Wrap in aluminum foil and place on grill and heat 10 minutes, turning once or twice.

Finalist in 1982 Recipe Contest: RITA PHISTER, Riverside, CA

The chile, garlic and Cheddar filling in this braided bread is the surprise ingredient that brought this contestant to the finals in the 1982 Gilroy Garlic Recipe Contest.

SOUTHERN CALIFORNIA'S BEST BREAD IN THE WEST

1 envelope active dry yeast
¼ cup warm water
½ cup milk
2 eggs
¼ cup soft butter *or* margarine
3 tablespoons sugar
1½ teaspoons salt
1½ teaspoons ground cumin
3½ cups all-purpose flour
   Green Chile Filling (recipe below)
½ cup grated Cheddar cheese

In large bowl of electric mixer, dissolve yeast in warm water. Blend in milk, eggs, butter, sugar, salt and cumin. Blend in 2 cups flour, 1 cup at a time. Beat on medium speed of mixer 3 minutes, scraping bowl often. With heavy-duty mixer (or with wooden spoon) blend in remaining flour to make a soft dough. Turn out onto floured board, and knead until smooth, 5 to 10 minutes. Place in greased bowl, turn over, and cover. Let rise in warm place until doubled, about 1½ hours. Meanwhile, prepare Green Chile Filling. When dough has risen, punch down and turn out onto floured board. Roll to a 9x30-inch rectangle. Crumble filling over dough to within 1 inch of edges. Starting from long side, roll up tightly. Moisten edge with water and pinch together firmly to seal. Using a floured sharp knife, cut roll lengthwise in halves. Carefully turn cut sides up. Loosely twist the two strips together, keeping cut sides up. Transfer to greased and floured baking sheet, and shape to 10-inch circle. Pinch ends firmly together. Let rise in warm place, uncovered, until

puffy looking, about 45 to 60
minutes. Bake at 375 degrees 15
minutes. Sprinkle with ½ cup Cheddar cheese and bake 5 minutes
longer, until browned. Makes 1
10-inch twist.

Green Chile Filling
  1 large onion, chopped
  8 cloves fresh garlic,
    chopped
  1 tablespoon butter
  2 cups grated Cheddar
    cheese
  1 can (7 oz.) diced green
    chiles

Saute onion and garlic in butter
until soft but not browned. Cool. Mix
in 2 cups Cheddar and chiles. Cover
and chill.

BUSY DAY GARLIC CASSEROLE BREAD

If baking bread seems like a chore, try this easy casserole bread, rich
with the flavor of garlic and oregano.

Recipe contest entry: Dorothy Pankratz, Santa Clara, CA

  1 envelope active dry yeast
  1 cup cottage cheese,
    heated
  4 cloves fresh garlic,
    pressed
  1 unbeaten egg
  1 tablespoon oil
  1 tablespoon oregano
  2 teaspoons sugar
  1 teaspoon seasoned salt
  ¼ teaspoon baking soda
2½ cups flour

Soften yeast in ¼ cup water. Combine in large mixing bowl with cottage cheese, garlic, egg, oil,
oregano, sugar, salt and soda. Add
flour and blend well. Let rise until
double. Stir down and turn into a
greased casserole. Let rise 30
minutes. Bake for 40 minutes at 350
degrees.

Finalist in 1981 Recipe Contest: PATRICIA BISSINGER, Livermore, CA

The garlic in this fragrant bread is baked right in, so 1981 finalist Patricia Bissinger gives a warning with her recipe: "When the aroma of garlic perfumes the air you can anticipate company in the kitchen, if there is anyone else in the house, so be prepared for group participation until the last crumbs disappear."

BACON-GREENS-AND-GARLIC BREAD

2 envelopes active dry yeast
1 teaspoon sugar
½ cup warm water
½ cup fresh parsley
½ cup fresh basil
1½ cups buttermilk
4 pieces thick-sliced lean bacon
6 cloves fresh garlic
¼ cup bacon drippings
5 to 5½ cups unbleached flour
2½ teaspoons salt
¼ teaspoon black pepper, freshly ground
1 large egg, beaten
1 egg white
2 teaspoons sesame seeds

Combine yeast, sugar, and warm water in large mixing bowl. Let stand about 5 minutes until yeast is bubbly. Meanwhile, chop parsley and basil fine. Heat buttermilk just until lukewarm. Dice bacon fine and fry until crispy. Peel and mince garlic. Add to ¼ cup bacon drippings and saute a few seconds until the aroma of garlic perfumes the air; set aside. Add 2 cups flour to yeast mixture along with buttermilk, bacon-garlic drippings mixture, parsley, basil, salt, pepper and whole egg. Beat hard with a spoon until thick and elastic. Continue to beat in enough of the remaining flour to make a firm dough. Knead on a well-floured surface until smooth and elastic. Place in a greased bowl, turning to grease top. Cover and let rise in warm oven about 20 minutes. (To warm oven, turn oven to lowest setting for 1 minute, then turn off.) Punch down dough, divide into 2 parts and shape into 12-inch-long loaves or into round loaves. Place on greased cookie sheet. Brush with egg white and sprinkle with sesame seeds. Slash top of loaves every 1½ inches. Cover and let rise until doubled, about 30 minutes. Bake in moderately hot oven, 375 degrees, for 25 to 30 minutes, until golden brown and hollow sounding when tapped on bottom. Cool on wire rack. Serve with whipped butter and a smile.

Finalist in 1982 Recipe Contest: PATRICIA BISSINGER, Livermore, CA

This bread recipe is from a second-time finalist in the Recipe Contest, a very creative cook whose entry won high praise from all who sampled it. It is also excellent cold. "Enjoy! Enjoy!" said Ms. Bissinger, and we did, we did!

KRUSTY GARLIC KUCHEN

Dough:
- 1 envelope active dry yeast
- 1½ cups warm water
- 3 cups unbleached flour
- 1 cup whole wheat flour
- ¼ cup grated Parmesan cheese
- 1 egg, lightly beaten
- 2 tablespoons vegetable oil
- 1 teaspoon garlic salt

Sprinkle yeast over warm water and let stand until bubbly. Meanwhile, measure all remaining dough ingredients into food processor bowl. Add yeast mixture and process just until dough forms a ball. Turn out onto floured surface and knead until dough is soft and no longer sticky. Shape into a ball, place in greased bowl, cover and let rise in warm place while preparing topping.

Garlic Topping
- 1 head fresh garlic, minced (10 to 12 cloves)
- 2 tablespoons vegetable oil
- 1 cup sour cream
- 2 eggs, lightly beaten
- ½ teaspoon salt
- Minced chives *or* green scallion tops

Peel and mince garlic cloves. Saute 3 to 5 minutes in oil over low heat, until soft but not browned. Remove from heat and cool slightly, then combine with sour cream, eggs and salt.

Press dough into bottom and up sides of greased 10x15x1-inch pan, forming rim around edges. Crimp edge (*or* cut rim to decorate edge). Spread Garlic Topping evenly into pan and sprinkle with minced chives. Bake at 400 degrees 20 to 24 minutes until edges are well browned and creamy garlic topping is light golden. Serve slightly warm, cut into strips as bread or appetizer. Makes 8 to 10 servings.

Finalist in 1980 Recipe Contest: DAVID LEHMANN, Palo Alto, CA

Choose your own filling for this huge, gusty turnover. A type of folded over pizza, it was a favorite of many tasters in the Great Garlic Cook-off audience. Can be eaten either hot or cold, and also packs well for a picnic.

CALZONE

Pizza Dough
2 envelopes active dry yeast
1 teaspoon sugar
¼ cup warm water (100 degrees)
4 cups warm water
⅓ cup olive oil
1 teaspoon salt
1½ cups nonfat dry milk powder
12 cups unbleached white flour

Pizza Sauce
1 head fresh garlic
⅓ cup olive oil
1 can (29 oz.) heavy tomato puree
1 can (28 oz.) peeled Italian tomatoes, diced *or* 2 lb. fresh peeled tomatoes, diced
1½ tablespoons dry whole basil
1½ tablespoons dry whole oregano
½ teaspoon salt
1 teaspoon crushed hot red pepper

Fillings
Cheeses: wholemilk Mozzarella, ricotta, Bel Paese, Parmesan, Romano
Ham (prosciutto) *or* sausage, sliced thin
Onions and/or mushrooms, sliced and sauteed with garlic
Marinated artichoke hearts *or* black olives

Stir first 3 ingredients together in a warm quart bowl in a warm kitchen. Set aside to proof. The yeast will start working quickly if it is good.

Stir next 4 ingredients and 6 cups of the flour together in a large warm bowl. Then add the yeast mixture and stir in 3 more cups of flour slowly. Continue to add flour gradually, stirring very vigorously. When dough is too stiff to stir, dump out on a lightly floured board and knead until smooth and elastic (10-15 minutes) adding just enough flour to keep dough from sticking. The 12-cup estimate of flour can vary greatly. You can use half whole wheat flour, but the dough will not be as elastic. This should make about 6 pounds of dough. Cut into ½-pound pieces for individual calzone or pizzas. Form into balls, rub with olive oil, and allow to rise in a warm place on plates or a pan large enough so they won't touch and stick together. Let rise until double in size.

Separate and clean the cloves of garlic. Slice them thinly, crosswise. Place with oil in a kettle large enough to hold all the sauce. Heat gently until the garlic is sizzling in the oil. Do not let the garlic brown. Pour the tomato puree and the tomatoes into the kettle. Stir in the basil, oregano, salt and red pepper. Simmer 15 minutes, stirring often, and allow to cool. Enough for a dozen individual calzone or 3 to 4 large pizzas.

Making Calzone: To form a calzone crust, take a ½-pound ball of risen pizza dough and place on a floured board. Pound out flat with hands, being careful to keep the round shape. Use a rolling pin if you need to. The dough should be evenly thin and as big around as a dinner plate. Spread pizza sauce over the whole dough, except for an inch border around the edge. Put grated cheeses and other fillings on half the sauced area. Use any combinations you like, but be careful not to pile too much on. Fold the other side of the dough over the fillings, and seal the edges together by pressing the borders firmly with your fingers. Rub a little olive oil over the top of the calzone. Put a tablespoon of sauce or cheese on the very top for decoration, or to denote what is inside.

Bake on an oiled pan or baking sheet in a 450-degree oven until the crust is golden brown on sides and bottom (8 to 18 minutes, depending on your oven). Each calzone will make a meal for someone hungry. Serve with wine or beer and a green salad. Calzone pack well to be eaten cold on a picnic.

Finalist in 1979 Recipe Contest: BARBARA SPELLMAN, Morgan, CA

Barbara Spellman, a home economics teacher, became a Garlic Contest finalist with this delightful recipe. Elegant and buttery, these lovely croissants get their appealing flavor from the creamy garlic butter that is mixed into the dough.

CROISSANTS D'AIL   *Garlic Crescents*

Garlic Butter
   3 to 8 cloves fresh garlic
   1 quart boiling water
   4 tablespoons butter

Place unpeeled cloves of garlic in boiling water for 5 seconds. Drain, peel and rinse under cold water. Bring to a boil again for 30 seconds; drain and rinse. Pound into a smooth paste in a mortar or put through a garlic press. Soften butter and mix with the garlic paste. Set aside.

Croissant Dough
   4 cups flour
   6 tablespoons sugar
   2 teaspoons salt
   2 oz. yeast, softened in ½ cup warm water for about 20 minutes
   1 cup water *or* milk (plus or minus a little)
   ¾ cup butter
   1 egg

Sift together the flour, sugar and salt in a large mixing bowl. Add the softened yeast. Gradually add the water (milk) until the mixture forms a ball (you may need to vary this 1 cup of liquid more or less depending upon the moisture level of the flour). Continue kneading in the bowl or on a lightly floured pastry cloth until a smooth, elastic dough is formed. Place about ⅓ of the dough back in the bowl, and add the garlic butter to it. When this is mixed into the dough, add the remaining ⅔ of the dough. Mix thoroughly. On a lightly floured cloth, roll the dough into a rectangle about ⅜ inch thick. Place ¾ cup butter (soft enough to spread) in the center of the dough. Bring each side up and over the butter. Seal the center and ends of the dough. Fold the dough into thirds; turn and roll to the size of the original rectangle. Repeat this process two more times. Fold the dough into thirds. Allow the dough to rise at room temperature until double. Place on a baking sheet and refrigerate 45 minutes to 1 hour, until dough is chilled. Remove from the refrigerator and roll into a rectangle about 10 inches by 20 inches. Cut into 10 rectangles about 4 inches by 5 inches. Cut each of these rectangles in half diagonally. Roll each piece of dough, beginning at the wide end; curve to crescent shape; place on an ungreased baking sheet and allow to rise until doubled in size (about 2 hours). Paint with egg mixed with a small amount of water and bake in 400-degree oven for 10 to 15 minutes, depending upon desired browness. *Optional:* Before rolling dough into crescent shape, sprinkle with freshly chopped parsley mixed with Parmesan cheese.

MAMMA'S SFEENJUNEE

Frank, Josephine and Merrie Jo Fees, who entered their mother's recipe in the Garlic Recipe Contest, described this bread as easy, filling, and wonderfully aromatic . . . and healthful! Mamma even stuck whole cloves into the dough.

Recipe contest entry: Fees family, Honolulu, HI

1⅓ cups very warm water
 1 envelope active dry yeast
 1 teaspoon sugar
 3 tablespoons olive oil
 4 cups flour
 1 teaspoon salt
 1 lb. Italian sausage (*or* Polish sausage, ham *or* cooked pork)
 4 or 5 cloves fresh garlic
 ½ teaspoon Italian seasoning *or* oregano
 ½ cup black olives

Pour water into large bowl, sprinkle yeast over, add sugar and allow to sit for a few minutes while it bubbles. Stir in 2 tablespoons olive oil. Combine flour and salt and add to yeast. Mix well. Knead for about 10 minutes, cover and set in warm place to rise for 1 to 1½ hours. Meanwhile, remove skin from sausage and fry until cooked and crumbly. Drain off grease. Cut each garlic clove lengthwise into 6 slivers. Place in cup and cover with remaining 1 tablespoon oil and seasoning. Cut olives in half and add to sausage. When dough has risen, pat into a greased 9x9x2-inch pan and evenly sprinkle the garlic-oil over. Force sausage mixture down into dough 1 teaspoon at a time. Bake at 375 degrees for 25 minutes or until golden. Makes 8 to 10 servings.

Regional Winner 1984 Recipe Contest: GLEN PETERSON, Omaha, NE

This sensational and savory garlic bread is made with thawed frozen white bread dough. It's quick and easy and attractive to serve. If you prefer, you can bake it in two 9x6-inch loaf pans rather than the Bundt pan.

GARLIC CLOVE BREAD

2 loaves frozen white bread dough, thawed
⅓ cup butter, melted and cooled to lukewarm
¼ teaspoon basil
2 tablespoons chopped parsley
1 small onion, chopped
5 cloves fresh garlic, minced

Cut or snip off pieces of dough about the size of an English walnut. Place into a greased 10-inch Bundt pan. Combine the melted butter, basil, chopped parsley, onions, and minced garlic. Pour over dough. Cover and let rise until double in size (about 1½ hours). Bake in 375-degree oven until golden brown (about 30 to 35 minutes). Cool in pan for 10 minutes and then remove from pan and serve.

HOBO BREAD

This bread is baked in a coffee can. It's terrific with stew, and good reheated later. Slice into rounds and pop into the toaster—that is, *if* there are any leftovers.

Recipe contest entry: Jacqueline McComas, Frazer, PA

Butter to grease 2 1-lb. coffee cans
4 cups self-rising flour
½ cup grated Cheddar cheese
1 tablespoon dry basil or 2 tablespoons fresh basil
¼ cup butter
½ cup finely chopped fresh parsley
3 *or* 4 cloves fresh garlic, chopped
2 tablespoons honey
2 tablespoons chopped chives
½ cup milk
1 can (12 oz.) beer

Generously butter cans. In mixing bowl, combine flour, cheese and basil. In saucepan, heat butter, parsley, garlic, honey and chives until butter melts. Remove from heat and add milk. Add beer and IMMEDI-ATELY add to dry ingredients. Combine gently ONLY until moistened. Divide dough evenly into the cans and bake at 350 degrees for 30 to 40 minutes or until tops are very brown. Slice into rounds and serve with plenty of butter. Makes 2 loaves.

Finalist in 1980 Recipe Contest: JACKIE HOWARD, Morgan Hill, CA

Sourdough bread is transformed into a family-pleasing sandwich loaf. An imaginative entree for a hot summer day, it can be prepared ahead of time and either reheated or served cold for a picnic outing.

COUNTRY PICNIC LOAF

1 loaf rounded sourdough French bread
3 cloves fresh garlic, chopped fine
1 medium-sized red onion, chopped fine
4 tablespoons olive oil
6 eggs, whipped
1 whole green pepper, coarsely chopped
1 can (3 oz.) small shrimp
¾ cup chopped leftover ham *or* pork
8 slices of Italian hard salami, diced
2 or 3 dashes garlic powder
1 teaspoon chili powder
Dash coarse ground black pepper
6 slices Muenster *or* American Swiss Cheese

Cut sourdough bread in half horizontally and scoop out enough bread on upper and lower sections with a sharp knife to form a dishlike loaf. (Reserve removed bread to add to a meat loaf or for making croutons.) Sprinkle bottom loaf inside with garlic and onion; then drizzle olive oil over all. Set aside. In non-stick fry pan sprayed with non-stick vegetable shortening, saute whipped eggs; add green pepper, then stir in shrimp, ham or pork and salami. When the eggs are almost set, add garlic powder, chili powder and pepper. (Add no salt as salami and spices will be adequate.) Stir until all ingredients are hot and the eggs have set. Spoon mixture over garlic and onions in bottom half of loaf, filling completely. Cover with overlapping slices of cheese, and top with remaining half loaf. Wrap tightly in foil and keep warm. This can be made ahead of time and then warmed in 350-degree oven for about 30 minutes. Slice in pie-shaped wedges and serve with fresh fruit in season or a crisp green salad with a garlic, olive oil and fresh lemon juice dressing. Makes 6 to 8 servings.

GARLIC FOCACCIA

Northern Italy's answer to "pizza," this "cake which is not sweet" has many variations. To the basic Focaccia add artichoke hearts, preserved sweet red peppers, olives, mushrooms, cheese or anchovies. Delicious hot from the oven, it also keeps well.

Recipe contest entry: Carolyn Ragsdale, Paso Robles, CA

½ cup chopped fresh garlic
⅓ cup olive oil
3 cups biscuit mix
1 cup milk *or* buttermilk
½ cup grated Parmesan
    cheese

Gently saute garlic in oil until yellow, about 10 minutes. Pour through strainer and reserve both garlic and oil separately. Combine biscuit mix, garlic and milk. Pour a generous third of the oil into a 7x11-inch baking dish or pan. Spread the oil around to cover the dish. Turn dough into dish, pat out evenly with floured fingers. Poke holes into dough every 2 inches with a tool such as a pointed knife blade or wooden skewer to make small holes. Pour remaining oil over top of dough and spread evenly with the fingers. Sprinkle Parmesan over the top and bake at 400 degrees for 24 minutes. Makes 8 to 10 servings.

NOTE: For stronger garlic flavor, do not cook garlic. Add to the dough raw and bake as usual.

Let's face it, is there a mortal soul who can deny that this cousin of the onion is not one of the most important seasoning agents known to man?

Home Economics Reading Service
Washington, D.C.

Third Prize Winner 1980 Recipe Contest:

JEANNE HOWARD, Monterey Park, CA

Fascinating Yorkshire pudding popover with pizazz! A quick, glorious accompaniment to roasts, steaks and stews. Makes even the simplest of meat dishes seem extra special.

GOLDEN GARLIC CLOUDS

Shortening, bacon grease *or* fat drippings
2 eggs
½ cup whole milk
6 or more cloves fresh garlic *or* 1 teaspoon garlic powder
1 teaspoon dried bouquet garni, well crushed
½ cup all-purpose flour, unsifted
½ teaspoon salt
⅛ teaspoon baking powder

Preheat oven to 450 degrees. Be sure all ingredients are room temperature. Prepare large muffin pan (preferably cast iron) by greasing generously with either shortening, bacon grease or fat drippings from roast. Heat in oven until fat *spits*. Beat eggs well. Add milk and mix together either by electric mixer or by hand. If using fresh garlic, peel and put through garlic press and add the resulting juice. If using garlic powder, sift with dry ingredients. Sift dry ingredients together, add to milk mixture and beat until thoroughly blended. Remove muffin pan from oven and quickly pour in batter to about ½ full. Immediately return to oven and bake 20 minutes *without opening oven*. Makes about 8 large clouds. For double recipe, double all ingredients except use only 3 eggs (not 4). The secret in the preparation is the preheating of the pans. The secret in the eating is the delicious surprise of the garlic and herbs.

Sauces/Marinades

Spinach Pesto	315
Marie's Aioli	315
Aioli	316
Skordalia	317
Steak Sauce Elizabeth	317
Louie's Special Marinade	318
Patricia's Marinade	318
Garlic Barbecue Dressing	319
Leo's Garlic Barbecue Sauce	319
Quick 'n' Easy Barbecue Sauce	320
Teriyaki Sauce	320

Third Prize Winner 1981 Recipe Contest: PENNY LOCKHART, Gilroy, CA

This recipe may seem a heresy to the pesto purist, but by using readily available fresh spinach and parsley in this full-flavored sauce, it can be prepared and enjoyed the year round. It (like pesto) is delicious over almost anything: pasta, mushrooms, French bread, sauteed vegetables, even liver.

SPINACH PESTO

6 cloves fresh garlic
1 bunch fresh spinach
1 cup fresh parsley leaves
⅔ cup freshly grated Parmesan cheese
½ cup walnut pieces
4 flat anchovy fillets
1 tablespoon dried tarragon
1 teaspoon dried basil
1 teaspoon salt
½ teaspoon pepper
¼ teaspoon anise *or* fennel seed
1 cup olive oil

Peel and crush garlic. Wash, dry and chop spinach. Trim and discard stems from parsley, Turn all ingredients except oil into food processor fitted with the steel blade. Blend until mixture is smooth. With motor running, add the oil in a thin stream (as when making mayonnaise). When all oil has been added, taste and add additional seasoning as desired. Cover and refrigerate. Sauce will keep about 1 week. Makes about 2 cups.

MARIE'S AIOLI

This pungent mayonnaise can be used as a dip or salad dressing or to dollop on raw oysters, steak tartare or seviche.

Recipe contest entry: Marie Spence, El Paso, TX

2 tablespoons fine dry bread crumbs
2 tablespoons wine vinegar
6 cloves fresh garlic, minced
3 egg yolks
½ teaspoon salt
Pinch of white pepper
½ cup olive oil
1 tablespoon lemon juice

Soak crumbs in vinegar; drain. Mash crumbs and garlic to a smooth paste, preferably in a mortar and pestle. Beat in yolks one at a time with salt and pepper. Then, beating vigorously, add ¼ cup olive oil, a few drops at a time. Continuing to beat, mix in the remaining oil by teaspoonfuls. Add lemon juice and mix thoroughly. Makes about 1 cup.

AIOLI

Probably the most famous garlic sauce of all is aioli, the golden, garlic mayonnaise of Provence. So celebrated is this versatile French sauce that certain days are set aside in many villages for feasts that last from noon until after sundown as platters of vegetables, fish, hard-cooked eggs and bread are carried in for dipping up the smooth, garlicky delight.

4   large cloves fresh garlic
2   large egg yolks
1   teaspoon dry mustard
¼   teaspoon salt
¼   teaspoon white pepper
1   cup olive oil*
1½ tablespoons fresh lemon juice

Have all ingredients at room temperature. Combine garlic, egg yolks, mustard, salt and pepper in blender jar. Cover and blend at medium speed until smooth. With motor running, remove cover and slowly pour in half the oil in a small, steady stream. Stop the motor, and scrape down sides of jar. Cover and turn to medium speed. Uncover and add lemon juice, then remaining oil in slow stream as before, stopping motor to scrape down sides of jar occasionally as sauce thickens. Chill. Serve with hot or cold fish, cold meat or vegetables. Makes 1⅓ cups.

To prepare sauce with hand or electric mixer: Use a narrow, deep bowl (a 1-quart glass measure makes a good container, or use smaller bowl supplied with large electric mixer). Beat in oil very slowly, especially at the beginning, being sure oil is completely blended before adding more. When thick, crush garlic cloves over sauce and mix well. Chill.

* Use half salad oil, if less strong flavor is desired.

SKORDALIA   *Greek Garlic Sauce*

A sauce of fresh garlic has been blended together in the Greek islands since the days of the Argonauts, when, it is said, the searchers after the Golden Fleece passed bowls of *skordalia* around their banquet tables. Sometimes nuts are included. Use ⅓ cup blanched almonds, if you like.

Courtesy of: Katherine Pappas, Gilroy, CA

6 medium potatoes
4 cloves fresh garlic, crushed
2 teaspoons salt
1 cup vegetable oil
½ cup white vinegar
3 egg yolks

Boil potatoes and put them through masher as for mashed potatoes. Add garlic and salt and let set for 10 minutes. Using mixer or food processor, mix potatoes and garlic, slowly adding the oil and vinegar, alternating each. (You may add more vinegar if you like a more tart flavor.) After ingredients are thoroughly mixed, add the egg yolks to make the mixture fluffy. Good on bread, crackers and fresh vegetables.

STEAK SAUCE ELIZABETH

This mushroom sauce is delicious over grilled steak.

Recipe contest entry: Darlene Perrin, San Jose, CA

1 medium red onion, chopped
4 cloves fresh garlic, minced *or* pressed
3 tablespoons olive oil
2 tablespoons butter
1 teaspoon sweet basil
½ teaspoon salt
½ cup beef broth
2 tablespoons flour mixed with water to make thin paste
1 lb. fresh mushrooms, sliced

Saute onion and garlic in oil and butter with basil and salt until onion is tender. Add broth and bring to boil. Reduce heat and add flour mixture. Stir until sauce thickens. Add mushrooms and cook until tender. Do not overcook. Serve over grilled steak. Makes enough for 4 servings.

LOUIE'S SPECIAL MARINADE

If you're lucky enough to have some fresh game, you'll want to marinate it using this special recipe, a delectable blending of flavors.

Courtesy of: Louis Bonesio, Jr., Gilroy, CA

2   cups dry wine
2   cups vinegar
½   cup catsup
2   medium onions,
     quartered and sliced
8 to 10 whole cloves
8 to 10 drops Tabasco
     sauce
4   cloves fresh garlic,
     crushed
3   bay leaves
2   teaspoons coarse black
     pepper
½   teaspoon thyme
½   teaspoon dry mustard
½   teaspoon oregano

Combine all ingredients until well blended. Do *not* use a metal container for the marinade, but crockery, glass or plastic. The use of so many ingredients may seem wasteful until you realize that the marinade may be used two to three times. How much or how little you should prepare depends on the amount of meat, so let your experience be your guide. It is advisable to turn the meat occasionally in the marinade.

The marinade may be used for venison and other antlered game, such as elk and antelope, as well as for domestic meats, such as beef and lamb. Most times 24 hours is more than enough for the meat to marinate. If you prefer the gamey flavor, then shorten the time. Since the gamey taste in venison is carried in the fat, it should be removed prior to cooking.

The lean meat should be cooked with a small amount of pork fat, butter or oil to replace the natural fat that has been removed.

PATRICIA'S MARINADE

A "super good" marinade for meat or poultry.

Recipe contest entry: Patricia Canova, S. Weymouth, MA

½   cup soy sauce
¼   cup salad oil
6   cloves fresh garlic,
     minced
2   tablespoons honey
2   teaspoons dry mustard

Mix all ingredients together and use as marinade for meat or poultry. Makes about 1 cup.

Four good and garlicky barbecue sauces, with any kind of meat.

GARLIC BARBECUE DRESSING

Recipe contest entry: Mirta Richards, Cerritos, CA

2	cups hot water
⅔	cup vinegar
½	cup oil
15	whole peppercorns
10	cloves fresh garlic, crushed
4	bay leaves, crushed
1½	tablespoons oregano
1	tablespoon parsley
1	tablespoon salt
1	teaspoon rosemary

Mix all ingredients in a jar with a tight fitting lid and shake well. Refrigerate overnight or longer—the longer the better. Baste meat several times while cooking.

LEO'S GARLIC BARBECUE SAUCE

Courtesy of: Leo Goforth, Gilroy, CA

¾	cup salad oil
¾	cup olive oil
5	cloves fresh garlic, pressed
4	sprigs fresh rosemary
2	tablespoons red wine vinegar
1	teaspoon oregano
1	teaspoon salt
1	teaspoon black pepper
¼	cup lemon juice
1	teaspoon Tabasco sauce
1	teaspoon Worcestershire sauce

Blend all ingredients 1 hour before using. For chicken and ribs, add 4 tablespoons catsup.

QUICK 'N' EASY BARBECUE SAUCE

1 cup catsup
½ cup wine vinegar
1 teaspoon Worcestershire sauce
1 teaspoon instant minced onion
½ teaspoon seasoned salt
¼ teaspoon garlic salt
¼ teaspoon barbecue spice
⅛ teaspoon black pepper

Combine all ingredients and mix well. Makes 1½ cups.

TERIYAKI SAUCE

1 cup soy sauce
¼ cup brown sugar, packed
2 tablespoons lemon juice
1 teaspoon ground ginger
½ teaspoon garlic powder
¼ teaspoon onion powder

Combine all ingredients in jar. Shake to mix well and dissolve sugar. For a marinade, let stand in sealed jar overnight. Makes about 1 cup.

Miscellaneous

Garlic Pancakes with Ham Sauce   324
Sicilian Garlic Roll   325
Happy Heart Garlic "Cheese" Pie
    with Garlic-Tomatoe Sauce   326
Garlic Chip Cookies   327
Sicilian Gems   328
Garlic Pudding   329
Garlic Relish   330
Garlic Dill Pickles   330
Paul's Pickled Peppers   331
Hungarian Salami   331
Garlic Butters   332
Savory Italian Seasoning Salt   333
Our Best Wurst   334
Ron's Deluxe Garlic Sandwich   334
Homemade Dog Biscuits   335

QUICK AND EASY RECIPE IDEAS

Garlic goes with all dishes, if you give it a chance. Be innovative. Garlic and scrambled eggs? It perks up sluggish morning appetites. Add garlic to soups, salads, and entrees of every kind. And top toast with a garlic spread for a zesty brunch treat.

One recipe contest entrant suggested a flavorful English muffin and garlic treat that is used in her household for colds, flu or bronchitis. Butter toasted English muffin halves and sprinkle with a minced clove of garlic. Spread with grated cheese, then top with three more cloves of minced garlic. Broil until cheese melts and the garlic is toasted and crispy. Eat with parsley on the side or sprinkle chopped parsley on top of the muffin before eating. Whether or not these garlic muffins give aid to various ailments, their flavor appeal is likely to perk up poor appetites.

Another contest entrant suggests eating garlic with breakfast cereal. She starts with three small cloves of fresh garlic and chews them quickly. Then she eats the cereal immediately afterwards. "The cereal removes the sting of the garlic and precludes any smell on your breath," she says. Her reason for eating the garlic is to regulate her blood pressure.

Finalist in 1983 Recipe Contest:

JOHN KEITH DRUMMOND, San Francisco, CA

Cooking the garlic until it is soft changes its flavor from pungent to sweet and nut-like—a very good addition to pancakes and a pleasant complement to the smokiness of the ham sauce. Serve for breakfast, brunch, lunch or even a light supper.

GARLIC PANCAKES WITH HAM SAUCE

½ lb. butter
3 tablespoons rubbed sage
3 large heads fresh garlic
2 cups self-rising flour, approx.
2 eggs
2 tablespoons oil
3½ cups milk
9 large cloves fresh garlic, minced
1 lb. lean ham, minced

Mix together 12 tablespoons (1½ sticks) butter and sage; reserve. Remove as much outer skin from garlic as possible without piercing the cloves' covering. Set garlic in saucepan, cover with water and boil gently about 45 minutes or until cloves are quite soft. Remove from heat. When cool enough to handle squeeze each clove to remove cooked garlic by grasping clove at the tip and pulling down toward base. In mixing bowl, beat garlic with fork until smooth. You should have about 1 cup of garlic. Add to garlic about same amount (at least 1 cup) flour, eggs, oil and 1½ cups milk to make pancake batter. Add minced garlic to batter and set aside. Melt remaining 4 tablespoons butter and keep warm. While waiting for batter to work, place half the sage butter (6 tablespoons) in saucepan, add 6 tablespoons flour to make a roux and cook at medium temperature, stirring frequently, to brown. Meanwhile in skillet, place 2 tablespoons of remaining sage butter and add ham. Heat through, but do not burn. When roux is nicely browned, add remaining 2 cups milk. Allow to thicken, stirring frequently. Add ham and skillet drippings and mix to make ham sauce. Keep warm. Heat griddle or clean skillet and grease lightly with a bit of remaining sage butter. Drop batter by spoonfuls onto griddle to make silver dollar-size pancakes. Serve with melted butter and ham sauce. Makes 2 dozen pancakes.

Finalist in 1985 Recipe Contest: ROXANNE E. CHAN, Albany, CA

This is a real Mediterranean treat . . . perfect as a first course or as part of a buffet.

SICILIAN GARLIC ROLL

Sauce:

4 tomatoes, peeled, seeded and chopped
⅓ cup olive oil
¼ cup chopped fresh basil leaves
4 cloves fresh garlic, peeled and finely minced
1 tablespoon balsamic vinegar

Roll:

2 large heads fresh garlic, separated into unpeeled cloves
   Boiling water
2 cups ricotta cheese
1 raw egg
½ cup currants
4 sheets phyllo dough, covered with damp towel to prevent drying out
¼ cup melted butter
½ cup toasted pine nuts

In bowl, combine all sauce ingredients and set aside to blend flavors. Cover unpeeled garlic cloves with boiling water and cook until cloves are soft. Peel and mash. Combine garlic with ricotta and egg; mix well. Stir in currants. Place 1 sheet of phyllo dough on a damp cloth. Brush with butter. Place a second sheet over the first and brush with butter. Repeat with 2 additional sheets. Spread ricotta mixture over the top sheet. Top with pine nuts. Lift towel gently away from you to form a roll. Pick up towel and put roll on a buttered baking sheet. Prick in several places and bake at 350 degrees for 35 minutes or until the roll is golden. Cool. Place sauce in small glass bowl and put in center of platter. Slice roll and arrange attractively around bowl. Makes 6 servings.

HAPPY HEART GARLIC "CHEESE" PIE WITH GARLIC-TOMATO SAUCE

Here's a recipe for those on a low-fat, low-cholesterol diet. Not only does the garlic add great flavor it has also been credited by some in the medical community with lowering cholesterol in the blood.

Recipe contest entry: Carol Granaldi, Sacramento, CA

2 egg whites
1 teaspoon fresh lemon juice
1 pkg. (14 oz.) firm tofu, mashed well
1 cup chopped onion
4 tablespoons safflower oil
½ cup chopped cooked mushrooms *or* 1 can (8 oz.) drained
⅓ cup minced fresh parsley
¼ cup dry bread crumbs
6 cloves fresh garlic, minced
½ teaspoon plus a pinch of dried oregano
Salt and pepper to taste
1 can (1 lb.) crushed tomatoes
½ teaspoon crushed dried basil
Dash cayenne

In large mixing bowl, beat egg whites until foamy; add lemon juice and tofu. Stir well. Saute onion in 2 tablespoons oil until golden brown. Add to tofu mixture along with mushrooms, parsley, bread crumbs, half the garlic, pinch of oregano and salt and pepper to taste. Stir to mix thoroughly. Spray 8-inch glass pie plate with low-fat, no-cholesterol pan spray. Pour mixture in and spread evenly. Bake at 350 degrees for 30 to 40 minutes until lightly golden in color or knife inserted in center comes out clean. Remove and let cool about 10 minutes. Meanwhile prepare sauce. Saute remaining garlic in 2 tablespoons oil until golden, then add tomatoes, ½ teaspoon oregano, basil, cayenne and salt and pepper to taste. Stir well, and bring to bubbling. Reduce heat and simmer for about 15 minutes. Cut pie into 4 wedges and top each with sauce. Makes 4 servings.

Finalist in 1984 Recipe Contest: MICHELE SCIORTINO, San Diego, CA

Cookies made with garlic? Well, why not? Everyone who tasted them agreed they were delicious and would even be better with more garlic!

GARLIC CHIP COOKIES

10	cloves fresh garlic
	Boiling water
½	cup maple syrup
1	cup butter, softened
¾	cup brown sugar
¾	cup sugar
2	eggs
1	teaspoon vanilla
½	teaspoon salt
2¼	cups chocolate chips
½	cup chopped nuts
2½	cups flour
1	teaspoon baking soda

Drop garlic cloves into boiling water for about 5 minutes until tender. Peel and chop garlic and soak in maple syrup for 20 minutes. Meanwhile, cream butter, sugars, eggs and vanilla together until light and fluffy. Combine flour, baking soda and salt. Add to cream mixture. Then stir in chocolate chips and nuts. Drain garlic and add to cookie batter. Blend well. Drop cookie batter by tablespoons onto ungreased cookie sheet about 2 inches apart. Bake at 375 degrees for 8 to 10 minutes, until lightly browned. Remove from oven and cool on racks. Yield: 5 dozen cookies.

SICILIAN GEMS

Chocolate-coated garlic cloves? Why not! The recipe's originator says, "Garlic is very good for you! Particularly for high blood pressure." These little Sicilian Gems are a wonderful way to get your family to eat garlic and enjoy it!

Recipe contest entry: Mrs. Margaret Buccery, Palos Verdes, CA

3 large heads fresh garlic (about 30 cloves)
Ice water
½ lb. sweet dark chocolate
1 tablespoon Grand Marnier *or* liqueur of your choice
Ground walnuts (optional)

Separate and peel cloves of garlic. Soak in ice water to seal in flavor and juices while you are preparing the chocolate. Melt chocolate in double boiler or fondue pot; add liqueur and blend well. Dry garlic cloves and dip until completely covered in the chocolate-liqueur mixture. Allow to harden, and serve on a small elegant dish at the end of the meal, with cappuccino. These are the "piece de resistance" at the finale of a long and sumptuous Italian meal! (They may also be rolled in ground nuts before they harden, but they are just as good plain.)

There are many miracles in the world to be celebrated and, for me, garlic is among the most deserving.

Professor Leo Buscaglia

GARLIC PUDDING

During the First Garlic Festival, Digger Dan's, a Gilroy restaurant, featured this unusual dessert on their menu. Although the recipe calls for quite a lot of garlic, it is a light and flavorful dessert.

Recipe contest entry: Judith M. Bozzo, Gilroy, CA

2 heads fresh garlic
1½ cups cold water
1 cup sugar
1 envelope unflavored gelatin
¼ cup lemon juice
1 teaspoon lemon peel, grated
2 egg whites
¼ teaspoon nutmeg
Custard Sauce (recipe below)
¼ teaspoon salt
¼ cup lemon juice

Wrap garlic heads in foil and bake until done (soft). Remove from foil and boil in water until flavor is transferred from bulbs to water and water is reduced to about 1¼ cups garlic water. In saucepan combine sugar, gelatin and salt. Add ½ cup garlic water; stir until dissolved and remove from heat. Add remaining ¾ cup garlic water, lemon juice and lemon peel. Chill until partially set. Turn into large bowl. Add egg whites and beat with electric mixer until mixture begins to hold its shape. Turn into mold. Chill until firm. Unmold and garnish with sprinkles of nutmeg and custard sauce.

Custard Sauce
4 egg yolks, beaten
¼ cup sugar
2 cups milk
Dash salt

In heavy saucepan, mix egg yolks with sugar, milk and salt. Cook over low heat until mixture coats spoon. Cool and serve.

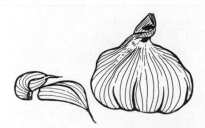

GARLIC RELISH

Garlic relish adds that extra little touch to dress up simple entrees. With its tomato and eggplant flavor, enhanced with fish paste and garlic, this versatile relish is savory as well as easy to prepare.

Recipe contest entry: Birgita Muller, Los Angeles, CA

1 large or 2 small eggplant
2 large tomatoes
4 cloves fresh garlic
    Salt
1 teaspoon fish paste *or* marmite
1 large onion, thinly sliced
1 tablespoon vegetable oil
1 teaspoon brown sugar
2 teaspoons chili powder

Slice eggplant, sprinkle with salt and set aside for 30 minutes. Cut up tomatoes and remove seeds. Crush garlic and mix with fish paste. Brown onion slightly in oil. Add fish paste, garlic, sugar and chili powder. Add eggplant and mix all together, blending well. Add tomatoes and cook gently for 5 minutes. Taste and add salt if necessary. Put mixture in a bowl in steamer and steam for 20 minutes.

GARLIC DILL PICKLES

When cucumbers are plentiful, put up a batch or two of crunchy dill pickles. They're great for sandwiches and to garnish potato, tuna and other salads.

7 lb. medium-size cucumbers
6 thick onion slices
4 tablespoons dill seed
3 teaspoons crushed red pepper
¾ teaspoon dehydrated garlic
1 quart vinegar
2 quarts water
½ cup salt

Wash cucumbers and pack into 6 hot sterilized quart jars. To each jar add 1 slice onion, 2 teaspoons dill seed, ½ teaspoon crushed red pepper, and ⅛ teaspoon garlic. For a stronger flavor, use ¼ teaspoon garlic in each jar. Combine remaining ingredients and bring to a boil. Pour, boiling hot, over cucumbers, leaving ¼-inch space at top. Seal at once.

PAUL'S PICKLED PEPPERS

If Peter Piper picked a peck of pickled peppers, he'd want to put up a batch with garlic, as in the recipe below.

Courtesy of: Paul Pelliccione, Gilroy, CA

3 lb. green peppers (7 to 9 large), seeded
Boiling water
2½ cups distilled white vinegar
2½ cups water
1¼ cups granulated sugar
8 cloves fresh garlic, peeled
4 teaspoons salad oil
2 teaspoons salt

Cut peppers lengthwise into ¾-inch strips, place in bowl and cover with boiling water. Let stand 5 minutes; drain. Combine vinegar, water and sugar in saucepan; boil 5 minutes. Meanwhile pack peppers into 4 hot sterilized pint jars. To each jar add 2 cloves garlic, 1 teaspoon salad oil and ½ teaspoon salt. Immediately pour in boiling syrup to cover peppers, one jar at a time. Fill to within ⅛ inch of top. Seal at once. Makes 4 pints.

Second Prize Winner 1981 Recipe Contest:

AMBER BURNEY, Ventura, CA

"I'm a garlic fiend," says Amber Burney. "I'm very sure I use 10 heads a month—not cloves, heads." This scrumptious salami contains eight fresh garlic cloves and when chilled, resembles a firm pate. Delicious!

HUNGARIAN SALAMI

8 cloves fresh garlic, minced
2 lb. ground beef (33% fat)
1 tablespoon Hungarian paprika
1 tablespoon salt
1 tablespoon coarsely ground black pepper
1 tablespoon onion powder
1 tablespoon dill seed
1 tablespoon chopped fresh basil (*or* 1 teaspoon dry)
1 teaspoon liquid smoke
1 teaspoon whole coriander seed
1 teaspoon whole pickling spice
1 teaspoon mustard seed

Combine all ingredients and mix well. Shape into 2 logs, each about 10 inches long. Cover and refrigerate overnight. Uncover, place on broiling pan and bake in a very slow oven 225 degrees for 2 hours. Cool before slicing. Makes 2 logs salami.

GARLIC BUTTERS

Garlic butters are easy to make and add an extra-special epicurean touch to many dishes. Slather some on bread slices before adding the filling for rich, zesty sandwiches. Brush loaves of French or Italian bread with garlic butter and broil or bake for mouth-watering garlic bread. Use as a spread to perk up simple canapes.

Melt garlic butter over vegetables or grilled meat for incomparable flavor enhancement or heat some in a skillet to saute shrimp, lamb or other meats or vegetables. Use in sauces, to flavor soups, and don't forget escargots—it's not possible to cook these tender morsels without garlic butter!

Make extra garlic butter to keep on hand in the refrigerator (or freezer for longer storage). You'll be surprised at how many new uses you'll discover if you have some readily available.

Hint: Chill garlic butter, roll into logs, cover with plastic wrap and chill till firm. Slice off as needed.

For a novel party idea, gather friends together to make garlic butter. Everyone can take turns peeling garlic cloves and creaming butter. Each guest will have some nice garlic butter to take home afterwards. What to serve at your garlic party? All sorts of garlicky goodies, of course, from appetizers to salads to the entree, even a garlic dessert if you're daring!

Try one of these combinations for garlic butter.

BASIC GARLIC BUTTER

½ cup butter
 2 to 3 cloves fresh garlic,
    pressed *or* finely minced

Cream butter. Add garlic and beat until fluffy. Makes ½ cup.

Garlic Herb Butters:
Add freshly chopped chives, shallots or parsley to basic garlic butter, or select herbs and spices from the spice shelf—Italian herb seasoning, basil, or dill, for example.

Garlic Cheese Butters:
Add shredded or grated cheese of your choice to basic garlic butter.

Quickie Garlic Butter:
Use ¾ teaspoon garlic powder instead of fresh garlic. Add ¼ teaspoon salt and a dash black pepper. Let stand for 30 minutes for flavors to blend.

Easy Melt Garlic Butter:
Instead of creaming basic garlic butter, just heat butter and garlic over low heat until butter melts. Do not brown!

Extra Garlicky Butter:
Mash 6 cloves (or use dehydrated equivalent) of fresh garlic into ½ cup butter.

Delicate Garlic Butter:
Blanch and drain 4 cloves of fresh garlic and pound together; combine with ½ cup fresh butter or margarine. Pass the mixture through a fine sieve.

Party Time Garlic Butter:
Moisten 1 teaspoon of instant granulated garlic with an equal amount of water. Place in a mixer bowl with 1 lb. softened butter or margarine. Beat until very creamy. Let stand about 20 minutes to blend falvors. Butter may also be melted over hot water or in a food warmer and spread with a pastry brush. Makes enough garlic butter for 100 medium pieces of French or Italian bread or 200 slices of bread or bun halves for sandwiches.

Finalist in 1981 Recipe Contest: MRS. DOMENI ROMANO, Fresno, CA

Italians are great users of garlic in their cooking. Mrs. Romano has developed this recipe not only for her own use but to give as a small gift to friends and relatives who are also creative cooks.

SAVORY ITALIAN SEASONING SALT

4 whole dried red chile peppers
¼ cup dehydrated minced garlic
½ cup dehydrated minced onion
¼ cup dried oregano leaves
¼ cup dried basil leaves
¼ cup dried parsley leaves
¼ cup salt
2 tablespoons dried rosemary (optional)

With blender turned on at low speed, add ingredients in order listed. Cover and turn on high speed to pulverize and blend well. Store in shaker container with tight lid. Use for seasoning steaks, roasts, vegetables, soups, stews and salads, adding seasoning to suit taste. Makes about 1 cup.

OUR BEST WURST

This homemade salami recipe makes 4 pounds, enough for 50 people when sliced as a snack. Freezes well for later use.

Recipe contest entry: Bob and Sylvia Solterbeck, Hooks, TX

10 jalapeno peppers, minced (optional)
5 cloves fresh garlic, minced
¼ cup curing salt
4 tablespoons dry red wine
2 tablespoons brown sugar
1 tablespoon *each* chili powder, Italian seasoning and coarse ground black pepper
1 teaspoon *each* ground cumin and oregano
5 lb. lean ground beef

Combine all ingredients except beef thoroughly, then mix into beef. Refrigerate mixture for 24 hours to allow flavors to mingle. Form into 4 rolls. Wrap in aluminum foil and bake in 225-degree oven for 4 hours, turning every hour. Remove foil and place on broiler pan or rack to allow excess liquid to drain. Then rewrap and refrigerate or freeze. Makes 4 1-lb. sticks. Recipe may be doubled if desired.

RON'S DELUXE GARLIC SANDWICH

The ultimate comfort food!

Recipe contest entry: Ronald Dobbins, Sacramento, CA

2 tablespoons crunchy peanut butter
2 slices wheat *or* other bread
3 to 4 cloves fresh garlic, sliced
2 tablespoons Marie's Ranch Dressing

Spread peanut butter on one slice of bread. Place garlic slices on peanut butter and cover with remaining slice of bread which has been spread with Ranch Dressing. Makes 1 serving. "Enjoy," says Mr. Dobbins.

HOMEMADE DOG BISCUITS

The following testimonials came from those who tested this recipe: "My 10-year-old Samoyed preferred them to those purchased at the store." "My daughter's 7-year-old, large dog liked them." "My son-in-law's 5-year-old beagle, a finicky eater, loved them." They are an excellent, nutritious treat for the family dog and won't hurt the small children in the family if they happen to eat one.

Recipe contest entry: G.C. Bemis, Pebble Beach, CA

3½ cups all-purpose flour
2 cups whole wheat flour
2 cups bran
1 cup rye flour
1 cup grits *or* cornmeal
½ cup nonfat dry milk
1 tablespoon dehydrated minced *or* powdered garlic
4 teaspoons salt, optional (salt substitute may be used)
1 pkg. dry yeast
¼ cup warm water
2 cups tomato juice (salt free, if desired)

Combine all dry ingredients. Dissolve yeast in warm water and add tomato juice. Mix with dry ingredients. Dough should be very stiff. Knead dough for about 3 minutes. Roll out on floured board to ¼- to ½-inch thickness. Cut to desired size with knife or cookie cutters. Place on ungreased cookie sheet and bake at 300 degrees for 1 hour. Turn off oven. Leave biscuits overnight or at least 4 hours to harden. Makes about 7 dozen cookie-size biscuits.

Good Things to Know About Garlic

KNOW YOUR GARLIC!

Fresh garlic may be creamy white or have a purplish-red cast, but whatever the color, it should be plump and firm, with its paperlike covering intact, not spongy, soft or shriveled.

Dehydrated or other forms of processed garlic should be purchased in tightly sealed containers, preferably from markets where there is sufficient traffic to ensure that the spices are fresh.

HOW BEST TO STORE

Fresh garlic keeps best in a cool, dry place with plenty of ventilation. It should not be refrigerated unless you separate the cloves and immerse them in oil, either peeled or unpeeled. If the garlic isn't peeled, the cloves will hold their firmness longer, but peeling will be more difficult. Fresh garlic which is held in open-air storage for any length of time will lose some of its pungency and may even develop sprouts. The garlic is still usable, but will be somewhat milder and more will be needed to achieve the same strength of flavor in a dish being prepared.

Dehydrated forms of garlic should be stored with other spices in as cool and dry a place as possible, definitely not above or next to the kitchen range or sink or in front of a window with exposure to the sun. Keep tightly sealed. Processed garlic which requires refrigeration after opening should, of course, always be stored in the refrigerator to maintain its quality.

HOW TO PEEL

If you are peeling only a few cloves, simply press each clove against the cutting board with the flat side of a heavy kitchen knife or press between the thumb and forefinger to loosen the skin first. If your recipe calls for a larger quantity of garlic, drop the cloves in boiling water for just a minute and drain quickly. They will peel quite easily. If you have a microwave oven, you can cook the cloves for 5 seconds or so to achieve the same effect.

MUST GARLIC BE PEELED?

Not necessarily. You can cook unpeeled garlic in a hot pan—it won't burn easily—then slip off the skins when the garlic is soft. Or, if the garlic is to be cooked in a soup or sauce and then the whole cloves discarded, there is certainly no necessity to peel them. And, if you are preparing a dish such as "Forty Clove Chicken," cook the cloves unpeeled and then simply press the soft garlic out of the skin with your fingers or with knife and fork as you eat it.

WHICH TO USE

Whether you use fresh, dehydrated, or processed garlic is a matter of personal choice. Fresh garlic fans note that garlic flavors food differently, depending on how it is used. Fresh uncooked garlic is most pungent when pureed, crushed or finely minced. For milder garlic flavor, keep cloves whole or cut in large pieces. Whole cloves cooked for a long time with roasts, stews or soups have a surprisingly sweet, nutlike flavor. It is very important when cooking with fresh garlic not to burn it. When garlic is burned, it has a very bitter flavor and must be discarded or it will ruin the flavor of the dish. Remember, when sauteing garlic in oil, keep the heat fairly low and cook it until it is just very lightly browned.

Other forms of garlic vary somewhat in their flavoring characteristics, but you can generally plan on the following substitutions:

1 average-size clove = ⅛ teaspoon dehydrated, powdered,
of fresh garlic   minced or chopped garlic
                                              or
                               ½ teaspoon garlic salt. (*Caution:* when using garlic salt in recipes calling for fresh garlic, decrease the amount of salt called for.)

GARLIC ODOR

Several techniques help to control the odor of garlic on the hands that results from peeling or chopping. Disposable plastic gloves can be worn while performing this chore. Or you can rub the fingers with salt and lemon juice afterwards, then rinse under cold water. The best solution we have found is to rub the fingers over the bowl of a stainless steel teaspoon under running water for a few moments. There is a chemical reaction which takes place that does indeed eliminate the odor from the fingers. The more garlic chopped, the longer it will take to remove the odor, but it can be done! Garlic odor on the breath is most easily controlled by eating fresh parsley. Parsley has been called "nature's mouthwash" by garlic lovers because of its effectiveness. Chewing on a coffee bean or two also seems to do the trick.

TO CHOP OR PRESS?

There are some who swear by their garlic press and others who claim that using a garlic press makes the fresh garlic taste bitter. It is certainly a quick and easy method of mincing garlic; however, you do lose some of the pulp which means that hand-chopped gives a better yield and less waste. Again, the choice is yours. If you choose to chop the garlic by hand, here's a tip from the wife of a garlic grower: Add the salt required for your recipe directly into the minced garlic while it is still on the cutting board. The salt will absorb the juices and make it easier to scoop the tiny garlic pieces off the board.

GARLIC FLAVORED OIL, VINEGAR OR SALT

It's easy to flavor with garlic by adding peeled whole cloves of garlic to bottles of oil or vinegar for two or three days before using. To make garlic salt, just bury 3 peeled and pressed garlic cloves in half a cup of salt. Add fresh ground pepper and ground ginger to taste, if you like. Let stand for a few days in a screw-top jar. Remove garlic and use the salt as desired to flavor soups, meats, salads, etc.

GARLIC BUTTER

Make logs of garlic butter and freeze them to have on hand to melt on broiled meats or to mix into fresh cooked vegetables or spread on bread. Just add mashed garlic cloves or the equivalent in dehydrated or processed garlic to suit your taste to sticks of butter (about 6 cloves fresh garlic per stick is recommended). If you wish, add a few herbs and salt lightly. Form into logs, wrap in plastic and freeze. Slice off as needed.

BAKED WHOLE HEADS

One of the most popular ways to serve fresh garlic is to bake whole heads to serve as an hors d'oeuvre with crunchy bread or as an accompaniment to meat or vegetables. Peel as much of the outer skin away as possible, leaving the cloves unpeeled and the head intact. Place heads in covered casserole or on a piece of heavy aluminum foil, drizzle with olive oil, dot with butter, salt and pepper to taste and bake covered at 350 degrees for about 45 minutes or until cloves are soft and can be squeezed easily out of their skins onto bread or other foods.

Clove. One of the several segments of a bulb, each of which is covered with a thin, papery skin.

Crushed. A term which refers to fresh garlic which has been smashed by the broad side of a knife or cleaver on a chopping board or with a rolling pin between several thicknesses of waxed paper.

Dehydrated. Any of several forms of garlic from which the moisture has been removed. Dehydrated garlic is available minced, powdered and granulated.

Fresh. The term used to describe garlic which has not been dehydrated. Actually "fresh" garlic is allowed to "cure" in the field before harvesting just until the papery skin, not the cloves, becomes dry.

Garlic Braid. A garland of fresh garlic braided together by its tops. Braiding is done while the garlic is still only partially cured with some moisture remaining in the tops and before the tops are removed in harvesting. When they become fully dried, they are too brittle to braid. Originally devised as a convenient storage method, garlic braids are quite decorative and have become popular in this country as a kitchen adornment. Serious garlic lovers like to use them for cooking purposes, cutting off one bulb at a time from the braid. Care should be taken if the braid is to be preserved as a decoration that it is not handled carelessly. The papery covering of the bulb is fragile and will break easily when the garlic itself has shriveled after a year or so.

Granulated. A dehydrated form of garlic that is five times stronger than raw garlic. Its flavor is released only in the presence of moisture.

Juice. Garlic juice may be purchased commercially or prepared by squeezing fresh cloves in a garlic press, being certain not to include any of the flesh. Juice blends easily for uniform flavor.

Minced. This term is used for both dehydrated and fresh garlic. Generally called for when small pieces of garlic are desirable as in soups, sauces or salad dressings. Fresh garlic may be minced using a sharp knife on a chopping board. If the recipe calls for salt, add it to the garlic while mincing. It will prevent the garlic from sticking to the knife and absorb the juices otherwise lost in the mincing process. Finely minced garlic, as called for in most French recipes, tends to disappear into the finished dish. For a more robust flavor, mince more coarsely as called for in many Chinese dishes. Large amounts of garlic can be minced using a blender or food processor.

Powdered. Powdered garlic is available commercially. When using powder in recipes with a high acid content, mix with water (two parts water to one part powder) before adding. Powdered garlic can be made from fresh by slowly drying peeled garlic cloves in the oven. When very dry, pound or crush until fine and powdery. Pass through a sieve and pound any large pieces, then sieve again. Store in sealed jars in a dry place.

Pressed. A term for garlic which has been put through a garlic press. There are many different types of presses available, some even "self-cleaning." When using a garlic press, it isn't necessary to peel the garlic clove. Simply cut it in half and place in the press. Then squeeze. The skin will stay behind, making the press easier to clean. Remember to clean your press immediately after use before the small particles which remain behind have a chance to dry.

Puree. A term for garlic which has been cooked at high heat and then pressed through a sieve. Available commercially or made at home. It is excellent to have on hand to blend into soups, sauces or to spread on slices of bread to serve with hors d'oeuvres.

Garlic Salt. Available commercially, it is usually a blend of approximately 90% salt, approximately 9% garlic and approximately 1% free-flowing agent. When using garlic salt in recipes calling for fresh garlic, decrease the amount of salt called for.

Garlic is enveloping the country.

Twin Falls Idaho Times News

No one is indifferent to garlic. People either love it or hate it, and most good cooks seem to belong to the first group.

Faye Levy
Los Angeles Herald Examiner

Cooking Equivalents Table

Kitchen Measure

     3 teaspoons = 1 tablespoon
     2 tablespoons = 1 fluid ounce
  16 tablespoons = 1 cup
     8 ounces = 1 cup or ½ pound
  16 ounces = 1 pound
     2 cups = 1 pint
     2 pints = 1 quart
     4 pints = 2 quarts or ½ gallon
     8 pints = 4 quarts or 1 gallon
     4 quarts = 1 gallon

Metric Measure

     1 ounce = 28.35 grams
     1 gram = .035 ounce
     8 ounces = 226.78 grams or ½ pound
  100 grams = 3½ ounces
  500 grams = 1 pound (generous)
     1 pound = ½ kilogram (scant)
     1 kilogram = 2¼ pounds (scant)
     ¹⁄₁₀ liter = ½ cup (scant) or ¼ pint (scant)
     ½ liter = 2 cups (generous) or 1 pint (generous)
     1 quart = 1 liter (scant, or .9463 liter)
     1 liter = 1 quart (generous, or 1.0567 quarts)
     1 liter = 4½ cups or 1 quart 2 ounces
     1 gallon = 3.785 liters (approximately 3¾ liters)

RECOMMENDED USE PROPORTIONS

As cooks become more confident in the use of garlic and discover what wonders its flavor can perform with simple meat and vegetable dishes, they tend to use larger and larger quantities. For the beginner, who may be uncertain about how much garlic to use when experimenting with familiar recipes, we offer the following proportions of fresh or dehydrated garlic. Keep in mind that these are on the low side and most who really enjoy the flavor of garlic will want to use a great deal more.

Meats: For each 2 pounds of pork, beef, lamb or other meats, use ⅛ to ¼ teaspoon garlic powder, or 1½ to 2 teaspoons garlic salt, or 2 to 3 cloves fresh garlic.

Sauces: For 3 cups barbecue, tomato or other sauce, use ⅛ to ¼ teaspoon garlic powder, or 2 to 3 cloves fresh garlic.

Soups: To 3 cups meat stock or vegetable soup, add ⅛ teaspoon garlic powder, or 2 cloves fresh garlic.

Pickled foods: Per quart of kosher-style dill pickles or per pint of dilled green beans, add ⅛ to ¼ teaspoon dehydrated chopped or minced garlic, or 2 to 3 cloves fresh garlic.

Relishes: To 2 pints of chutney or relish, add ⅛ teaspoon dehydrated minced garlic, or 2 cloves fresh garlic.

Index

A

APPETIZERS / ANTIPASTI
also see chapter index 19
Antipasto Aglio 45
Quick and Easy Appetizers 21
Artichokes
Artichoke and Carrot Frittati 101
Artichoke and Garlic Frittata 102
Artichoke Hearts Marinati 38
Artichoke Pie 99
Artichokes alla Rosina 140
California Gourmet Garlic Loaf 297
Cream of Artichoke Soup 64
Garlic Artichoke Dip 45
Stuffed Artichokes Castroville 141
Very Garlic Artichokes 142
Avocado
Avocado Bisque 64
Creamy Garlic Guacamole 39
Garlic Guacamole 40
The Greatest Guacamole Ole! 39

B

Barbecue Sauce
Garlic Barbecue Dressing 319
Leo's Garlic Barbecue Sauce 319
Quick 'N' Easy Barbeque
Sauce 320
Beef
Angela's Milanese 187
Beef Stew Bonesio 189
Beef Teriyaki 195
Buffet Meat Loaf 204
Caballero Casserole 192
Charcoal Grilled Steak 185
Chili Verde (Mexican Stew) 190
Chow Yuk 196
Dr. Jensen's Uncensored
7-clove Hash 203
Flank Steak Ole 179
Flautas al Bau 194
Garlic Beef Enchiladas 191
Garlic Festival Pepper
Beefsteak Sandwiches 12
Gilroy Chili 194
Gilroy Meat-and-Potatoes
Quiche 197
Green Garlic Chili 192
Herbed Minute Steaks 187
Herbed Pot Roast with
Eggplant and Tomatoes 183
John's Neapolitan Beef Entree 188
Larry's Favorite Beef in Beer 186
Lena's Meatballs 204

Meatball Soup, California Style 66
Mighty Good Moussaka 221
Pacific Post Roast 184
Pot Roast a la Gilroy 182
Quickie Cube Steaks 188
Roast Tenderloin San Benito 181
Roast with Garlic / Dill Sauce 180
Spit-Roasted Rolled Rib 181
Steak and Mushrooms San
Juan 184
Tamale Party Pie 193
Tijuana Jail Chili 193
Tortilla Loaf 190
Wayne's Bulgogi 195

BREADS
see chapter index 293
Gourmet Alley Garlic Bread 9
Quick Tips for Making Garlic
Bread 295
Broccoli
Best Broccoli 143
Garlic-Broccoli Soup 65
Italian Broccoli 142
Rosie's Broccoli Salad 86
Butters, Garlic 332

C

Calamari
see Squid
Calzone 304
Carrots
Ali Baba's Carrots 145
Capered Carrots and Zucchini 146
Garlic-Cheese Filled Carrots 144
Transylvanian Carrots 146

CHEESE / EGGS
see chapter index 95
Aphra de Jacques 27
Slender Cheesy Spread 40
Speedy Garlic Cheese Bread 298
Stinky Cheese 41
Chicken
101 Garlic Chicken 236
Bob's Garlic Chicken 229
Broiled Garlic and Lemon
Chicken 244
Burgundy Chicken Mozzone 243
California Chicken 232
Chicken a la Brazil 255
Chicken alla Toscano 259
Chicken and Sausage Ragout
alla Rosina 264

Chicken Curry with Peaches ... 260
Chicken in Garlic Mushroom
   Sauce ... 241
Chicken Karma ... 261
Chicken Mama's Way ... 245
Chicken Maui ... 253
Chicken Peperonata ... 233
Chicken Pizzaiola ... 258
Chicken Rosemary ... 244
Chinesey Chicken Wings ... 254
Crepes Poule a la Garlic ... 262
Digger Dan's Chicken ... 246
Forty-Clove Chicken Filice ... 240
Franco-Syrian Chicken ... 257
French Garlic Chicken a la
   Ingram ... 258
Garlic Chicken with
   Artichokes and
   Mushrooms ... 243
Garlic Chicken with Plum
   Sauce ... 251
Garlic Soup with Chicken ... 60
Garlic-Chicken Phyllo Rolls ... 237
Garlic-Glazed Chicken for a
   Gang ... 246
Garlicky Pasta Chicken Salad ... 83
Gilroy Chicken Paprika ... 260
Gin-Gar Chicken ... 240
Gypsy Garlic Chicken ... 256
Herbed Cheese and Chicken in
   Puff Pastry ... 263
Hodge-Podge Chicken Bake ... 254
Joycie-A's Chicken Provincial ... 230
Kelly's Asian Chicken ... 249
Kiss Me Now-Chicken ... 234
Mediterranean Chicken
   Breasts ... 238
My Own Breathtaking
   Cacciatore ... 259
Nehls' Saffron Chicken ... 248
Nofri's Garlic Chicken ... 247
Phony Abalone ... 265
Pollo al Ajullo ... 255
Shanghai Chicken on
   Shanghai Rice ... 250
Spicy Garlic Chicken ... 231
Stuffed Chicken Breasts a l'Ail ... 235
Thirty-Clove Chicken ... 241
Uncle Hugo's Chicken ... 247
Vermouth Garlic Chicken ... 242
Wild Rice and Chicken ... 245
Woking Garlic Chicken ... 252
Clams
   Baked Stuffed Garlic Clams ... 23
   Clams Sailor Style ... 287
   Cockles in Garlic Sauce ... 288
   Garlic Clams ... 287
   Marion and Linda's Baked
      Stuffed Clams ... 24

Cookies, Garlic Chip ... 327
Cornish Game Hens
   Helen's Baggy Henny ... 266
Crab
   California Crab Dip ... 48
   Dungeness Crab Dijonnaise ... 288
   Helen's Seafood Treat ... 291
   Mixed Seafood Saute ... 291
Croissants d'Ail ... 306

D

Dips
   Aioli ... 316
   Bagna Cauda ... 52
   California Crab Dip ... 48
   Creamy Garlic Guacamole ... 39
   Dave's Favorite Garlic Dip ... 46
   Dip with a Zip ... 49
   Dragon Dip ... 43
   Eggplant Dip Solano ... 46
   Fresh Garlic Vegetable Dip ... 48
   Garlic Artichoke Dip ... 45
   Garlic Guacamole ... 40
   Garlic Herb Dip ... 47
   Garlic Veggie Dip ... 49
   Manny's Portuguese Garlic Dip ... 46
   Marie's Aioli ... 315
   Mexi-Gilroy Garlic Dip ... 47
   People Always Ask for this
      Recipe Party Dip ... 44
   Roasted Garlic Puree Dip ... 43
   Skordalia ... 317
   Tennent Garlic Dip ... 49
   The Greatest Guacamole Ole! ... 39

DRESSINGS
   see chapter index ... 77
   Aioli ... 316
   Garlic French Dressing ... 91
   Georgette's French Dressing ... 92
   Green Goddess Dressing ... 91
   Italian Sweet-Sour Dressing ... 93
   Jeanne's Low-Fat Creamy
      Garlic Dressing ... 90
   Karen's Fresh Pears with
      Garlic-Roquefort Dressing ... 90
   Marie's Aioli ... 315
   Party-Perfect Garlic Dressing ... 92
   Tart 'N' Tangy Italian Dressing ... 93

E

EGGS / CHEESE
   see chapter index ... 95
   Egg Salad with Garlic
      Dressing ... 83
Eggplant
   Basque-Style Eggplant
      Casserole ... 151

Eggplant Delight   149
Eggplant Dip Solano   46
Eggplant Parmigiana   151
Eggplant Pasta Fantastico   109
Eggplant Salad Trinidadelish   87
Epicurean Eggplant Bake   147
Garlic Eggplant   150
Herbed Pot Roast with
  Eggplant and Tomatoes   183
Light 'N' Lovely Eggplant
  Casserole   149
Marinated Eggplant   148
Rose Emma's Eggplant Relish   38
Vegetables Veracruz   172
Escargots Carmela   22
Escarole Garlic Soup with Chick
  Peas   62

F

Fish
  Alla Tamen Fillet of Sole
    Roll-Ups   277
  Baked Codfish Gilroy Style   273
  Baked Trout Montbarry   274
  Bass and Swiss Chard   272
  Fillets Neapolitan   276
  Grilled Fish with Garlic Salsa   271
  Herb-Broiled Salmon Steaks   276
  Mouth-Watering Baked Fish   272
  Sharon's Garlic Monkfish   277
  Supersonic Fish Stew   292
  Trout Cantonese a la Gow   275
  Trout Saute alla Rosina   273
Focaccia, Garlic   311
Frittata
  Artichoke and Carrot Frittata   101
  Artichoke and Garlic Frittata   102
  Garlic Frittata   101
  The Gubsers' Green Bean and
    Garlic Frittata   103

G

GOURMET ALLEY
  also see chapter index   7
Green Beans
  Dilled Green Beans   155
  Garlic Green Bean Salad   88
  Garlic Green Beans   154
  Greek Beans   156
  Green Beans Asadoor   155
  Green Beans au Garlic   153
  Val and Elsie's Julienne Beans   156

H

Hash, Dr. Jensen's Uncensored
  7-Clove   203

L

Lamb
  Chad's Garlic Lamb   215
  Crusty Lamb con Ajo   217
  Curried Lamb Chops   220
  Diane's Barbecued Mexican
    Lamb Chops   219
  Garlic-Stuffed Leg of Lamb
    with Cabernet Sauce   212
  Garlicious Lamb Roll-Ups   216
  Gloria's Lamb Stew   222
  Good 'N' Garlicky Kebabs   218
  Lamb Shanks a la Basque   213
  Lamb Shanks Divine   218
  Lamb Shanks with Barley and
    Garlic   211
  Marinated Grilled Leg of Lamb   217
  Mrs. Joseph Gubser's
    Barbecued Lamb   219
  Rack of Lamb Breadbin   214
  Ragout of Lamb   220
Lobster
  Jambalaya a la Creole   290
  Renne's Seafood fra Diavolo   289

M

MEATS
  see chapter index or see, beef,
    lamb, oxtails, pork, rabbit,
    tripe, veal   177

MISCELLANEOUS
  see chapter index   321
  Quick and Easy Recipe Ideas   323
Mushrooms
  Garlic Mushroom Casserole   157
  Garlic Mushrooms Morgan Hill   35
  Garlicky Mushrooms Supreme   157
  Gourmet Alley's Stuffed
    Mushrooms   10
  Italian Sausage Stuffed
    Mushrooms   35
  Mushrooms a la 'Rissa   37
  Mushrooms of the Auvergne   36
  Pesto Mushrooms   34
  Zucchini and Mushroom Hors
    d' Oeuvres   34

N

Nuts
  Garlic-Spiced Walnuts   53
  Peanuts and Slivers   50

O

Olives
Great Garlic Olives   51
Ripe Olives with a Hint of
Garlic   51
Oxtails, Sherried   224
Oysters Gilroy   22

P

Pancakes, Garlic with Ham
Sauce   324

PASTA / RICE
see chapter index   105
Pesto
Pasta con Pesto alla Melone   112
Pasta con Pesto alla
Pelliccione   9
Pesto Mushrooms   34
Pesto Quiche   97
Spinach Pesto   315
Pheasant in a Bag   268
Phyllo, Garlic-Chicken Rolls   237
Pickles, Garlic Dill   330
Pies
Artichoke Pie   99
Garlic Goddess Cheese Pie   98
Garlic Pie   162
Mushroom Crust Florentine
Pie   100
Popcorn
Garlic Popcorn Balls   54
Garlic-Basil Popcorn   54
Pork
Adobo   210
Annabelle's Pork in Vinegar   210
Annabelle's Portuguese Pork
in Orange Juice   210
Garlic Spareribs   206
Orange-Garlic Pork Chops   207
Pork and Chicken Los Arcos   208
Pork and Green Chiles   209
Spareribs a la Gilroy   205
Spicy Chops and Cabbage   209
Sumptuous Spareribs   207
Tenth Anniversary Ribs   206
Potatoes
Baked Garlic Potatoes   158
Delicious Potatoes   160
Garlic Jalapeno Potatoes   160
Garlic Potatoes with Cheese
Sauce   159
Hollister Vegetable Casserole 171
Mama's Potato Soup   67
Potato-Garlic Puree   162

Roasted Garlic Potatoes   161
S.O.S. (Super Omnipotent
Spuds)   161
Shrimply Garlic Potato Salad   85

POULTRY
see chapter index or see,
chicken, squabs, cornish
game hens, turkey, pheas-
ant, quail   227
Prawns
see shrimp

Q

Quail, Oven-Fried   268
Quiche, Pesto   97

R

Rabbit
Conejo a la Chilindron   225
Rabbit with Lentils   223
Ratatouille
Gilroy Ratatouille   153
Nina's Ratatouille   152
Relish
Garlic Relish   330
Rose Emma's Eggplant Relish   38

RICE / PASTA
also see chapter index   105
Rice a la Najar   280
Shanghai Chicken on
Shanghai Rice   250
Wild Rice and Chicken   245

S

SALADS / DRESSINGS
see chapter index   77
Salami, Hungarian   331
Sandwiches
Country Picnic Loaf   310
Garlic Festival Pepper
Beefsteak Sandwiches   12
Parsley-Garlic Finger
Sandwiches   30

SAUCES / MARINADES
see chapter index   313
Sausage
All-American Egg Rolls   25
Chicken and Sausage Ragout
alla Rosina   264
Italian Sausage Soup   69
Italian Sausage Stuffed
Mushrooms   35

Limas and Sausage Italiano 205
Sausage and Rice, Swiss Style 135
Texas Surprise 28
Scallops
Garlic Scallop Saute 286
Mixed Seafood Saute 291
Scallops and Mushrooms
Brochette 285
Scallops Gilroix 285
Scallops in Garlic Mushroom
Sauce 286
Supersonic Fish Stew 292

SEAFOOD
see chapter index or see,
clams, crab, fish, lobster,
oysters, scallops, shrimp,
squid 269
Shrimp
Garlic Shrimp 278
Garlic Shrimp au Gratin 279
Garlic Shrimp Salad 84
Garlic-Shrimp Hors d' Oeuvre 24
Helen's Seafood Treat 291
Jambalaya a la Creole 290
Mixed Seafood Saute 291
Renee's Seafood fra Diavolo 289
Rice a la Najar 280
Roger's Scampi 278
Scampi in Butter Sauce 13
Shrimp Appetizer Supreme 25
Spicy Marinated Shrimp for a
Crowd 85
Succulent Sauteed Shrimp 280
Supersonic Fish Stew 292
Tipsy Garlic Shrimp 279
Snow Peas Canton 174
Souffle, Sabrina's Garlic 103

SOUP
see chapter index 55
Spinach
Big Daddy's Big-On-Flavor
Spinach Treats 164
Cheesy Spinach 163
Creamy Garlic Spinach Soup 61
Garlic-Spinach Snacks 30
Spinach Casserole 163
Spinach Fettuccine with
Artichoke Sauce 121
Spinach Pesto 315
Spinach Salad 82
Spinach-Garlic Pasta with
Garlic-Onion Sauce 107
Spreads
Auntie Peggy's Garlic Spread 41
Creamy Garlic Herb Cheese 42
Mock Caviar 51
Slender Cheesy Spread 40

Stinky Cheese 41
"Too Easy" 42
Squabs a la Santa Cruz 265
Squid
Baked Squid Sicilian 282
Calamari del Mediterranean 282
Calamari, Festival-Style 11
Insalata di Calamari 284
Marinated Squid alla Rosina 283
Squid Gilroy for Two 283
Stuffed Calamari 281

T

Teriyaki Sauce 320
Tofu
Mock Oyster Stir-Fry 171
Tomatoes
Garlic Butter Crumb Tomatoes 167
Garlicky Tomato Saffron Soup 58
Tomatoes a la Clare 166
Tomatoes a la William 166
Tripe
Scandinavian Tripe Salad 81
Tripe a la Louis 226
Turkey Breast, Oyster Sauce
with Peas and Mushrooms 267

V

Veal
Scaloppine al Limone 198
Veal Cutlet Parmigiana 200
Veal Fricassee with Garlic 202
Veal Garlic Chop 198
Veal Parmigiana 201
Veal Shanks with Garlic 199

VEGETABLES
see chapter index or see,
vegetable by name 137
Quick and Easy Recipe Ideas 139
Central Coast Stir-Fry
Vegetables 10

Z

Zucchini
Capered Carrots and Zucchini 146
Hollister Vegetable Casserole 171
Mock Oyster Stir-Fry 171
Myrna's Stuffed Zucchini 168
Vegetables Veracruz 172
Zesty Zucchini Saute 168
Zippy Zucchini Fritters 170
Zucchini alla Pelliccione 170
Zucchini and Mushroom Hors
d'Oeuvres 34
Zucchini Appetizer Angelino 32
Zucchini Leaves 169
Zucchini Zap! 169

Notes

— **NOTES** —